ANGLISTIK UND ENGLISCHUNTERRICHT

Herausgegeben von
Gabriele Linke
Holger Rossow
Merle Tönnies

Band 92

CHRISTIAN LUDWIG
ELIZABETH SHIPLEY (Eds.)

Mapping the Imaginative I

Teaching Fantasy and Science Fiction in the EFL Classroom

Universitätsverlag
WINTER
Heidelberg

Bibliografische Information der Deutschen Nationalbibliothek

Die Deutsche Nationalbibliothek verzeichnet diese Publikation in der Deutschen Nationalbibliografie; detaillierte bibliografische Daten sind im Internet über *http://dnb.d-nb.de* abrufbar.

Herausgeber:

Prof. Dr. Gabriele Linke
PD Dr. Holger Rossow
Prof. Dr. Merle Tönnies

Gedruckt mit Unterstützung der
Ernst-Reuter-Gesellschaft der Freunde, Förderer und
Ehemaligen der Freien Universität Berlin e.V.

ISBN 978-3-8253-4720-8
ISSN 0344-8266

Imprimé en Allemagne · Printed in Germany
Druck: Memminger MedienCentrum, 87700 Memmingen

Gedruckt auf umweltfreundlichem, chlorfrei gebleichtem und alterungsbeständigem Papier

Den Verlag erreichen Sie im Internet unter:
www.winter-verlag.de

Contents

List of Illustrations

Christian Ludwig (Berlin) and Elizabeth Shipley (Karlsruhe)

Mapping the Field of Teaching Fantasy and Science Fiction

Popular culture has gained a firm place in the English as a foreign language (EFL) classroom. Nevertheless, two edited volumes on teaching fantasy and science-fiction texts seem like a bold endeavour. There are, of course, some stellar classics, such as Mary Shelley's *Frankenstein; or, The Modern Prometheus* (1818), Lewis Carroll's *Alice's Adventures in Wonderland* (1865), H.G. Wells' *The Time Machine* (1895) and *The War of the Worlds* (1898), and, to mention one modern classic, Margaret Atwood's *The Handmaid's Tale* (1985), which have made it into school curricula. The majority of fantasy and science-fiction (f&sf) texts, including films and TV series, however, are still kept outside classrooms in spite of growing academic recognition of the genres. This is particularly surprising since science fiction is what could be called the literature of the future, offering students the unique opportunity to critically discuss a cornucopia of issues through the lens of future or alternative realities.

The aim of this edited work is twofold: to provide readers with a brief introduction to science fiction and fantasy and to encourage them to discover some of the potential the two genres have for the foreign language classroom. In the first section, we will attempt to define science-fiction and fantasy literature. The following section will then be devoted to some of the reasons for including f&sf in the contemporary (and future) EFL classroom. In addition to more tangible language learning objectives that can be achieved by working with science fiction and fantasy, for example, developing students' reading and audio-visual skills, the two genres also hold vast potential when it comes to fulfilling other curricular demands such as developing students' empathy, critical awareness, or inter- and transcultural competence. We will keep these considerations deliberately short in order not to anticipate the colourful kaleidoscope of ideas and suggestions in the articles collected in these volumes, and conclude by providing a brief overview of the contributions to this volume.

Many attempts have been made to define science fiction, but it remains a contested genre, which is why some even go as far as to propose that sf is not a genre but a "field where different genres and subgenres intersect".[1] What most definitions of science fiction have in common is that they see sf somehow connected to a reality that is different from our own, i.e. the future or alternative realities. According to Heinlein, science fiction represents a "realistic speculation about future events".[2] For Kafka, the present seems more important than the future when she argues that sf is a "commentary on people and societies as we find them today, as well as extrapolating from this to give us a view of some possible alternative futures".[3] For the purpose of this article, we will stick to the definition of sf suggested by Grady in 1979 as "speculative fiction which takes into account life as it presently exists and provides the reader with possible alternatives which might exist at some future time based on ideas generated by contemporary problems or concerns".[4] Despite many crossovers such as George Lucas' *Star Wars* (1977-), the fantasy genre traditionally delineates itself from science fiction in that it depicts a fictive, fantastic world, often containing magical elements and fantastic creatures. Or as Shippey has it: "if science fiction deals with what is known not to be true, but not known to be beyond possibility, fantasy in its modern sense deals with what is known or very generally thought to be impossible".[5] In a similar vein, Hunt argues that "all fiction [...] is in a sense fantasy [...] [as] fiction narrates and makes sense of things in a way that is unavailable in reality".[6] Taking into account Shippey's significant observation that "[m]odern definitions of fantasy accordingly often find difficulty in being both broad enough to take in what is an extremely prolific genre and narrow enough to say anything useful",[7] for the purpose of this introduction, we refer to Hume's seminal definition according to which "[f]antasy is any departure from consensus reality, an impulse native to literature and manifested in innumerable variations".[8]

One of the first sf magazines to extend into the mainstream literary tradition, as well explicitly intertwine the two genres of fantasy and science fiction, was *The Magazine of Fantasy and Science Fiction* (1949), in which many well-known fantasy and science-fiction writers have been published.[9] The professional association for American writers of science fiction and fantasy (Science Fiction and Fantasy Writers of America

[SFWA], founded in 1965) is another case in point. Sometimes the term science fiction is used as the broader term for all genres of the fantastic, as reflected in the title of the prestigious Science Fiction Research Association (SFRA), founded in 1971, and one of its academic journals *Science Fiction Studies* (1973-).

Bookstores for science fiction usually contain fantasy as well. The Stockholm Science Fiction Bokhandeln, a well-known bookstore in the old part of Stockholm, shown in the figure, is clearly using the word science fiction in this broader sense as the juxtaposed figures of dragon and spaceship so clearly illustrate. One is reminded of a quip by Ursula K. Le Guin, a writer of both science fiction and fantasy (and many other genres such as children's literature and mainstream realism, making it difficult for non-specialist bookstores to decide what section to put her books in). As Reid writes, she was not "patient with the academic definitions of literary genres" and once dismissed "the differentiation between science fiction and fantasy as 'elves over here, robots over there'".[10] This is nicely represented spatially by the shop sign in the image below, which shows us instead of elves and robots, 'dragons over here, spaceships over there', giving the book shopper immediate visual information how the phrase 'science fiction' is to be interpreted in this place of business. This also supports the hypothesis that "readers of one genre tend also to read in the other".[11] The commonly used short forms f&sf, and sf&f are a vivid illustration of how the two genres are intertwined.

Fig. 1: Shop Sign of the Stockholm Science Fiction Bokhandeln[12]

One can only speculate that one of the reasons for this mutual interest is the fact that not only fantasy, as Gates, Steffel, and Molson propose, is defined "in a personal way, depending on "[our] own life stories, experiences, hopes, dreams, and fears"[13] but also science fiction. Science fiction and fantasy, however, are not only almost inseparable in terms of readership but also in their ways of telling a story. Both genres are famously noted for arousing a "sense of wonder."[14] Moreover, they both share the element of worldbuilding, as authors of both genres create worlds that have an internal logic, almost without any exception deviating from the logic of our 'real' world, while, at the same time, being grounded in real-life stories, events, or other extrapolations of the present. The idea of worldbuilding is closely related to the concept of mapping as maps play an important role in many worldbuilding endeavours. As Ekman posits:

> [A] map is in itself a claim that whatever is on it somehow exists. Every map creates a world, or part of a world [...]. The map of a secondary world is a powerful suggestion that the mapped world exists, at least in some sense.[15]

The maps of fantasy, which, according to Mathews, are "circumscribed only by imagination itself", [16] can "bring an imaginary place into existence"[17] and move it from the imaginary into the realm of the real. We have chosen the metaphor of mapping for the title in the hope that its explorations of the imaginative will be of use.

So far we have discussed science-fiction and fantasy literature as genres. In the following, we will concentrate on their potential for the modern English as a foreign language classroom.

At first glance, the history of teaching science fiction and fantasy appears to be rather short, having its origins in 1953 when Sam Moskowitz taught the first course on science-fiction literature at the City College of New York.[18] However, such a history would only look at courses which focus on fantasy and science fiction as genres, excluding all courses in which texts which might be categorised under f&sf were read as part of another genre such as Gothic Literature or Children's Literature, or as part of a survey course on, say, seventeenth-century or eighteenth-century literature.[19] Furthermore, as Kincaid notes, there is

> no starting point for science fiction. There is no one novel that marks the beginning of the genre … Brian Aldiss famously named *Frankenstein* by Mary Shelley, and his suggestion has been taken up by a number of later commentators. Other strong contenders include H.G. Wells, or Edgar Allen [sic] Poe, or Jules Verne. Gary Westfahl has nominated Hugo Gernsback as the true father of science fiction. Still others (including myself) have gone back to Thomas More's *Utopia*.[20]

Thus, one might well say that the origins of teaching f&sf go back to the origins of teaching literature. The last few decades, however, have seen a growing number of scholarly publications and teaching resources which address the teaching of fantasy and science fiction as genres, appreciating their potential within and beyond the university classroom. Since literature about teaching science fiction and fantasy began to appear, their place has not only been seen in the literature classroom[21] but also in science, critical literacy, and rhetoric classes.[22] Another seminal purpose is using such texts for learning English as a foreign language. The literature about this is fairly recent and mostly practice oriented. Publications in Germany for the secondary classroom include the two issues of *Der Fremdsprachliche Unterricht Englisch*, one focusing on science fiction and one on fantasy, the *Praxis Englisch* issue on utopia and dystopia as well as the collection of texts and a teacher's guide on science fiction and dystopia by Christian Ludwig.[23] However, the potential of these genres for EFL learning needs to be explored further.

What all f&sf texts have in common is that "authors explore the concerns of their times by mapping them on to invented worlds, whether they be political dystopias, fabulous kingdoms or supernatural dimensions".[24] Thus, those texts not only allow us to imagine futuristic and fantastic societies and see things we would never see otherwise, but, more importantly, to contemplate current social, political, and technological developments. If foreign language teaching endeavours to prepare students for the world (and not just for the next exam), then there is no logical reason to exclude f&sf from the curriculum. While this does not necessarily mean that it would motivate students per se, most will agree that speculative fiction's tremendous entertainment value should also be harnessed for the classroom.

Science fiction portrays future or alternative societies, allowing the reader to see what life on earth, in space, on faraway planets, or in alternative universes is or will be like. Similarly, fantasy narratives take us to worlds that, depending on the subgenre, resemble the Middle Ages, pre-medieval, or even pre-historic times, exploring the fabric of human society.

In other words, f&sf can be especially motivating for younger and teenage readers as the texts allow them to experience new (or alternative) worlds and cultures. Will human beings be able to travel between galaxies, discover new civilisations, live forever, or will human civilisation be wiped out by dark alien forces? These questions imply what science fiction is about: change. Advances in science and technology allow us to live longer, travel faster, and communicate with almost everyone in the world. However, the accelerating advances in science and technology (Will invisibility, telepathy, and teleportation be one day possible?) also shake the very foundations of our society. Suddenly, questions such as whether androids should have human rights become relevant and are no longer distant thought experiments as in Asimov's "Bicentennial Man" (1976). In fact, reading Asimov's sf novella or watching the film adaptation in the foreign language classroom compels us to grapple with such 'basic' questions and helps us to consider and adopt a position on robotic life forms. The same is true for fantasy where genres such as low and high fantasy, science fantasy, urban, epic, dark, or animal fantasy take us to worlds which allow us to explore cultural, social, and psychological factors in our development as a species. The first Old English epos *Beowulf* may serve as an example here. Modern remakes of the epos in form of picturebooks, computer games, TV series, or blockbusters take us to what is today Scandinavia, depicting the fight of the warrior Beowulf against the evil monster Grendel and his mother and later against a fire-breathing dragon. The tale not only allows us to learn more about social values such as honour, tenacity, and vigour as well as the firm belief in destiny, but also about the increasing mix of Christian and Norse traditions.

Let us look at some more key elements which make speculative fiction, an umbrella term frequently used to refer to both science fiction and fantasy, the perfect genre for the classroom. As far as fantasy is concerned, the genre (and the same seems to be true for science fiction)

> allows us to explore major life mysteries without being limited by size, time, or space. More specifically, fantasy literature, like all other forms of myth, springs from the human need to understand the struggle of good versus evil.[25]

Of course, it goes without saying that speculative narratives should undergo the same 'quality test' as any other literary text, film, or series. The fact that so many of us are drawn towards possible visions of the future should also have a motivating effect inside the classroom, or as Rand and Verner argue: "[s]ince material is concerned with the student's future, relevance is built in and motivation is high".[26] Moreover, the admittedly varying degree of realism allows us to reflect on an endless number of issues also relevant for the foreign language classroom, including gender and sexuality, race, social class, discrimination, the posthuman, forced labour, drugs and addiction, genetic research, terrorism, the right to life and death and many, many more. As Sawyer and Wright emphasise in one of the best-known works on teaching science fiction:

> Its speculative nature, its incessant philosophizing on 'what if', invites a comparative speculative response; it requires engagement with thought-experiments that confront and often overturn passive acceptance of contemporary conditions; it has the capacity to stimulate, to unsettle, to provoke the reader into an intellectual response.[27]

If we put aside the topic-based approach for a moment, speculative fiction also holds vast potential when it comes to realising specific foreign language learning aims as specified in the Common European Framework[28] and national curricula across Europe and beyond. These include, inter- and transcultural learning, global learning, global citizenship, and many more. Each of the contributions in both volumes concentrates on one or several of these learning aims, also providing detailed lesson plans, project outlines, or course overviews which can be readily put into practice.

Moreover, the fact that speculative fiction is often about real-world developments and problems provides many opportunities for students to make sense of the text instead of analysing it. According to reader-response criticism, reading is about actively experiencing a literary text instead of identifying its central messages through a formal analysis. This is not to say that venturing into science fiction and fantasy in the classroom does not bring its own challenges. Novels, short stories, films, and songs about the future often place linguistic demands on the students. The languages created for science fiction help build new fictional worlds while, at the same time, they also create a new sociolinguistic context.[29]

This linguistic and cultural experience, however, is something we encounter every day when interacting with people from other cultures.

Last but not least, the growing fan fiction corpus provides numerous opportunities for student-centred activities such as creative writing. According to Jamison, fan fiction can be defined as "[w]riting that continues, interrupts, reimagines, or just riffs on stories and characters other people have already written about".[30] Through engaging with fan fiction, students get the opportunity to engage in processes of worldbuilding themselves, expressing their ideas about what tomorrow's (today's!) world should look like. They can, for example, write themselves into the piece of fiction, creating alternative universes, or combining different stories. Writing Harry Potter into *Star Wars* or changing the gender or ethnicity of one or more central characters compels students to change their perspective more than once.

Taking a glimpse into the future of teaching f&sf in the English classroom, we can assume that alternative and new media will play an increasing role.[31] Digital tools such as apps, video games, and virtual reality environments will allow students to experience these worlds in a more immediate, personal, and interactive way as these technologies are increasingly able to tell stories. Moreover, these tools not only enable students to read about or see alternative worlds but also to become an active part of the narrative. These tools are also examples of how the f&sf canon keeps expanding and reinventing itself.

For example, handheld devices such as smartphones or iPads are gradually moving into the realm of the foreign language classroom.[32] With them, a growing number of literature apps is now also available for educational purposes. Often, such apps provide a more engaging way of reading an old fantasy or science-fiction classic or contemporary text. While the literature apps currently on the market are diverse in nature, they often share some common features, such as an audio version of the text, additional information on the author and/or the text, and interactive features which allow students not only to experience the story virtually but also to actively engage with characters and the environment in which the action takes place. Often the stories are open-ended and/or allow readers to influence how the story develops. In addition to this, some apps allow teachers to create additional activities, such as questionnaires, to check comprehension, or provide tailor-made feedback.

Playing video games has become one of the top leisure time activities, especially among the younger generation. In contrast to realistic games, fantasy and science-fiction video games create opportunities for students to visit alien and future worlds or lost civilisations and "to create fantasy worlds for themselves where they [are] heroic, active, and respected".[33] In these worlds, they complete quests, face mythical beasts, and fight dark magic. In contrast to realistic games, fantasy games offer more freedom when it comes to worldbuilding as situations, events, and characters can basically be anything. Although Murray and Maher doubt that "the Fantasy dimension of gaming could ever achieve more than entertainment"[34], video games should not prematurely be excluded from formal foreign language learning contexts. As far as existing research is concerned, two broad directions can be distinguished: the use of video games/fan discourse in- and outside the classroom and the application of game mechanics, for example, achievement, immediate feedback, rewards, leaderboards, or social engagement loops in task design.[35] Regarding the former, video games provide authentic input which can help students develop their imagination, increase their empathy, and teach them about character development and multiple identities. Moreover, multiplayer online games (MMOs) create collaborative learning environments in which students are compelled to use the target language to communicate with other players to successfully play the game as players.[36]

Moreover, augmented and virtual reality systems offer another learning environment in which students can fully immerse in alien worlds by using life-like characters (avatars), role plays, location-based games, or virtual (augmented) reality treasure hunts. In other words, augmented and virtual reality systems have the power to reduce the distance between the reader/viewer and the narrative by teleporting students basically anywhere as they interact with each other and with virtual characters.[37]

The international contributions to this volume discuss a wide range of science-fiction and fantasy texts suitable for the classroom, illustrating the great potential of the genre for all age and ability groups in various educational and cultural contexts. This also includes primary school classrooms, which are hardly mentioned in existing publications on speculative fiction in foreign language learning. All articles do have a dual focus, in that they discuss speculative fiction as a genre as well as the pedagogical advantages and challenges of using f&sf texts in the foreign language classroom.

We hope that these discussions will contribute to the visibility and recognition of speculative fiction in both academia and the classroom, and serve as a springboard for further discussion.

The Contributions to this Volume

This two-volume work is conceived as a whole, the first volume reporting on teaching in the primary and secondary classroom and the second volume on university teaching. However, there is also considerable crossover. As many chapters have aspects that can be applied to more than one educational level, it is recommended that readers look at the entire work even if they are particularly interested in only one educational level. The first volume is divided into two main sections. Part one is dedicated to how science-fiction concepts can be introduced already at a very early age. "Of Megamag Mallet and Galactic Goggles: Science-Fiction Picturebooks in the Primary EFL Classroom" by Grit Alter focuses on the role of science-fiction picturebooks for the primary EFL classroom. Her contribution provides a detailed account of how science-fiction narratives provide numerous opportunities for exploring aspects of gender already with very young learners of English.

The second article to the first part of this volume by Christian Ludwig, "*The Three Little Aliens and the Big Bad Robot* in ELT", then reports on the results of a small-scale classroom project, exploring the learners' mental images of and attitudes towards robots. Considering the accelerating rate at which robots alter the way we live and work, the author of the article deems it indispensable to encourage students to explore the (future) role(s) of robots in our society as well as to critically reflect the social, political, and ethical implications this development has for our life.

Part two is then dedicated to exploring f&sf at secondary level, presenting a plethora of practical examples of how to introduce the genres and by doing so achieve learning goals which go far beyond educating scientifically literate individuals.[38] The article by Peter Hohwiller, "Teaching Michael Faber's *Under the Skin*", sets the scene for this section by discussing a real classic of psychological science fiction which has also been adapted for the screen. The novel's focus on otherness, sense of belonging, and misplacement but also more concrete issues such as vegetarianism or binary oppositions such as animal-human relationships, makes it suitable for pursuing a variety of curriculum-based learning goals. "Imagining Futures Beyond the Nation State: Mohsin Hamid's *Exit West* in the EFL Classroom" by Claudia Deetjen then serves as an example of how to explore themes surrounding migration through fantasy fiction. The contribution convincingly illustrates how the magic realism novel about a young couple on their flight from an unnamed country plunged in civil war can support students in grasping the global nature of the refugee situation. The following chapter by Liesel Hermes and Christian Ludwig, "John Marsden's *Tomorrow, When the War Began* – How War Can Change Young People's Lives", then explores the learning potential of John Marsden's highly successful Australian young adult novel. It depicts the lives of a group of teenagers in times of war when their country is invaded by an alien force. The article offers four different approaches to discussing the novel in class, combining the novel's young adult themes and its references to Australian history and culture as well as post- and neo-colonial ideas. Yet another article which concerns itself with visions of utopia and dystopia is the contribution by Almudena Machado-Jiménez, "When Heroes Meet Orwell: From Dystopia to Utopia in the EFL Classroom". The author argues that, through extrapolation, dystopian fiction provides countless opportunities for students to gain a critical view of the world they live in.

Posthuman critical theory is increasingly gaining attention. The article by Martin Štefl, "The Human/Machine: Science Fiction as a Primer for Critical Thinking in ESL Teaching for Secondary Students" tackles exactly that issue by drawing our attention to the ability of science-fiction texts to question the distinction between the human and machine, bringing epistemological questions to the forefront of classroom discourse. The article illustrates how posthuman encounters through a variety of sf narratives, such as pieces of art and films, can motivate students to critically rethink public conceptualisations of what it means to be human.

The fantastic is in the centre of attention in the article by Katalin Schober, "Performing Possible Worlds – How to Foster Empathy with Fantastic Literature". Arguing that many students are familiar with fantastic writings in their mother tongue, she introduces us to a variety of fantastic texts for lower secondary learners, illustrating their language and literary learning potential which can especially be harnessed by using drama pedagogy techniques. The next contribution "From Androids to Alternate Histories: Integrating Philip K. Dick's Fiction into the EFL Classroom" by Klara Stephanie Szlezák is dedicated to the oeuvre of one of the most famous sf authors of our time: Philip K. Dick. Szlezák suggests a comparative approach for discussing Dick in the classroom, allowing students to explore both 'typical' science-fiction themes as well as how some of his major works have been adapted for the screen.

The following contributions do not primarily focus on literary pieces of sf but on the science-fiction film and TV industry. Sarah Nele Geiger's "Teaching the *Planet of the Apes* Franchise in the EFL Classroom" introduces the reader to the world of *Planet of the Apes*, based on the French novel of the same name by Pierre Boulle. The novel and films tackle a wide range of issues such as animal rights, the human condition, and identity. A mega franchise is also the focus of attention in the following contribution. In "'The idea of gender – it is offensive to my people.' – Developing Students' Gender Competence with *Star Trek*: *The Next Generation*" by Christian Ludwig and Nadja Heß, the potential of *Star Trek* for the English as a foreign language classroom is discussed, arguing that the series allows for discussing a cornucopia of social, political, and ethical issues such as women's and gay rights, death sentence, or euthanasia. The discrimination and violence against transgender people in a faraway star system is a case in point, elucidating how sf TV series cannot only be conducive to developing students' audio-visual competence but also their gender and minority rights awareness. "Yet Another 'Giant Leap for Mankind': Teaching *The Martian* and a Human Mission to Mars to Students in Upper Secondary Education" by Dennis Weißenfels explores the learning potential of Ridley Scott's highly acclaimed 2015 science-fiction film *The Martian*. The film provides a plethora of discussion opportunities from learning more about the history of Mars explorations over the science aspects of space travel to the psychological, ethical, and religious but also economic implications of human missions to Mars.

Dealing with the fantastic and the unknown also invites us as teachers to teach creative writing with our students and to explore how both alternative worlds and narratives can be developed. The article by Jonathan Shipley entitled "Dinosaurian Legacy: The Role of Reptilian Sentients in Science Fiction and Fantasy" tackles exactly that issue by drawing on the experience of a writer who indulges in saurian cultures in his own writing. The article reports on a creative writing project from his own advanced secondary class where he asked students to imagine and write about a threatening non-human alien race as well as a scary monster of nightmare. The last article of section two by Jürgen Wehrmann "Teaching the Form of Science Fiction: Introducing and Using Critical Terminology in Analytical, Intertextual and Creative Tasks" convincingly proposes to focus on formal elements and narrative strategies of science-fiction texts, arguing that going beyond discussing the content of works such as Suzanne Collins' *The Hunger Games* offers a more holistic access to the diverse themes of such texts.

Notes

1 Seed, David (2011). *Science Fiction: A Very Short Introduction*. Oxford: Oxford University Press, 1.

2 Heinlein, Robert A. (1969). "Science Fiction: Its Nature, Faults and Virtues." *The Science Fiction Novel: Imagination and Social Criticism*. Ed. Basil Davenport. Illinois: Advent, 6.

3 Kafka, Janet (1975). "Why Science Fiction?" *The English Journal* 64, 46-53, 46.

4 Grady, Joan B. (1979). "Science Fiction: The Future in the Classroom." *Reading Horizons: A Journal of Literacy and Language Arts* 19.3, 193-196, 194.

5 Shippey, T. A. (2002). "Science Fiction and Fantasy." *Classics of Science Fiction and Fantasy Literature*. Ed. Fiona Kelleghan. Pasadena: Salem Press, 1-12, 8.

6 Hunt, Peter (2001). "Introduction: Fantasy and Alternative Worlds." *Alternative Worlds in Fantasy Fiction*. By Peter Hunt and Millicent Lenz. London: Continuum, 1-41, 10.

7 Shippey (2002), 8.

8 Hume, Kathryn (1984). *Fantasy and Mimesis. Responses to Reality in Western Literature*. New York: Methuen, 21.

9 Gunn, James (1992). *Inside Science Fiction: Essays on Fantastic Literature*. San Bernardino, CA: R. Reginald De Borgo Press, 18.

10 Reid, Suzanne Elizabeth (1997). *Presenting Ursula K. Le Guin*. New York: Twayne Publishers, 8.

[11] Kelleghan, Fiona (2002). "Introduction." *Classics of Science Fiction and Fantasy Literature*. Ed. Fiona Kelleghan. Pasadena: Salem Press, xix-xxii, xix.

[12] 2019 ©Christian Ludwig.

[13] Gates, Pamela S., Susan B. Steffel, and Francis J. Molson (2003). "Introduction." *Fantasy Literature for Children and Young Adults*. Eds. Pamela S. Gates, Susan B. Steffel and Francis J. Molson. Lanham, Maryland: The Scarecrow Press, 2.

[14] Kelleghan (2002), xix.

[15] Ekman, Stefan (2018). "Entering a Fantasy World through Its Map." *Extrapolation* 59.1, 71-87, 73.

[16] Mathews, Richard (2002). *Fantasy: The Liberation of Imagination.* New York: Routledge, 1.

[17] *Ibid.,* 85. See also Ekman, Stefan (2013). *Here Be Dragons.* Middletown, CT: Wesleyan University Press.

[18] Gunn (1992), 13.

[19] For a more detailed overview of how the teaching of science fiction relates to its appreciation, see *ibid*., 9-29.

[20] Kincaid, Paul (2005). "On the Origins of Genre." *Speculations on Speculation*. Eds. James Gunn and Matthew Candelaria. Oxford: Scarecrow Press, 41-54, 49.

[21] Sawyer, Andy, and Peter Wright (eds.) (2011). *Teaching Science Fiction.* New York: Palgrave Macmillan and Allen, L. David (1975). *The Ballantine Teacher's Guide to Science Fiction.* New York: Ballantine.

[22] Fabrizi, Mark A. (ed.) (2016). *Fantasy Literature: Challenging Genres.* Rotterdam: Sense Publishers; Hellekson, Karen et al. (eds.) (2010). *Practicing Science Fiction: Critical Essays on Writing, Reading and Teaching the Genre.* Jefferson, NC: McFarland.

[23] Lohre, Angelika (1994). "Science Fiction Stories." *Der Fremdsprachliche Unterricht Englisch* 28, 18-24; *Der Fremdsprachliche Unterricht Englisch Fantasy* 151 (2018); *Praxis Englisch* 3 (2017): *Space and Science Fiction, Utopia and Dystopia*; Ludwig, Christian (2018). *Envisioning Other Worlds: Science Fiction and Dystopia.* Berlin: Cornelsen.

[24] "Introduction: Fabulous Kingdoms and Supernatural Dimensions." *The Guardian* 22 Jan. 2009: n. pag. Web. 8 Oct. 2019 <https://www.theguardian.com/books/2009/jan/22/1000-novels-fiction-fantasy-introduction>.

[25] Gates, Steffel and Molson (2003), 2.

[26] Rand, Charlette, and Zenobia Verner (1976). "It'll Never Happen." *English*, 65.4, 65-66, 66.

[27] Sawyer and Wright (2011), 1.

[28] Council of Europe (2001). *Common European Framework of Reference for Languages: Learning, Teaching, Assessment*. Strasbourg: Council of Europe.

[29] Barnes, Lawrie, and Chantelle van Heerden (2008). "Virtual Languages in Science Fiction and Fantasy Literature." *Language Matters. Studies in the Languages of Africa* 37.1, 102-117.

[30] Jamison, Anne (2013). "Why Fic?" Fic. Why Fanfiction Is Taking Over the World. Ed. Anne Jamison. Dallas: Smart Pop, 17-24, 17.

[31] Florio-Hansen, Inez De (2018). *Teaching and Learning English in the Digital Age*. Paderborn: UTB.

[32] Falk, Simon (2019). *Mobile-Assisted Language Learning: Eine empirische Untersuchung zum Einsatz digitaler mobiler Endgeräte im Kontext des Fremdsprachenunterrichts*. Tübingen: Narr.

[33] Sanford, K., and L. Madill (2006). "Resistance Through Video Game Play: It's a Boy Thing." *Canadian Journal of Education* 29.1, 287-306, 294.

[34] Murray, Liam, and John Maher (2011). "The Role of Fantasy in Videogames: A Reappraisal." *Eludamos. Journal for Computer Game Culture* 5.1, 45-57.

[35] Prensky, Marc (2001). *Digital Game-Based Learning*. New York: McGraw Hill Companies.

[36] Poek, Bert Van (2017). "Critical Perspectives on the Collaborative Learning Potential of Digital Game-Based Learning in the Foreign Language Classroom." *Collaborative Learning and New Media*. Eds. Christian Ludwig and Kris Van de Poel. Frankfurt a. M.: Lang, 241-257.

[37] Ludwig, Christian (2020). "'The Future is Now' – Virtual Reality im Englischunterricht." *Englischunterricht in einer digitalisierten Gesellschaft*. Eds. Judith Bündgens-Kosten and Peter Schildhauer. Weinheim: Beltz Juventa, forthcoming.

[38] DeBoer, George E. (2000). "Scientific literacy: Another Look at Its Historical and Contemporary Meanings and Its Relationship to Science Education Reform." *Journal of Research in Science Teaching* 37.6, 582–601, 592.

Bibliography

Primary Texts

Asimov, Isaac (1991[1976]). "The Bicentennial Man." *Robot Visions*. New York: Byron Preiss Visual Publications, 245-290.

Atwood, Margaret (1998[1985]). *The Handmaid's Tale*. New York: Anchor.

Carroll, Lewis (2012[1865]). *Alice's Adventures in Wonderland.* London: Penguin.

Shelley, Mary (1994[1818]). *Frankenstein or, The Modern Prometheus*. New York: Penguin.

Star Wars. Creator George Lucas. 1977. 20th Century Fox.

Wells, Herbert George (2009[1895]). *The Time Machine*. Ed. Stephen Arata. New York: Norton.

Wells, Herbert George (2005[1898]). *The War of the Worlds*. New York: HarperCollins.

Secondary Literature

Allen, L. David (1975). *The Ballantine Teacher's Guide to Science Fiction.* New York: Del Rey.

Barnes, Lawrie, and Chantelle van Heerden, (2008). "Virtual Languages in Science Fiction and Fantasy Literature." *Language Matters. Studies in the Languages of Africa* 37.1, 102-117.

Council of Europe (2001). *Common European Framework of Reference for Languages: Learning, Teaching, Assessment*. Strasbourg: Council of Europe.

DeBoer, George E. (2000). "Scientific Literacy: Another Look at Its Historical and Contemporary Meanings and Its Relationship to Science Education Reform." *Journal of Research in Science Teaching* 37.6, 582–601, 592.

Ekman, Stefan (2013). *Here Be Dragons.* Middletown, CT: Wesleyan University Press.

--- (2018). "Entering a Fantasy World through Its Map." *Extrapolation* 59.1, 71-87.

Fabrizi, Mark A. (ed.) (2016). *Fantasy Literature: Challenging Genres*. Rotterdam: Sense Publishers.

Falk, Simon (2019). *Mobile-Assisted Language Learning: Eine empirische Untersuchung zum Einsatz digitaler mobiler Endgeräte im Kontext des Fremdsprachenunterrichts*. Tübingen: Narr.

Florio-Hansen, Inez De (2018). *Teaching and Learning English in the Digital Age*. Paderborn: UTB.

Der Fremdsprachliche Unterricht Englisch 151 (2018). *Fantasy.*

Gates, Pamela S., Susan B. Steffel and Francis J. Molson (2003). "Introduction." *Fantasy Literature for Children and Young Adults*. Eds. Pamela S. Gates, Susan B. Steffel and Francis J. Molson. Lanham, Maryland: The Scarecrow Press.

Grady, Joan B. (1979). "Science Fiction: The Future in the Classroom." *Reading Horizons: A Journal of Literacy and Language Arts* 19.3, 193-196.

Gunn, James (1992). *Inside Science Fiction: Essays on Fantastic Literature.* San Bernardino, CA: R. Reginald De Borgo Press.

Heinlein, Robert A. (1969). "Science Fiction: Its Nature, Faults and Virtues." *The Science Fiction Novel: Imagination and Social Criticism*. Ed. Basil Davenport. Illinois: Advent, 6.

Hellekson, Karen et al. (eds.) (2010). *Practicing Science Fiction: Critical Essays on Writing, Reading and Teaching the Genre*. Jefferson, NC: McFarland.

Hume, Kathryn (1984). *Fantasy and Mimesis. Responses to Reality in Western Literature*. New York: Methuen.

Hunt, Peter (2001). "Introduction: Fantasy and Alternative Worlds." *Alternative Worlds in Fantasy Fiction.* By Peter Hunt and Millicent Lenz. London: Continuum, 1-41.

"Introduction: Fabulous kingdoms and supernatural dimensions." *The Guardian* 22 Jan. 2009: n.pag. Web. 8 Oct. 2019 <https://www.theguardian.com/books /2009/jan/22/1000-novels-fiction-fantasy-introduction>.

Jamieson, Anne (2013). "Why Fic?" *Fic. Why Fanfiction Is Taking Over the World.* Ed. Anne Jamieson. Dallas: Smart Pop, 17-24.

Kafka, Janet (1975). "Why Science Fiction?" *The English Journal* 64, 46-53.

Kelleghan, Fiona (2002). "Introduction." *Classics of Science Fiction and Fantasy Literature*. Ed. Fiona Kelleghan. Pasadena: Salem Press, xix-xxii.

Kincaid, Paul (2005). "On the Origins of Genre." *Speculations on Speculation*. Eds. James Gunn and Matthew Candelaria,. Oxford: Scarecrow Press, 41-54.

Lohre, Angelika (1994). "Science Fiction Stories." *Der Fremdsprachliche Unterricht Englisch* 28, 18-24.

Ludwig, Christian (2018). *Envisioning Other Worlds: Science Fiction and Dystopia.* Berlin: Cornelsen.

--- (2020). "'The Future Is Now' – Virtual Reality im Englischunterricht. *Englischunterricht in einer digitalisierten Gesellschaft*." Eds. Judith

Bündgens-Kosten and Peter Schildhauer. Weinheim: Beltz Juventa, forthcoming.

Mathews, Richard (2002). *Fantasy: The Liberation of Imagination.* New York: Routledge.

Murray, Liam, and John Maher (2011). "The Role of Fantasy in Videogames: A Reappraisal." *Eludamos. Journal for Computer Game Culture* 5.1, 45-57.

Poek, Bert Van (2017). "Critical Perspectives on the Collaborative Learning Potential of Digital Game-Based Learning in the Foreign Language Classroom." *Collaborative Learning and New Media*. Eds. Christian Ludwig and Kris Van de Poel. Frankfurt a. M.: Lang, 241-257.

Praxis Englisch 3 (2017). *Space and Science Fiction, Utopia and Dystopia.*

Prensky, Marc (2001). *Digital Game-Based Learning*. New York: McGraw Hill Companies.

Rand, Charlette, and Zenobia Verner (1976). "It'll Never Happen." *English Journal* 65.4, 65-66.

Reid, Suzanne Elizabeth (1997). *Presenting Ursula K. Le Guin.* New York: Twayne Publishers.

Sanford, K., and L. Madill (2006). "Resistance Through Video Game Play: It's a Boy Thing." *Canadian Journal of Education* 29.1, 287-306, 294.

Seed, David (2011). *Science Fiction: A Very Short Introduction*. Oxford: Oxford University Press.

Shippey, T. A. (2002). "Science Fiction and Fantasy." *Classics of Science Fiction and Fantasy Literature*. Ed. Fiona Kelleghan. Pasadena: Salem Press, 1-12.

Grit Alter (Regensburg)

Of Megamag Mallet and Galactic Goggles: Science-Fiction Picturebooks in the Primary EFL Classroom

1. Introduction

This contribution explores science-fiction (SF) picturebooks for young readers to unfold the potential this seemingly unusual combination of genre and book format presents for English language teaching (ELT). Similar to science-fiction novels for adults, science-fiction picturebooks look back on a long tradition. Yet, one aspect that has been criticized in view of these publications is the low percentage of female protagonists within such texts for young readers. Hence, Underwood and Hunt's picturebook *Interstellar Cinderella*[1] (2015) takes center stage in this essay. This galactic adaptation of the Brothers Grimm's *Cinderella* fairy tale is framed in a fairy world and society which still contains mean step-mothers, jealous step-sisters, and a lonesome prince. However, it reverses and transcends the traditional fairy tale role of the girl in a beautiful dress and crown who merely accompanies and decorates the prince. Instead, Cinderella takes on the active role of a rocket engineer who finds herself at the court of the prince, yet, and by her own choice, as his chief mechanic. Dressed in a work suit and wearing galactic goggles, she refuses to become his wife and rather applies her megamag mallet to repair rockets.

Babette Cole's *Princess Smartypants* (1997) and Deborah Underwood's *Part-time Princess* (2013) are but two similar texts that reverse traditional gender roles in fairy tale texts. The general potential of such texts lies with offering (young) readers a different image of a princess who exerts agency based on her free will, skills and competences, and strong sense of self. Reading and reflecting such texts invites the audience to critically perceive gender roles in further literary and non-fiction texts and domains such as advertisements, their communities, and society as a whole. *Interstellar Cinderella* is specific in so far as it additionally occupies a space which has commonly been associated with males, i.e., male scientists and explorers. In terms of ELT, the picturebook can be used to create imaginative classrooms which foster literary literacy by employing cooperative and collaborative approaches and creative writing projects.

This introduction is followed by general insights into the genre of science fiction. Two aspects will be of particular importance: a) science fiction and gender, and b) science fiction for children. Both aspects lay the foundation for a detailed discussion of the primary text *Interstellar Cinderella*. The final part suggests ideas of how this science-fiction picturebook can be implemented in primary ELT. It will be argued that a galactic adaptation of a fairy tale such as *Interstellar Cinderella* lends itself to not only introduce science fiction as a genre to primary ELT, but that the way it overcomes traditional gender roles offers important role models needed in a children's cultural world in which women too often subordinate themselves to or are subordinated by men.

2. Science-Fiction Picturebooks

Any attempt to define the genre of SF leads to complex debates. In their elaborations of the subject, Baker and Roberts refer to various scholars and authors of SF who have tried to do so but could not establish a common understanding of this genre. The genre SF "resists easy definition"[2] because of its complexity, hybridity, and its "sub-generic diversity".[3] According to Suvin's seminal definition, SF is a "literary genre whose necessary and sufficient conditions are the presence and interaction of estrangement and cognition, and whose main formal device is an imaginative framework alternative to the author's empirical environment".[4] There are certain elements of newness or points of difference which create these other worlds and "differentiate the world portrayed in science fiction from the world we recognise around us".[5] Suvin labels this point of difference a novum, which is "grounded in a discourse of possibility […] and which renders the difference a *material* rather than just a conceptual or imaginative one".[6] In science fiction, such a novum does not necessarily have to be science or technology, but can also be "something material, such as a spaceship, a time machine or a communications device; or it might be something conceptual, such as a new conception of gender or consciousness". [7] Even though this understanding of SF is often used as a foundation for further elaborations on the genre, SF cannot be limited to this, as the mere variety of texts and the many sub-genres indicate. In the context of this essay, however, it shall suffice to direct interested readers to Baker's and Roberts' publications.

Similar to the difficulty of defining SF for older readers, it is also challenging to establish an all-embracing definition of science-fiction picturebooks. Still, children should know basic characteristics of science fiction, particularly when such texts are read in ELT. Certainly, SF for children differs from SF for a teenage and adult audience. Hence as Mendlesohn observes, some of children's SF "is science fiction only by courtesy. Aliens and robots are reduced to the level of icon and take the place of fairies, elves and monsters". [8] Simultaneously, "[c]hildren's picture books and science fiction have at their heart something in common; they aim to encourage the reader to explore the universe",[9] or at least their own worlds through bottomless imagination and creativity. This indicates that SF is closely related to fantasy in that both can contain elements of each other, be it that "children's fantasy contains SF elements" or that "children's SF is written with a disregard for scientific accuracy [...], which effectively renders it fantasy".[10]

Moreover, I concur with Von Der Lohe who argues that such a definition should then also be child friendly,[11] for which one could turn to children's dictionaries and lexica. For example, kids.wordsmyth.com, an online dictionary for children that provides child-oriented explanations, defines science fiction as "fiction in which scientific findings, capabilities, or speculations provide an essential basis for the imagined events"; [12] learnersdictionary.com offers "stories about how people and societies are affected by imaginary scientific developments in the future"[13] as the entry for science fiction.

In her critical essay "A World of Their Own: Exploring the Spectrum of Science Fiction Elements in Children's Picture Books", Von Der Lohe points out that it is worthwhile to "recognize and systematically archive SF-themed picture books in order to facilitate further exploration of this scholarly terra incognita".[14] Based on her extensive research, she differentiates science-fiction picturebooks into categories such as fantasy SF,[15] anthropomorphic SF,[16] fairy tale SF,[17] marvelous machinery, [18] plausible SF, [19] imagination SF, [20] informational SF, [21] and realistic SF[22] as well as blurred boundaries[23] for texts which do not fit into a single category.

Interstellar Cinderella, the picturebook that takes center stage in this essay, not only invites readers to travel to space and explore marvelous robots, rockets, and tools, but to also meet a powerful and self-reliant female protagonist. One of the most revealing and praiseworthy plot twists in this fairy tale adaptation is its reversal of gender roles. While this may come as a surprise in a galactic adaptation of a fairy tale, such empowerments of female protagonists are quite common in SF. In fact, feminist SF has been established as a separate sub-genre and field of academic research. It mainly focuses on questions of social issues and how society constructs gender roles, power of and opportunities for women and men to participate equally in social life. Because SF as a form of speculative fiction allows us to consider how else the world may be, this also includes considering how else the world could be in terms of shifted gender roles and the distribution of power among different genders. A notable example is Ursula K. Le Guin's *The Left Hand of Darkness* (1969), in which the society is set on a planet on which the inhabitants have no fixed gender.[24]

Studies such as McCabe's "Gender in Twentieth-Century Children's Books" (2011)[25] reveal that there has been a strong imbalance of gender representation in picturebooks with male characters far outnumbering female characters. Weitzmann's study (as early as 1972) reveals that this is in so far problematic, as picturebooks "play an important role in early sex-role socialization because they are a vehicle for the presentation of societal values to the young child"[26] and thus evoke specific schemes and scripts of gendered behavior:

> Through books, children learn about the world outside of their immediate environment: they learn about what other boys and girls do, say, and feel; they learn what is right and wrong; and they learn what is expected of children their age. In addition, books provide children role models - images of what they can and should be like when they grow up.[27]

The extensive research by scholars such as Mary Ritchie Key,[28] John Stephens,[29] and Karen Coats[30] confirms that male characters, be it as protagonists, on covers, in illustrations, or even as animals, far outnumber female characters. As their studies show, male roles are more active and feature characters traits such as cleverness, adventure, and independence;

males are transgressive, think analytically, and earn money. Compared to that, females are onlookers, victims, need help to achieve their goals, are obedient, and emotional. As gender identity and gender constancy emerge before children are six years of age,[31] it is essential to offer young boys and girls reading material in which they can identify with a variety of ways in which gender can be performed.

Thus, picturebooks such as *Part-time Princess* (2013)[32] or *Princess Smartypants* (1997)[33] seem to pay tribute to the need for female protagonists who are as strong, confident, and self-reliant as their male counterparts. These adaptations of traditional fairy tales reverse the traditional role of the female protagonist. When her parents invite several suitors as potential husbands, Smartypants sets challenging tasks for them, none of which can be solved by any of the princes. Instead of marrying one of them, she prefers her rather unusual pets, a toad for example, and remains single.

3. *Interstellar Cinderella*

In view of Von Der Lohe's categorization of SF picturebooks mentioned above, *Interstellar Cinderella* fits into the category of fairy tale SF. Von Der Lohe identifies these texts as reexaminations of "fairy tales by using science fiction".[34] In the sample text discussed here, Underwood transfers the Brothers Grimm's "Cinderella" (1812) to intergalactic space. The following paragraphs analyze this adaptation in terms of the plot, protagonists, and the moral at the end of the picturebook. As the way in which *Interstellar Cinderella* performs gender differs decisively from the traditional fairy tale, gender will be analyzed in more detail in view of how Cinderella develops agency and voice.

The plot of the picturebook follows the main idea of the Brothers Grimm's text: Cinderella lives with her step-mother and step-sisters. When invited to the prince's ball, they take off without her. Despite an unsolvable task, she still manages to go to the ball, she meets the prince, and he selects her as his future wife. The informed reader recognizes that this short summary omits certain details that are decisive for the plot. This is not done accidentally, as the similarities already stop here. The book does not reveal that Cinderella is generally treated as a servant rather than a family member, there is no indication of a father-figure who shows affection to the girl, and, most importantly, there is no happy marriage in the end. As will be argued, the ending is still happy, albeit re-written to a feminist turn.

Even though the plot in this science fiction adaptation is reduced to specific elements, it is also extended. This regards Cinderella's positioning within the story and the self-confident twist at the end. The first opening[35] of the text introduces the reader to Cinderella, sitting outside in a desert-like environment with small volcanic craters, a spaceship structure in the background, and star formations in the sky depicting spaceships. Dressed in a plain purple dress, a green apron, and work gloves, she holds a screw-wrench in her hand, dreaming of "fixing fancy rockets",[36] a tool box right beside her. She is accompanied by Murgatroyd, a mouse, whose tail is a power cord ending in a plug, thus indicating that it is a robot. While she does chores such as fixing "the robot dishwashers and zoombrooms",[37] it does not seem as if she is forced to do this. Even so, the reader can draw conclusions about her happiness from the design of the respective page. It reveals a part of the house; one-third of the page is dedicated to a staircase with furniture and decorations in the background. This part is in dark green, blue, and red tones and contains the verbal text which refers to the chores for which Cinderella is responsible. The main part of this opening shows the space underneath the staircase. Brightly illuminated by a bulb on the robot mouse's back, the room contains Cinderella's bed, a lamp, a space poster on the wall, and a few books. The girl sits there and "stud[ies] ship repair".[38] Based on the rather different color code of warm orange, yellow, red, purple, and blue tones and Cinderella's content facial expression, one could infer that this is where she is happy. The placement of the verbal text supports such a reading as the chores are placed in the dark part of the house, i.e., where the family lives, and the text revealing Cinderella's private activity is placed in the part of the page that shows her room. Even when the verbal text indicates that the private reading is done late at night, the chores are not contextualized in any time of the day, thus limiting an interpretation as to when these are done.

Similar to the original story, Cinderella is excluded from the family's outing to meet the prince and needs to rely on help to finally get there. Here, it is the prince's "Royal Space Parade"[39] to which the family is invited. Cinderella's stepmother seems to be sorry that the girl cannot join them as there would not be enough space in the ship. She may still come, though, if she manages to repair another spaceship. Yet, the stepmother's facial expression as well as the fact that they take Cinderella's tool box with them[40] show that she is not that sorry after all. Whereas in the original story, pigeons help Cinderella to get to the ball, Murgatroyd "sen[ds] out a cosmic SOS".[41] Murgatroyd's cosmic SOS is answered by a fairy godrobot who provides Cinderella with new tools and a space suit in atomic blue and decorated with jewels.[42] She also restricts Cinderella's time frame for joining the space parade until midnight; then, the power gem will no longer work and her ship no longer fly. The girl repairs the ship and takes off to join the parade.

The remaining plot is a twist to the story that transcends the common gendered positioning of a (future) princess in fairy tales. From the outset of the picturebook, Cinderella's focus is on spaceships and she is interested in repairing them. It thus seems unlikely that her desire to join the parade stems from meeting the prince. The plot evades the construction of traditional gender roles common in fairy tales where a girl longs for royal Mr. Right solely to escape poverty and enter the seemingly affluent lifestyle in a castle, and the girl being picked by the prince solely based on her looks. Compared to superficially reducing character traits to beauty, *Interstellar Cinderella* equips the girl with a strong interest in technology and with agency. This is also revealed when she arrives at the parade during which "each starship made her swoon".[43]

There is a short incident where the plot seems to fall back on the traditional princess-meets-prince story when the prince's ship arrives and Cinderella's "heart was filled with yearning".[44] However, the verbal text is quick to unveil that this yearning is connected to the "ship of Cinderella's dreams!"[45] Her passion for and know-how of repairing spaceships will soon be decisive because the prince's spaceship catches fire. As his "chief mechanic quit!",[46] Cinderella uses her sonic socket wrench to repair it, which earns her an invitation to the "Gravity-Free Ball" at "Galactic Hall".[47] She does join, but instead of dancing together, Cinderella and the prince talk about rocket ships and get to know each other by discovering mutual interests rather than admiring each other's outward appearance. Yet, similar to the original story, time flies and Cinderella's power gem and spacesuit will soon vanish. She takes off in a hurry and the prince forgets to ask how to remain in touch. Still, a happy end is on the horizon as she forgets her socket wrench, which then becomes the prince's tool to find her. He sets out through outer space and searches for her, recognizing that he has not really seen her face behind her space goggles and the helmet. Visiting houses and seeking the girl who can repair a spaceship with the tool, he also arrives at Cinderella's home. While Cinderella's step-sisters try their best – and fail –, Cinderella herself is trapped in the attic where her step-mother tied her with space rope. Again, she can rely on the help of Murgatroyd, who bites through the rope. As the prince has already taken off from the house, she quickly repairs and puts on a jet pack and flies after him.[48] She catches up with him, says that the wrench belongs to her, and the prince – surprise – asks her to be his wife.

Yet – and this is the main adaptation to the original fairy tale – throughout the story, Cinderella has been established as a self-confident girl who has her own will and a strong interest in tools and technology. Thus, her answer may come as a surprise for readers who are attached to the original happy ending. For those who are aware of the gender critical adaptation of *Interstellar Cinderella,* her answer is an obvious conclusion: "I'm far too young for marriage, but I'll be your chief mechanic!"[49] In the final opening, Cinderella is dressed in a work suit, sits on the edge of a broken spaceship, and the prince hands her the tools she needs. The background displays a variety of ships, steered by diverse creatures. This is where she wants to be, "amid a fleet of sparkling ships", allowing her to voice the last words of the picturebook "My stars! Dreams do come true!"[50] Cinderella establishes herself as a proud and self-confident young woman and, thus, it is also her voice that occupies the final lines of the book. Her competences set her apart from others, not her beauty (which does not mean that she is not pretty, but whether or not is just not important). It is not only her verbal act, but also her outward appearance as a professional mechanic that contribute to her agency.

Similarly, the visual design of the picturebook transcends the image of a pink and glittery princess so often found in children's books. The images in *Interstellar Cinderella* are mainly held in earthy tones of shades of brown, red, blue, and green; screaming bright pinks, purples, or further hyper-friendly colors are not employed. Even so, Cinderella's space suit does sparkle, but in muted tones of blue which allow her to appear more serious, self-confident, and less confined to established gender roles. The shape of her body adds to the emancipatory tone of the picturebook in that she is not super skinny, but healthy and strong, which is necessary in order to work on spaceships. When she wears the spacesuit and her helmet, these items are added to her body shape rather than substituting for it. Compared to other science-fiction picturebooks,[51] this also adds to the scientific accuracy of the text.

The alternate rhyme scheme of the verbal text adds a playful tone to the story. At times, this even appears to be cheeky, for example, when the stepsisters try to repair the spaceship:

> He gave the sonic socket wrench
> to one, then to the other.
> Alas, they couldn't fix the ship
> (and neither could their mother).[52]

This fresh tone is also present at the end of the picturebook when Cinderella refuses to marry the prince and employs a smart argumentation about her age and professional career to take a stand.

4. *Interstellar Cinderella* in the EFL Classroom

As the analysis above reveals, the galactic adaptation of Cinderella does not revolve around the typical princess-story in which an almost voiceless young girl in a fancy dress is looking for a husband and which focuses on superficial beauty. In this picturebook, merit and competences as well as intellect and following one's own dreams independent of patriarchal world views take center stage.

Interstellar Cinderella carries potential for advanced learners at the upper secondary school level. They could engage in a political and gendered critique of how fairy tales and society construct female protagonists in literary texts and beyond. This could then be extended to include popular culture and the children's toys industry, which is strongly geared towards creating and pleasing girls' constructed desire to be princesses. Toy stores very often differentiate between a girl's and a boy's section, offering fluffy and ready-made toys to play with for girls, while boys' shelves contain toys for which constructing the toy itself is part of the game.[53]

This gender debate can be introduced to the advanced English classroom when students analyze the prevalent discourse in traditional Disney princess movies in which the princesses are obedient and pretty daughters who do what fathers tell them, who may have dreams of their own but forget about these as soon as a handsome prince comes along. They marry and, despite their dream of freedom, are caught in the control and demands of their husbands. A prototypical example is Disney's version of *The Little Mermaid*, in which Arielle suffers from her father's control over her every move but is willing to give up the one feature that sets her apart from others, her voice, to marry a man she hardly knows (1989, based on Hans-Christian Andersen's fairy tale *The Little Mermaid*, 1837). Even so, more recent movies such as *Brave* (2012) introduce female figures who are more successful in balancing a self-confident appearance and strong will with caring and empathic traits.[54]

Such issues of gender inequality and patriarchal oppression within stories that are often named after the princess but leave all power to the male counterparts can very well be topical in advanced ELT. In this context, advanced students may read *Interstellar Cinderella* as a counter narrative and delineate how Underwood equips Cinderella with voice and agency, for example, based on a comparison to Cinderella picturebooks that are closer to the Brothers Grimm's version of the fairy tale.

Yet, as the book is a picturebook mainly intended for younger learners, the following section introduces teaching ideas for the age group of eight to twelve-year-olds and a language level of A1 and A1+ according to the *Companion Volume* to the *Common European Framework*.[55]

4.1. *Interstellar Cinderella* in the EFL Primary Classroom

The primary EFL classroom mainly focuses on listening and speaking skills embedded in activating and playful approaches to language learning (rhyme, song, role play) and storytelling.[56] These can also be productively employed in the teaching suggestions below. Rather than offering a strict lesson plan teachers should follow, the activities suggested here unfold the huge potential of using the picturebook with young learners and are divided into the common three-step approach of pre-, while-, and post activities. The ideas are far from exhaustive but offer creative, process-, and product-oriented suggestions that teachers may adjust to their own learner groups and extend with their own ideas.

4.1.1. Pre-activity I: The Original Children's Tale

- The teacher asks the learners whether they know any fairy tales, explains the term 'fairy tale' by offering images of examples and introduces the phrase 'once upon a time' as a central marker of these texts.
- The teacher draws the learners' attention to the traditional Cinderella and asks whether they know this fairy tale. In the plenum, teacher and learners retell the fairy tale together, supported with picture cards showing central elements of the plot; important words and phrases are collected on the blackboard.
- Learners receive a stack of cards showing images of the common Cinderella story and, based on the prior activity, put the cards into the correct order and match these with simple phrases and sentences referring to the content of the images. Based on this, they retell the story in pairs or small groups.
- The teacher may ask learners whether they know any other versions of this tale, i.e., from other cultural backgrounds. Learners may use German for this reflection.

These tasks elicit learners' pre-knowledge and prepare them for the topic and language items they will encounter in the following. The learners are familiarized with the common children's version of Cinderella and understand central phrases of the fairy tale.

4.1.2. Pre-Activity II: Introducing the Picturebook

- The teacher shares the cover of the picturebook *Interstellar Cinderella* with the class and asks for clarifications of the term 'interstellar' which the learners are able to derive from the images. The learners elicit that this Cinderella-story is set in space. By talking about the image, teacher and learners clarify lexis to talk about the cover (for example, space, stars, planets, tool, robot mouse).
- The teacher shows an image of a familiar Cinderella (for example, Disney) and Interstellar Cinderella. The learners compare both, supported by the teacher, who offers terms and phrases on cards, which learners attach to the matching image (white vs. blue and green,

dress vs. suit of a mechanic, long blond hair vs. pink hair, crown vs. tools and goggles).

- The teacher shares the peritext with the learners and asks them to find names for the tools and their function. This could also be done as a matching task or using German or a first language respectively. This multilingual approach could lead to creative reformulations and multilingual inventions of new terms for these imagined tools.
- Based on these reflections, learners share ideas about how the plot of this *Interstellar Cinderella* story could develop. In order to support this, the teacher could provide different images of possible endings of the story, or learners could draw these themselves and formulate a single sentence about the content.

These tasks familiarize learners with a different version of Cinderella and invite them to compare this new Cinderella with the one they may know. By pointing out differences between both, they become aware of the modern tone of this picturebook. Engaging with the tools shown in the peritext of the book appeals to their imagination and focuses the galactic setting. Learners hypothesize how the story could unfold.

4.1.3. While Activities: Reading the Book Together

- The teacher reads the book out loud. The reading process can be interrupted to clarify the meaning of terms and the development of the plot, mainly by sharing the illustrations.
- While reading the picturebook out loud, the teacher selects decisive points in the plot and asks the learners how they think the story continues, for example, when the stepmother and stepsister leave for the ball and take Cinderella's tool kit with them or when the prince asks Cinderella to marry him. In case such hypothesizing was implemented during the pre-phase, this needs to be adjusted accordingly. The teacher should mention again that this is a different Cinderella story and that it may be very different from the original texts to appeal to the learners to think outside the common fairy tale box and activate their imagination.
- The teacher reads out the book again, this time asking students to fill in the rhyme words at the end of a stanza. As a scaffold, the respective words could be offered on the blackboard (maybe not in the correct order) or given on cards which students need to attach to the correct

rhyme. This can also be done as pair work when learners have adapted copies of the pages.

- The learners reflect on the end of the book, for example, whether they think Cinderella is happy with her decision or which adventures the two of them will have in the future.
- In case learners hypothesized about the end of the book, they can now compare their own ideas and drawings to the actual end of the book. They can reflect how their own ideas differ from the original and evaluate which ending they like better and why.

With these tasks, the learners meet a different kind of Cinderella. They engage in a shift of gender representation and recognize that marrying a prince is only one option for Cinderella to be happy. In the further reflection of the book (and depending on whether this was implemented in the pre-phase or not), teacher and learners can continue the comparison of the original Cinderella and Interstellar Cinderella in terms of their clothes, the colors, and what sets them apart from others. Such rather basic thoughts allow introducing a gender critical perspective already on a primary school level. While learners can be asked which image of Cinderella they like better, it may conceptually be too demanding to have learners employ a gender critical perspective for their argumentation.

4.1.4. Post Activities

The learners

- Practice reading the book with expression out loud, for example, in groups or with the whole class with every student reading a few lines. This could also be part of a picturebook performance within the class or for the school.
- Create a role play based on the book, either the whole book in groups or selected scenes for each group.
- Draw other galactic tools and explain their function.
- Invent robots which improve house- or schoolwork (for example, a homework machine that does homework or a handwriting machine). They draw a picture and present their creations in front of the group, or collect them in a folder or booklet.
- Re-write and illustrate another fairy tale in space (for example, "Intergalactic Red-Riding Hood").

These activities invite students to creatively work with *Interstellar Cinderella* and to transfer their experiences with this adaptation of a fairy tale to other fairy tales with which they are familiar. Designing other tools, machines, or robots allows them to creatively engage with the genre of science fiction even when the term as such may only play a minor role.

4.2. Holistic Competence Orientation

In general, these teaching ideas create a primary ELT classroom that employs pair and group work in which learners need to cooperate and collaborate to achieve a common goal. Listening to this picturebook, reading and retelling it together, the learners develop listening, speaking, and reading competences and develop an awareness of certain gender roles implemented in children's culture, albeit, and taking the learners' age into consideration, on a rather fundamental level. As the teaching ideas involve pair and group work and employ learners' imagination, these implicitly differentiate the learning process and allow learners to contribute to the learning process and product according to their interests and abilities. Having young learners reflect on the positioning of male and female protagonists and having them pay attention to the way in which both are dressed or the color code employed to represent them, also in comparison with other fairy tales they know, can function as a first step toward developing literary literacy.[57] Despite their young age and basic language competences and when provided with respective scaffolding, even young learners can be enabled to compare the representation of princesses in visual texts and thus discover intertextual references or reflect on the color coding of respective depictions and thus develop aesthetic and stylistic competences.

5. Conclusion

The discussion of *Interstellar Cinderella* and the teaching suggestions for the EFL primary classroom reveal that this picturebook can offer an enjoyable reading experience for young learners. Beyond reading for pleasure, it can be used to introduce science fiction and to stimulate a critical engagement with traditional gender roles. Even though the overall idea of this SF picturebook text may not be very original – spaceships and space travel are common *nova* in SF texts –, it illustrates how humans could live in space, inhabiting remote planets, living in space houses, and using spaceships and rockets for transport. While not all the details may be logical (for example, Cinderella's house from the inside and the outside), the picturebook picks up on actual physics, in that the protagonists need spacesuits and helmets when outside in space, and in that it distinguishes between gravity and weightlessness.

Apart from prevalent science fiction features, *Interstellar Cinderella* adds to the gender critical discourse and can be read as a gender sensitive answer to the image of princesses established by writers such as the Brothers Grimm and Hans-Christian Anderson as well as respective film adaptations by Disney and Pixar. By giving Cinderella a voice and ownership of her decisions, Underwood creates a self-confident female heroine who refuses to marry and transform into the role of a princess who merely decorates her prince. Rather than subordinating her needs and desires to his gaze, Interstellar Cinderella bases her future on her competences. Thus, in comparison to former fairy tales, the picturebook disrupts gender schemas as readers are provoked to refresh and restructure their expectation of a princess and script of a fairy tale. The schema of a princess is changed as princesses do not have to marry in order to be happy or wear a glamorous dress to be pretty. *Interstellar Cinderella* redefines gender roles and gender identities still prevalent in most princess stories, despite slight changes.[58] Mechanisms of reducing female protagonists to silent roles and superficial beauty as in *The Little Mermaid* (for example, Disney 1989) or *Sleeping Beauty* (for example, Disney 1959), are here transcended by repositioning the female protagonist and the prince to spaces both are able to define for themselves. The prince is not given the power to decide Cinderella's fate. He needs to find another princess if he wishes to get married. Underwood's feminist adaptation is successful in introducing a female protagonist who pursues her happiness beyond marriage and beauty, but with a focus on her skills, competences, and self-esteem.

Notes

1 Underwood, Deborah, and Meg Hunt (2015). *Interstellar Cinderella.* San Francisco: Chronicle Books LLC.

2 Roberts, Adam (2000). *Science Fiction*. New York: Routledge, 1.

3 Baker, Brian (2014). *Science Fiction*. London: Palgrave, 3.

4 Suvin in Roberts (2000), 7.

5 Roberts (2000), 6.

6 *Ibid*., 7 (emphasis in the original).

7 Roberts, Adam (2005). *History of Science Fiction*. New York: Palgrave, 1.

8 Mendlesohn in Von Der Lohe, Amanda R. (2013). "A World of Their Own: Exploring the Spectrum of Science Fiction Elements in Children's Picture Books." *The Eaton Journal of Archival Research in Science Fiction* 1.2, 96-117, 98.

9 Von Der Lohe (2013), 108.

10 Nicholls in Von Der Lohe (2013), 98.

11 Von Der Lohe (2013), 98.

12 "Science Fiction." Def. *Kids Wordsmyth* (n.d.). Web. 10 March 2019 <https://kids.wordsmyth.net/we/?ent=science+fiction>.

13 "Science Fiction." Def. *Merriam-Webster Learner's Dictionary* (n.d.). Web. 10 March 2019 <http://learnersdictionary.com/definition/science%20 fiction>.

14 Von Der Lohe (2013), 96.

15 *Ibid*., 98.

16 *Ibid*., 99.

17 *Ibid*., 101.

18 *Ibid*., 103.

19 *Ibid*., 104.

20 *Ibid*., 105.

21 *Ibid*., 107.

22 *Ibid*., 108.

23 *Ibid*., 102.

24 Cf. Shipley, Elizabeth (2007). "Science Fiction of Other-Genderedness in the EFL Classroom." *Gender Studies and Foreign Language Teaching.* Eds. Helene Decke-Cornill and Laurenz Volkmann. Narr: Tübingen, 227-242.

25 McCabe, Janice et al. (2011). "Gender in Twentieth-Century Children's Books: Patterns of Disparity in Titles and Central Characters." *Gender & Society* 25.2, 197-226.

26 Weitzmann in Coats, Karen (2018). "Gender in Picturebooks." *Routledge Companion to Picturebooks*. Ed. Bettina Kümmerling-Meibauer. Routledge: New York, 119-127, 120.

27 *Ibid.,* 120-121.

28 Key, Mary Richtie (1971). "The Role of Male and Female in Children's Books: Dispelling All Doubts." *Wilson Library Bulletin* 46, 167-176.

29 Stephens, John (1996). "Gender, Genre and Children's Literature." *Signal* 79, 17-30.

30 Coats, Karen (2018).

31 *Ibid*., 122.

32 Underwood, Deborah, and Cambria Evans (2013). *Part-time Princess*. New York: Disney Hyperion.

33 Cole, Babette (1997). *Princess Smartypants*. London: Puffin.

34 Von Der Lohe (2013), 101.

35 The pages of a picturebooks are usually not numbered. Therefore, the term opening refers to a double page in a picturebook, counted from the beginning of the story.

36 Underwood and Hunt (2015).

37 *Ibid*., opening 2.

38 *Ibid*., opening 2.

39 *Ibid*., opening 3.

40 Cf. *ibid*., opening 4.

41 *Ibid*., opening 4.

42 Cf. *ibid*., opening 5.

43 *Ibid*., opening 6.

44 *Ibid*., opening 6.

45 *Ibid*., opening 6.

46 *Ibid*., opening 6-7.

47 *Ibid*., opening 8.

48 *Ibid*., opening 14.

49 *Ibid*., opening 15.

50 *Ibid*., opening 16.

51 Cf. Von Der Lohe (2013).

52 *Underwood* and Hunt (2015), opening 13.

53 This was the result of critical discussions in three consecutive BA seminars at Innsbruck University from the summer term 2016 till the summer term 2018.

54 Hurley, Dorothy L. (2005). "Seeing White: Children of Color and the Disney Fairy Tale Princess." *The Journal of Negro Education* 74.3, 221-232.

[55] Council of Europe (2018). *Common European Framework of References for Languages: Learning, Teaching, Assessment. Companion Volume with New Descriptors.* Strasbourg: Council of Europe.

[56] Elsner, Daniela (2010). *Englisch in der Grundschule unterrichten*. München: Oldenbourg.

[57] Alter, Grit, and Ulla Ratheiser, (2019). "A New Model of Literary Competence for the New CEFR Descriptors." *ELTJournal* 73.4: 377-386. Web. 25 February 2020 <https://doi.org/10.1093/elt/ccz024>.

[58] Cf. Hurley (2005).

Bibliography

Primary Texts

Andersen, Hans-Christian (1837). *The Little Mermaid.* Copenhagen: C. A. Reitzel.

Brave. Dir. Mark Andrews and Brenda Chapman. 2012. Walt Disney.

Cole, Babette (1997). *Princess Smartypants.* London: Puffin.

Grimm, Jacob, and Wilhelm Grimm (1812). *Kinder- und Hausmärchen. Gesammelt durch die Brüder Grimm.* Berlin: Realschulbuchhandlung.

Le Guin, Ursula K. (1969). *The Left Hand of Darkness.* New York: Ace Books.

The Little Mermaid. Dir. Ron Clemens and John Musker. 1989. Walt Disney Pictures.

Sleeping Beauty. Dir. Clyde Geronimi. 1959. Walt Disney.

Underwood, Deborah, and Meg Hunt (2015). *Interstellar Cinderella.* San Francisco: Chronicle Books LLC.

Underwood, Deborah, and Cambria Evans (2013). *Part-time Princess*. New York: Disney Hyperion.

Secondary Literature

Alter, Grit, and Ulla Ratheiser (2019). "A New Model of Literary Competence for the New CEFR Descriptors." *ELTJournal* 73.4: 377-386. Web. 25 February 2020 <https://doi.org/10.1093/elt/ccz024>.

Baker, Brian (2014). *Science Fiction*. London: Palgrave.

Coats, Karen (2018). "Gender in Picturebooks." *Routledge Companion to Picturebooks*. Ed. Bettina Kümmerling-Meibauer. Routledge: New York, 119-127.

Council of Europe (2018). *Common European Framework of References for Languages: Learning, Teaching, Assessment. Companion Volume with New Descriptors.* Strasbourg: Council of Europe.

Elsner, Daniela (2010). *Englisch in der Grundschule unterrichten.* München: Oldenbourg.

Hurley, Dorothy L. (2005). "Seeing White: Children of Color and the Disney Fairy Tale Princess." *The Journal of Negro Education* 74.3, 221-232.

Key, Mary Richtie (1971). "The Role of Male and Female in Children's Books: Dispelling All Doubts." *Wilson Library Bulletin* 46, 167-176.

"Science Fiction." *Kids Wordsmyth* (n.d.). Web. 10 March 2019 <http://kids.wordsmyth.net/we/?ent=science+fiction>.

"Science Fiction." *Merriam-Webster Learner's Dictionary* (n.d.). Web. 10 March 2019 <http://learnersdictionary.com/definition/science%20fiction>.

McCabe, Janice et al. (2011). "Gender in Twentieth-Century Children's Books: Patterns of Disparity in Titles and Central Characters." *Gender & Society* 25.2, 197-226.

Roberts, Adam (2000). *Science Fiction*. New York: Routledge.

--- (2005). *History of Science Fiction*. New York: Palgrave.

Shipley, Elizabeth (2007). "Science Fiction of Other-Genderedness in the EFL Classroom." *Gender Studies and Foreign Language Teaching.* Eds. Helene Decke-Cornill and Laurenz Volkmann. Gunther Narr: Tübingen, 227-242.

Stephens, John (1996). "Gender, Genre and Children's Literature." *Signal* 79, 17-30.

Von Der Lohe, Amanda R. (2013). "A World of Their Own: Exploring the Spectrum of Science Fiction Elements in Children's Picture Books." *The Eaton Journal of Archival Research in Science Fiction* 1.2, 96-117.

Christian Ludwig (Berlin)

The Three Little Aliens and the Big Bad Robot in ELT

1. Introduction

Humankind has been captivated by the idea of artificial beings for a long time, as their frequent appearances in ancient legends and fairytales impressively show. Here, Hephaestus' metal beings (*automatones*) in Greek mythology or Leonardo DaVinci's 15th century mechanical knight are only two of many examples. Up until recently, they have only been a myth and an element of science fiction. Lang's expressionist science-fiction utopia *Metropolis*, populated by (humanoid) robots, anticipated almost a century ago some of the present developments and ethical questions concerning the place of robots in our society where

> [r]apid technological advancement and reduced production costs of robots and robotic devices has led to a commercialized product environment in which robots are on the precipice of becoming ubiquitous home companions, health aides, and other social partners.[1]

This increasing ubiquity of robots in everyday life, "entering into human spaces and helping fill roles traditionally occupied by humans"[2] compel us to rethink our images of what robots look like, which legal status and rights they should be accorded, and how they should behave towards other (human) members of society. Isaac Asimov's science-fiction novella "The Bicentennial Man" (turned into a film of the same title in 1999) provides a plethora of illustrative examples of the challenges society will have to address with a growing presence of (increasingly humanoid) robots. Moreover, Phillips et al., reporting on the results of a study aiming to gain a better understanding of people's expectations of the appearance of different types of robots,[3] argue that "robot appearance powerfully influences how people interact with robots, and that this influence is strongly mediated by people's expectations about those robots".[4] Thus, it only seems a natural consequence to discuss roboethical questions such as 'What are robots?', 'Should robots be given employment rights?', or even 'Should robots be granted human rights?' also in English Language Teaching (ELT).

The present article sets out to tackle exactly these issues by presenting a small-scale learning project which was conducted in a year three class at a medium-sized comprehensive school (*Gemeinschaftsschule*) in northern Baden-Württemberg, demonstrating how the topic of robots can be discussed with young learners of English in an enjoyable and creative learning atmosphere. The project took place as part of a mandatory internship for students of English at the University of Education in Karlsruhe (Germany). Dealing with such an unusual topic allowed the interns to plan and design a lesson based on a traditional medium for the primary English classroom, while, at the same time, exploring a rather unusual topic. In addition to this, the project also sought to investigate the pupils' knowledge and perceptions of robots. The results of the project suggest that pupils between the age of eight and ten have diverse, though often not age appropriate, sources for their individual conceptions of robots which makes a suitable introduction to the topic at hand even more important.

The first section of this paper will look at the ubiquitous yet diverse representations of robots in popular culture. The ensuing section will then discuss the role of picturebooks in early foreign language learning, particularly focusing on reading authentic picturebooks. Then, the small-scale project will be outlined in more detail, arguing that science-fiction literature represents a worthwhile topic also for the primary English as a foreign language classroom for a plethora of reasons, not least considering the increasing demand for including global issues in the curriculum. Before the paper moves on to describing the implementation of the project in more detail and presenting some of the project's results, including a detailed lesson plan for the double lesson at hand, a brief summary of McNamara and Fearing's 2011 picturebook *The Three Aliens and the Big Bad Robot*[5] will be provided.

The next part will now look at the representations of robots in popular culture, mainly arguing that their increasing omnipresence in all areas of life makes it imperative to deal with the issue also in language learning.

2. "It is precisely because I am *not* human."[6] – Robots in Popular Culture

One can safely say that robots have secured a firm place in popular culture. One only has to think of the military insect and spider robots blockbusters such as Spielberg's *Minority Report* (2002), the police robots in Blomkamp's *Elysium* (2013), the robot villains in Larson's *Battle Star Galactica* (1978-80), or, to give one more example, robots that perform tedious or life-threatening tasks such as the Waste Allocation Load-Lifter, the eponymous character in Stanton's highly acclaimed computer-animated science-fiction film *Wall-E from Wall-E* (2008).

The term robot (robota = forced labour) goes back to Karel Čapek's play *R.U.R.* (1921)[7], in which artificial humans revolt against their human creators and ultimately destroy humankind. However, despite its omnipresence, the term robot, at least as it is used in popular culture today, is difficult to define and categorise as it often functions as an umbrella term for a whole variety of (humanoid-)mechanical entities, including, for example, organic humanoids, androids, and cyborgs.

As far as robots in science-fiction literature and film are concerned, there is no doubt that they differ vastly depending on the sf universe as well as the cultural, political, and historical context in which they were created. While in early works of science fiction, robots were presented as a menace to human existence, this changed in the mid-1930s when sf texts "featured benevolent robots subject to wholly unjustified attacks by humans conditioned to assume that robots must be evil".[8] This changed again in the aftermath of the atomic bomb, when "attitudes to robots in science fiction became noticeably more ambivalent"[9] and "many generic robot stories of the 1950s involved confrontation and conflict".[10] One example of this kind of story is Peter Phillips' "Lost Memory" (1952), in which a human is stranded on a planet entirely inhabited by robots. The robot scientists and the human fail to communicate with each other, leading to the astronaut's death when the robots, unaware of human existence, attempt to medically treat the 'fellow robot'.[11] Emerging robot technologies in the 1960s led to a growing awareness of robot existentialism, which was also reflected in the rapidly extending body of texts, featuring a multitude of robot images no longer restricted to the robot as the evil and sinister Other that tried to destroy humankind.

3. Reading Picturebooks in the Primary EFL Classroom

Stories and picturebooks, often used for storytelling,[12] constitute two of the oldest resources in primary English as a foreign language (EFL) classrooms in Germany. The power of stories, as Cameron points out, is generated "by their links into poetics and literature in one direction and to the warmth of early childhood experiences in another".[13] In addition to this, picturebooks are used for a multitude of purposes. Just to name a few examples, they can be used to "create a familiar frame and setting for discovering new lexical, syntactical, and phonological items".[14] Moreover, they also serve to develop multiple literacies such as visual or culture literacy. They also trigger motivation among pupils[15] and "invite primary children to identify with the protagonists and thus immerse themselves in the plots",[16] also inspiring young learners to use their imagination and come up with their own stories.[17] From a methodological point of view, picturebooks can often be used as a starting point for creative tasks.

Authentic picturebooks are mainly written for children with English as their first language. Thus, they allow authentic insights into the target language and culture, although they sometimes need modification as they would be too difficult for the German EFL classroom in the original form. Often, authentic picturebooks are based on traditional and often universal folk- and fairytales as well as stories from other cultures and languages which are known to the pupils. Thus, they provide a rich resource for the primary English classroom as they, for example, draw on the pupil's already existing knowledge of formulaic L1, plot structures, and binary oppositions.

4. *The Three Little Aliens and the Big Bad Robot*

The picturebook *The Three Little Aliens and the Big Bad Robot* is a modern retelling of the famous fable *The Three Little Pigs*, a famous children's story about three little pigs who build three houses of different materials when they are attacked by a wolf. The big bad wolf blows down two of the houses, while he is unable to destroy the third one which is made of brick, and, depending on the version, is either killed or chased away. The omnipresence of the fable through its inclusion in textbooks as well as various textbook, film, comics, and picturebook adaptations, not to forget the rich and varied classroom resources available for the story, makes it very likely that pupils have already encountered the fable in a different context.

The picturebook at hand transfers the fable's plot to outer space and replaces the three little pigs and the big bad wolf by three little aliens and a big bad robot respectively. Despite the fact that the main protagonists and setting have been changed, many prototypical elements of a fable, such as formulaic opening, an introduction of characters, description of setting, introduction of a problem, a series of events, the resolution of the problem, a closing and a moral,[18] are maintained.

The inside front cover displays the seven planets of our star system surrounded by some of the planets' moons as well as star clusters, remotely alluding to iconographic representations of the Milky Way. The opening page then introduces the three intrepid green little aliens, who sit in a cramped house in a "cosy crater"[19] on planet Mercury, the smallest planet, with their mama and a creature faintly resembling a dog. The introduction reads:

> Once there was a mama alien who had three little aliens. They were called Bork, Gork, and Nklxwcyz. Bork, Gork, and Nklxwcyz grew up in an old-fashioned house in a snug, cozy crater on a tiny little plane. As the eons passed, their house got too crowded.[20]

The stuffiness of the house becomes almost tangible when looking at the detailed illustration accompanying the text. The room is packed with furniture pieces, boxes, toys, and all sorts of other everyday objects. While the grown-up alien is simply referred to as mama, the three little aliens have alien names, one of which is impossible to pronounce as it consists of a seemingly random mix of consonants, contributing to the alienness of the characters. The appearance of the aliens is distinctively extraterrestrial, with two of them having three eyes and one of them only one eye placed in the middle of his cone-shaped head. However, they also have a remarkable human touch with all of them having two legs and two arms. The subordinate clause "As the eons passed" implies that their life span reaches far beyond ours. In addition, the three-eyed mother resembles a female being, having a cantilevered coiffure, painted lips, and eyelashes. While the mother is knitting, the three little aliens each pursue their now individual activities such as using the computer or reading.

As the story continues, the three little aliens are sent away by their mother in their jetpacks and they explore the universe looking for new homes. On their "far and fast" travel through space, they encounter various planets of our solar systems. They exclude Venus as it is "too hot" and Earth which is "too crowded". Although their mom had told them to stick together, the three little aliens each settle on their own planet: Bork on Jupiter, Gork on the rings of Saturn, and Nklxwcyz on the far away planet Neptune, where he is sure to be "safe from the Big Bad Robot". On the following double-page, Nklxwcyz is shown collecting different building materials such as star dust, solar panels, or a telescope, "everything he needed to make sturdy walls". Alluding to the original story of the three little pigs, Nklxwcyz house resembles the third's pig house made of bricks. Then the Big Bad Robot is introduced to the story. The depiction of the story's antagonist resembles the generic image of a robot, consisting of different metal parts, a disproportionally large torso and head. While the robot appears to be human like in some parts, it is machine like in others. It has two arms and two legs, but gripping tools instead of hands. Furthermore, its row of teeth is complemented by distinct non-human facial features such as five eyes and the absence of ears and nose. The robot is surrounded by onomatopoetic robot speak, such as "MEEP", "ORK", and "EEP". The evil and menacing nature of the robot is emphasised by the stark contrast between the bright and dark colours used for the three aliens and the robot respectively.

Bork, who stayed closest to home, is the first to encounter the robot. The discrepancy between the two extraterrestrial beings is underlined by the fact that the little alien appears tiny as she hides in her rover, while only the robot's lower legs are shown on the double-page. When Bork refuses to pull over, the robot threatens her, alluding to the original wording from the Three Little Pigs: "Then I'll crack and smack and whack your house down!" She has no other choice than to flee the planet as her rover is smashed to smithereens. When the robot is about to get her, she reaches Gork's satellite house, which is equally destroyed by the robot. Together, the two aliens escape and try to find their brother Nklxwcyz. In contrast to his brother and sister, who were too distracted by their swirly planet and surfing the rings to see the robot coming, Nklxwcyz already spotted the robot through its telescope and "flashed his solar panels halfway across the universe". When the robot fails to destroy the sturdy house, it tries to enter through the chimney but gets stuck and bursts into a million pieces. The aliens phone their mother who comes to tuck them in.[21]

5. The Project

The project was conducted in a year three class of a medium-sized German comprehensive school (*Gemeinschaftsschule*) in a small town in northern Baden-Württemberg during the summer term 2018. The class consisted of 24 pupils (thirteen boys, eleven girls), three of whom were not present on the project day and thus not able to participate in the project. The double lesson was mainly taught by an English student of the University of Education Karlsruhe, hereinafter referred to as Cornelia*, who had volunteered to be responsible for the lesson as part of her mandatory four-month internship, which she completed at the same school. The actual lesson, however, was actively supported by six more students, who also did their internship at the school at the time. The author was also present but did not intervene during the lesson. While the two lessons were mainly planned by Cornelia*, the planning process was closely guided by the author of this article as well as the other students of the group.

The idea for the present project originally derived from a tandem seminar, combining two classes, one focusing on science fiction and fantasy as a literary genre and the other on working with those texts in the EFL classroom. The large number of students who had registered for both courses confirmed the expectations that such a topic would be of great interest to the students. The classroom project was designed to capture the pupils' expectations about the appearance of a robot. In more detail, the main objectives of the project can be summarised as follows:

- to find out more about the pupils' sources of knowledge of robot existence;
- to gain a better understanding of pupils' *posteriori* images of robots and, last but not least,
- to look at the practical implementation of such a project/topic in the primary English classroom.

The double lesson started by reading Margaret McNamara and Mark Fearing's *The Three Little Aliens and the Big Bad Robot* together with the pupils. The project leaders were aware of the fact that seeing a (bad) robot beforehand would most likely influence the pupils' (already existing) imaginings of a robot, and thus make their creative responses less intuitive. However, the picturebook was vital in introducing the pupils to the new vocabulary related to the topic at hand.

6. The Implementation of the Project

The double lesson consisted of two 45-minute sessions, giving the teacher enough time to put everything into practice (cf. Appendix). After the good morning ritual, the main topic of the picturebook was introduced by connecting it to naming the different body parts in English, which the pupils had already learned in previous lessons. For this purpose, the teacher asked the pupils to imagine themselves as robots and then introduced herself as a mechanic who is responsible for checking their joints. Similar to the game Simon Says, the teacher then issued instructions, such as 'move your left leg' or 'lift your right arm' to the pupils, who were only allowed to follow the instructions if prefaced by 'the mechanic says'. In each round, the pupil who was eliminated from the game had to come to the front as the next mechanic. In the next step, Cornelia* introduced the main protagonists of the story relevant for understanding the picturebook as well as some key vocabulary, using pictures and word cards.

Then Cornelia* read out a slightly simplified version of the picturebook, omitting some advanced vocabulary, such as 'to blast' or 'clattered and scattered and shattered', in order to ensure a better understanding of the story. Moreover, the pupils' understanding of the plot was ensured by employing common storytelling techniques such as asking questions, using gestures, facial expressions, and sounds as well as using the picture cards and the images from the picturebook. After reading the picturebook, the pupils were assigned to five 'assembly tables'. At the beginning of the second lesson, the class was then told that they would create their own robot, each group creating one part of the robot's body, which would then be assembled towards the end of the lesson.

Towards the end of the lesson, the robot was assembled and put up in front of the blackboard. This way, all pupils had the opportunity to look at the robot. The pupils then presented the various body parts they had produced. Here, the more challenged students could use a worksheet for help, using pre-formulated sentences such as "The head of my robot has ___ eyes." or "The head of my robot has ___ ears."

The appearance of the robot clearly resembles the image of the robot from the picturebook. As there was a wealth of materials available to the pupils, it can be assumed that they built their individual robot parts based on the *Big Bad Robot* from the picturebook. Here, the fact that the robot created by the pupils is many-eyed supports this assumption. Despite the similarity in shape, the bright colours show a much more friendly-looking robot, hinting at the fact that the pupils' overall perception of the robot was not negative.

Before the teacher concluded the lesson by re-reading the picturebook, the pupils were asked whether they had encountered robots before. The pupils' answers showed that this was in fact true, although, admittedly, not necessarily from age appropriate sources. While one students said that he had known robots since early childhood, several students mentioned that they had rather encountered them coincidentally, for example, through films ("My sister watched a film about robots and I watched it with her."/"My dad plays a video game and it has a lot of robots in it".) Another student said that his dad "builds robots in his free time".[22]

Introduction	In this double lesson, the students get to know the story of *The Three Little Aliens and the Big Bad Robot* and, in a second step, create their own robot.
Objectives	To develop and practise: • oral skills by discussing issues surrounding space travel and non-human forms of life, • the vocabulary the language needed to describe a robot, • social skills needed to work together in a group.
Age	Primary school aged 8-10
Level	CEF level A1
Time	1 lesson of 90 mins. (or two lessons of 45 mins.each)
Materials/media	*The Three Little Aliens and the Big Bad Robot*, vocabulary flashcards, blackboard, craft material for putting

	together a robot, for example, old pieces of carton cables, and plugs, worksheet.
1. Introduction (5 mins.)	Play 'The Mechanic Says' (an adaptation of Simon Says) with the pupils repeating the body parts.
2. Pre-reading phase (10 mins.)	Introduce the main vocabulary needed to understand the picturebook as well as main characters.
3. Reading phase (20 mins.)	Pupils actively listen to the (simplified) story, unknown vocabulary is clarified, questions are used to secure the pupils' understanding of the story.
4. Post-reading phase (5 mins.)	Pupils summarise the story with the help of the flashcards and the teacher.
5. Group work (20 mins.)	Pupils are put into four groups (six groups for larger classes; each group puts together one part of the robot's body: head, torso, arms, legs) and are told that they can build their own robot.
Pre-presentation phase (15 mins.)	Pupils practice the description of their body part and the robot's abilities, e.g. "The head of our robot has three brown eyes, long, black hair, a small nose, etc."
Assembly phase (5 mins.)	Pupils assemble the robot with the help of the teacher.
Presentation phase (10 mins.)	Pupils describe the robot together as a group.

Table 1: Teaching *The Three Little Aliens and the Big Bad Robot*

7. Conclusion

It is safe to say that we are currently at an important juncture in the field of robotics, which also means that we need to think about how we envision the cohabitation of humans and (increasingly humanoid) robots in the future. Here, the English classroom provides numerous opportunities for fostering discussions of such vital topics in the foreign language. The sample project exemplifies how such a topic can be approached with young learners of English.

Notes

1 Phillips, Elizabeth, et al. (2017). "What Does a Robot Look Like? A Multi-Site Examination of User Expectations about Robot Appearance." *Proceedings of the Human Factors and Ergonomics Society 2017 Annual Meeting*, 1215-1219, 1215.

2 *Ibid.*

3 *Ibid.*

4 *Ibid.*

5 Other picturebooks on the topic at hand that the author can recommend include: Dyckman, Ame. *Boy + Bot* (2012), Yaccarino, Dan *Doug Unplugged.* (2014), DiPucchio, Kelly. *Clink* (2011), Scieszka, Jon. *Robot Zot!* (2009), Lester, Helen. *Wodney Wat's Wobot* (2011), Oliver, Mark. *Robot Dog* (2005), Yaccarino, Dan. *Doug Unplugs on the Farm* (2014), Corcoran, Mark. *Star Wars: The Mystery of the Rebellious Robot* (1979), Carrick, Paul. *Watch Out for Wolfgang* (2009), Cali, Davide. *Mama Robot* (2008).

6 The quote is taken from "The Measure of a Man", the ninth episode of the second season of *Star Trek: The Next Generation*, in which Captain Picard must prove that Data is a sentient being and not 'just' an android to protect him from disassembly. "The Measure of a Man." *Star Trek: The Next Generation.* Dir. Robert Scheerer. 1989. Broadcast syndication.

7 Cf. Stableford, Brian (2006). *Science Fact and Science Fiction: An Encyclopedia*. New York: Routledge.

8 *Ibid.*, 443.

9 *Ibid.*, 444

10 *Ibid.*

11 Phillips, Peter (1952). "Lost Memory." *Isaac Asimov Presents The Great SF Stories #14*. Eds. Isaac Asimov and Martin H. Greenberg. New York: Daw Books, 35-47.

12 Hempel, Margit (2015). "A Picture Book is Worth a Thousand Words: Picture Books in the EFL Classroom." *Learning with Literature in the EFL Classroom*. Eds. Werner Delanoy, Maria Eisenmann and Frauke Matz. Frankfurt am Main: Lang, 69-84, 69.

13 Cameron, Lynne (2001). *Teaching Languages to Young Learners*. Cambridge: Cambridge University Press, 160.

14 Hempel (2015), 69.

15 Elsner, Daniela (2010). *Englisch in der Grundschule unterrichten: Grundlagen, Methoden, Praxisbeispiele*. München: Oldenbourg Schulbuch Verlag, 119.

[16] Alter, Grit (2018). "Integrating Postcolonial Culture(s) into Primary English Language Teaching". *CLELEjournal* 6.1, 22-44, 26.

[17] Hempel (2015), 69-70; Elsner (2010), 119.

[18] Cameron (2001), 162.

[19] All quotes following in this section are from McNamara, Margaret, and Mark Fearing (2011). *The Three Little Aliens and the Big Bad Robot*. New York: Schwartz & Wade. The picturebook does not contain page numbers.

[20] *Ibid*.

[21] This summary illustrates that the story can also be used in CLIL classes, where topics such as the planet of our solar system or space travel could be discussed.

[22] All answers were translated by the author.

Bibliography

Primary Texts

Asimov, Isaac (1976). *The Bicentennial Man and Other Stories*. New York: Ballantine Books.

Battlestar Galactica. Creator Glen A. Larson. 1978. ABC.

The Bicentennial Man. Dir. Chris Columbus. 1999. Touchstone Pictures.

Cali, Davide. (2008). *Mama Robot*. Toronto: Tundra Books.

Čapek, Karel (2010 [1920]). *R.U.R.*: *Rossum's Universal Robots*. (David Wylie, *Trans*.). Rockville, Maryland: Wildside Press.

Carrick, Paul (2009). *Watch Out for Wolfgang*. Watertown, Massachusetts: Charlesbridge.

Corcoran, Mark (1979). *Star Wars: The Mystery of the Rebellious Robot*. New York: Random House.

DiPucchio, Kelly (2011). *Clink*. New York: Balzer + Bray.

Dyckman, Ame (2012). *Boy + Bot*. New York: Knopf Books for Young Readers.

Elysium. Dir. Neill Blomkamp. 2013. TriStar Pictures.

Lester, Helen (2011). *Wodney Wat's Wobot*. Boston, Massachusetts: HMH Books for Young Readers.

McNamara, Margaret, and Mark Fearing (2011). *The Three Little Aliens and the Big Bad Robot*. New York: Schwartz & Wade.

"The Measure of a Man." *Star Trek: The Next Generation*. Dir. Robert Scheerer. 1989. Broadcast syndication.

Metropolis. Dir. Fritz Lang. 1927. UFA.

Minority Report. Dir. Steven Spielberg. 2002. 20th Century Fox.
Oliver, Mark (2005). *Robot Dog*. London: Little Tiger Press.
Phillips, Peter (1952). "Lost Memory." *Isaac Asimov Presents The Great SF Stories #14*. Eds. Isaac Asimov and Martin H. Greenberg. New York: Daw Books, 35-47.
Scieszka, Jon (2009). *Robot Zot!* New York: Simon & Schuster Books for Young Readers.
WALL-E. Dir. Andrew Stanton. 2008. Walt Disney Pictures.
Yaccarino, Dan (2016). *Doug Unplugged*. Decorah, IA: Dragonfly Books.
--- (2014). *Doug Unplugs on the Farm*. Decorah, IA: Dragonfly Books.

Secondary Literature

Alter, Grit (2018). "Integrating Postcolonial Culture(s) into Primary English Language Teaching." *CLELEjournal* 6.1, 22-44.
Cameron, Lynne (2001). *Teaching Languages to Young Learners*. Cambridge: Cambridge University Press.
Elsner, Daniela (2010). *Englisch in der Grundschule unterrichten: Grundlagen, Methoden, Praxisbeispiele*. München: Oldenbourg Schulbuch Verlag.
Hempel, Margit (2015). "A Picture Book is Worth a Thousand Words: Picture Books in the EFL Classroom." *Learning with Literature in the EFL Classroom*. Eds. Werner Delanoy, Maria Eisenmann and Frauke Matz. Frankfurt am Main: Lang, 69-84.
Phillips, Elizabeth, et al. (2017). "What Does a Robot Look Like?: A Multi-Site Examination of User Expectations about Robot Appearance." *Proceedings of the Human Factors and Ergonomics Society 2017 Annual Meeting*, 1215-1219.
Stableford, Brian (2006). *Science Fact and Science Fiction: An Encyclopedia*. New York: Routledge.

Peter Hohwiller (Paderborn)

Teaching Michael Faber's *Under the Skin*

1. Introduction

Although largely unnoticed by literature pedagogy, *Under the Skin* offers considerable didactic potential. By discussing the novel's most promising motifs, this article will demonstrate how competences can be fostered and how issues meaningful to today's learners can be addressed through the novel. After an analysis of text and genre, this chapter focuses on the text's particular suitability for inclusion in the curriculum. In so doing, methodological implications for classroom use are discussed in detail.

2. Plot and Genre

Michael Faber (*1960) published *Under the Skin*, quite aptly, at the turn of the millennium. The novel deals with Isserley, an alien morphed into an alluring maneater, who pretends to seduce muscular men. Fleshly are her desires indeed – but in quite another sense of the term: working for the most powerful meat-processing cooperation of her planet, it is her job to procure supplies. And since human meat is *the* delicacy on her planet, it is hunky hitchhikers that Isserley is after. Once Isserley has lured her prey into her car, she drugs him and surrenders him to subterranean processing plants, where her victims are castrated, fattened and eventually slaughtered by a team of alien labourers.

Faber's novel allows the reader to accompany Isserley on her seemingly infinite journeys through the Scottish Highlands. Although Isserley executes some minor parts of her job rather poorly – she frequently struggles to go with the traffic flow – the years on the road have given her what could be labelled excellent killer instincts. Although left to her own devices when outside, Isserley manages to satisfy the cooperation's demands for human meat without fail. What is more,

Isserley has obviously fallen under the spell of the Highlands and their serenity, and she is enchanted by the local weather, flora, and fauna.

Throughout the course of the novel, it is gradually revealed that Isserley had deliberately been chosen for this job. Although the details are somewhat sketchy – Isserley's home planet is not directly presented in the novel – her place of origin seems to be strictly governed by social stratification: a ruling class is in full control, enjoying themselves and constantly craving human meat. It is their demand that the cooperation and Isserley satisfy. Unsurprisingly, most of the planet's population is ruthlessly exploited: they are sent to the so-called Estates where their hard underground labour secures them an untimely death and their oppressors even more affluence. Being popular with some members of this leisure class due to her stunning looks, Isserley had not been selected for the Estates but for her job in the so-called New Estates, the Scottish Highlands. Isserley's secondment comes at a price, though. Since the inhabitants of her planet are canine or vulpine four-feet creatures, Isserley had to undergo dramatic surgical changes – a metamorphosis that turned her, in hitchhikers' eyes, into an attractive human but in Isserley's eyes into an unattractive animal. Now all of a sudden Isserley's daily routine is disturbed. Amlis Vess, the son of the cooperation's founder, arrives at Isserley's place. Quite surprisingly, he is not the spoilt and superficial brat that Isserley expects, but a ruminative and responsible character. Most significantly, Amlis disapproves of his father's line of work, the meat business, and he even feels pity for Isserley's victims. It is, among other aspects, his advocacy for artificial meat that ultimately turns Isserley's world upside down. After Amlis' departure, she can no longer go through the motions of her job the way she used to.

The above summary already indicates that it is comparatively difficult to pin down *Under the Skin* generically. While there can be no doubt that it comprises classic elements of science-fiction literature, these properties are, more often than not, rather marginal. There is superior alien technology, and there is space travel – but the novel does not care to elaborate on what it looks like and how it works: the drug that Isserley uses to numb her victims is called 'icpathua' and what the novel reveals about the spacecraft that transports Amlis to Isserley's steading is that it is a 'ship' – it does not get any more specific than this. Regarding its treatment of science, Faber's novel is clearly on the soft side of the traditional science fiction spectrum.

Little is given away about Isserley's home planet either. However, as the reader puts all the pieces together, a dystopian picture of her planet's society is outlined. Apart from stratification and exploitation, it is determined by the key elements of dystopian societies: consolidation (the ruling class secures its position because it has access to human meat), experimentation (Isserley's surgical makeover), linguistic obfuscation (the *locus terribilis* to which the exploited are sent are the 'Estates') and, obviously, confrontation (Amlis' refusal to follow in his father's footsteps).

What *Under the Skin* does elaborate on a manifest level, though, is its extraterrestrial protagonists, Isserley and Amlis. One might even argue it is predominantly a science-fiction novel because of its alien *dramatis personae*. Most importantly, *Under the Skin* is a novel about the psychological consequences that a metamorphosis of an alien into a human being entails. Moreover, it also delves into the question of alien and human interaction, and, therefore, it touches on inter- or transcultural issues, too. By and large, *Under the Skin* could tentatively be labelled soft science fiction, set against a dystopian backdrop. What is also very interesting in terms of genre, is the novel's inter- or transcultural subtext. Isserley, the alien morphed into a human being, tries to understand what makes the *homo sapiens* tick. There are more narrative science fiction texts written in a similar vein. In the following, only texts suitable for the English as a foreign language (EFL) classroom are given. Ursula Le Guin's *The Left Hand of Darkness* (1969) is an example of what has been termed anthropological science fiction, since Le Guin, like Faber, provides a thick description of a society alien to the protagonists.[1] Faber's focus on the consequences of body transformation is also at the heart of James Tiptree's 1974 novella "The Girl Who Was Plugged In". Furthermore, both Tiptree and Faber set their texts against a dystopian background governed by capitalist interests. Although not a science fiction novel in a classical sense, Kazuo Ishiguro's *Never Let Me Go* (2005) bears striking resemblance to *Under the Skin,* as the Nobel Prize laureate, among a good many other things, negotiates the question of body identity, too.

This can easily raise doubts among teachers looking for new material: should a 300-page novel about the culinary choices of aliens really be read by students? Needless to say, *Under the Skin* has far more to offer, and its didactic potential is considerable due to – at least – four reasons.

To begin with, Faber's novel complies with curricular demands. Due to its linguistic and conceptual density, it is rather suitable for advanced learners of grade 11 and later, and the relevant curricular document for this age group are, on a federal level, the 2012 educational standards (*Bildungsstandards*). Characterised by a revaluation of the role of literary and non-literary texts in the EFL classroom,[2] the educational standards expect learners, for example, to deal with the perspectives given in texts and, possibly, to change their own perspectives.[3] By offering an alien-turned-human perspective on the *homo sapiens*, Faber's novel clearly has a tick in this box.

Most of the federal states have adopted the competence definition and/or the competence expectations of the educational standards. Some, for example Bavaria, Hamburg, and Rhineland-Palatinate, add that an in-class reading of at least one 20th or 21st century novel is obligatory in year eleven or later. Other federal states, for example Berlin or Hesse, link competences and obligatory topics. Faber's novel certainly meets these demands, too: it can be read against obligatory Hessian topics like "tradition and change" (Amlis' refusal to eat human meat) or Berlin topics like "science and technology – visions of the future".

Secondly, the novel's didactic potential is due to its balance between simplicity and density. Basically, there are only two round characters (Isserley and Amlis), one setting (the Highlands around the farm), one manifest plot line (Isserley's routine and its disruption), and a comparatively short time span is chronologically covered. This greatly adds to the novel's accessibility for foreign language learners.[4] Yet, at the same time, these readers are adequately challenged as far as the novel's language and core conflicts are concerned.

Thirdly, by teaching *Under the Skin* language awareness can be fostered[5] – and that is a domain which is not always at the heart of upper secondary (*Sekundarstufe II*) sequences and which some teachers might even find difficult to cater for. Two of the competence expectations listed in the language awareness section of the educational standards are relevant here: the reflection on the interplay between linguistic and cultural phenomena and the analysis of linguistic manipulation.[6] By having learners do just that, teachers can not only foster language awareness but also address the central motifs of Faber's novel. Isserley's culture has developed a distinct line of argument to justify their meat eating. Very much of it relies on language, though, particularly on labelling the *homo sapiens* an animal. The inhabitants of Isserley's planet consider themselves human, and by calling the *homo sapiens* either "animal", "beast", "brute", or "creature", a linguistic line is drawn between the species, between those who eat and those who are eaten and even between culture and nature.

Moreover, in their language, a *homo sapiens* is a 'vodsel' (a term reminiscent of the Dutch *voedsel*, meaning 'food' – possibly an ironic comment by the Dutch-born novelist). And their expression for 'human meat' is a *figura etymologica* of this very word: 'vodissin'. What is crucial here is that, in Isserley's culture, the *homo sapiens* has a telling name that unmistakably shows the purpose they serve.

When Isserley starts to question her job and tries to get a grip on her life again, she reassures herself of the righteousness of what she does:

> In the end, though, vodsels couldn't do any of the things that really defined a human being. They couldn't siuwil, they couldn't menishtil, they had no concept of slan. In their brutishness, they'd never evolved to use hunshur; their communities were so rudimentary that hississins did not exist; nor did these creatures seem to see any need for chail, or even chailsinn.[7]

Basically, it is said that the *homo sapiens* can be eaten because they do not have *signifiés* for some *signifiants* of Isserley's language – linguistic relativity killed the radio star. A last aspect that touches on language awareness (and text competence) is Faber's use of irony. It takes quite some time until it dawns on the reader that there is something wrong with Isserley and even more time until it is really clear that *Under the Skin* is about a kind of alien invasion. However, when re-reading the novel readers will be surprised to see how many vital clues are already given in the opening chapters. Isserley, for example, mentions the "alien innocence" of a hitchhiker, and when reading the logo of his t-shirt she has "no idea what on earth this might mean".[8] Moreover, returning empty-handed after a rather unsuccessful day, she wonders: "If she announced resolutely enough to the universe that she'd abandoned all hope, she might be offered something after all."[9] In a re-reading of the novel, it becomes clear that the above quotes are not to be merely taken metaphorically but literally. For Isserley, the hitchhiker is extraterrestrial, there are some things she does not understand on the blue planet, and she does engage in interstellar communication. On a similar, albeit darkly sarcastic level, re-reading the novel also reveals numerous examples of the *homo sapiens* being described with food metaphors and similes.[10] All in all, dealing with these intricate layers of irony, teachers can foster learners' language awareness – and the hermeneutic gains of re-reading are powerfully made clear – and this is more than just a didactic fringe benefit.

The fourth and last reason for the novel's didactic potential is its student orientation. The past years have shown an increased awareness of ecological issues, also in Germany – a trend that seems to be independent of gender, age, and class. In this process, food and traditional diets have also come under scrutiny, and vegetarianism and veganism have significantly gained in popularity due to ecological and ethical reasons. The availability and range of vegetarian or vegan products have tremendously changed, too. Statistically, most vegetarians can be found among young people aged 18 to 29, and most vegans are, on average, in their late 20s. Both vegetarians and vegans have high educational backgrounds.[11] Now these facts and figures underline what many teachers in Germany might have witnessed in their classrooms: today, young people, i.e. learners, have stronger inclinations towards plant-based diets. This is why Faber's novel might appeal to this generation in particular.

Last but by no means least, *Under the Skin* also turns the tables on carnivorous readers because it vividly showcases the cruelty of factory farming – with the haunting difference that it is humans who have taken the animal position. It is probably one of the strongest literary pleas for animal welfare of the two past decades.

4. Methodological Implications

Applying Klafki's basic questions and his axiom of didactic primacy[12] to the literature classroom, one might conclude that it is the literary text which determines the way it is taught. As far as *Under the Skin* is concerned, this question must then be answered: which methodological implications does the didactic potential of Faber's novel entail? Three answers to this question can be proposed.

Firstly, reflecting predominantly on human and alien interaction, *Under the Skin* largely centres on binary oppositions and a them-versus-us dichotomy. Two methodological conclusions can be drawn from this. The bipartite structure of the novel clearly invites comparative analyses in which similarities and differences are elaborated. These comparative analyses, in turn, lend themselves to pair work and to peer teaching because it is by having some students focus on, say, the descriptions of humans and some on the descriptions of animals that a natural information-gap is created and brought to its full communicative effect.

Secondly, by offering an implicit plea for vegetarianism, Faber's novel touches on controversial issues. Despite its possible appeal to contemporary learners, it is unlikely that its advocacy will be met with unanimous support in the classroom. Therefore, students must be given ample opportunity to discuss and possibly even debate the benefits and downsides of specific food choices.

Thirdly, by using complex patterns of irony that go largely unnoticed upon first reading, learners must be encouraged to read and re-read the novel. Although clearly not the standard reading approach in the EFL classroom, a sequence on Faber's novel should use the straight through approach – this is probably the most realistic way to have learners read it twice.[13]

5. Suggestions for the Classroom: Michael Faber's Novel *Under the Skin*

Objectives	Learners • acquire lexis relevant to describing the Scottish Highlands • analyse manipulative language use in literature and in contemporary Germany • analyse the interplay of language and culture • compare and contrast literary presentations of the self and of the other

	• discuss the ethic dimensions of meat-based and meat-free diets • use analytical and creative products to record their understanding of the novel • experience the advantages of re-reading literary texts
Age	Advanced learners (year 11 or later)
Level	CEFR level B2 and above
Time	10 lessons
Reading approach	Straight through approach: since re-reading is of supreme importance for the novel, at least one month before the sequence begins, students are asked to buy and to read the novel completely; the assignments of lesson 1, 3, 6 are, therefore, re-reading assignments
1st lesson: Isserley and her world(s) students have re-read chapters 1, 2, 3, 4 at home guiding assignment: underline important references to the different places of the novel	• students talk about the first four chapters in general – what they liked and disliked, open question etc. • jigsaw activity: students describe the different places so far mentioned in the novel and then they explain the relevance of a) country roads b) the farm c) the Highlands d) Isserley's former home
2nd lesson: Isserley and her world(s)	• classroom discussion on the results of the previous lesson so that all students have a sound understanding of who Isserley is and what her job is all about • concluding discussion on the use of irony in the first two chapters
3rd lesson and 4th lesson: the *homo sapiens* and Isserley's culture • students have re-read chapters 5, 6, 7, 8, 9 at home	• group work: students either exchange their findings about the *homo sapiens* or about Isserley's culture

• guiding assignment: underline passages describing the *homo sapiens* and Isserley's culture	• peer-teaching: students pair up so that now one *homo sapiens* expert and one expert on Isserley's culture work together; they inform each other about what they found out so far and then each pair designs a t-chart with different categories that contrasts Isserley's culture and the *homo sapiens* • differentiation: below-average learners can be given a t-chart that already contains categories like looks, diet, society, treatment of other species) • homework: Explain Isserley's position on the human/animal spectrum of the novel
5th lesson: language and manipulation	• presentation of homework is used to also talk about body identity – in Faber's novel and in contemporary Germany • chalk and talk discussion on a) food metaphors used for the *homo sapiens* b) how the *homo sapiens* is linguistically degraded c) whether linguistic degradation still exists in contemporary Germany
6th lesson: changes • students have re-read chapters 10, 11, 12, 13 at home guiding assignment: underline passages that show and that explain Isserley's change	• pair work: students design blackboard graphics that show and explain the changes that Isserley goes through • presentation: some graphics are presented, using document camera or overhead projector • differentiation: learners who might be too challenged by the above activity can be given an empty flowchart that only needs to be filled in with relevant passages
7th lesson: eating meat	• classroom discussion: is Faber's book a vegetarian plea?

	• homework: students design and conduct a survey about eating habits of friends and family
8th lesson: eating meat	• presentation of homework • classroom discussion on vegetarianism, veganism, factory farming, and meat-based diets • alternative for classes familiar with debates: a formal debate on the above topic is conducted
9th lesson: wrapping it all up	• students and teacher develop an abstract blackboard graphic that condenses the insights of the teaching sequence, particularly the use of irony; comments on genre are also given
10th lesson: an alternative cover	• students design an alternative dust jacket for *Under the Skin,* taking the insights gained in the teaching sequence into account

Table 1: Michael Faber's *Under the Skin*

6. Conclusion

In conclusion, it can be said that, for advanced students, *Under the Skin* is not only a good but also an unusual read that touches on aspects possibly not too often dealt with in the classroom. Faber's novel might be even more topical today than when it was first published as it touches upon a number of current societal discussions such as increasing the taxes on meat or the omnipresence of fake news in public discourse. Moreover, the novel comprises specific elements that address language awareness which should be fostered, particularly in the literature classroom. From a didactic point of view, *Under the Skin* therefore deserves more Teaching English as a foreign language (TEFL) attention.

Notes

1 Westphal, Gary (2005). *The Greenwood Encyclopedia of Science Fiction and Fantasy: Themes, Works, and Wonders*. Volume 1. Westport: Greenwood Press, 37.

2 Burwitz-Melzer, Eva, and Daniela Caspari (2017). "Text und Medienkompetenz." *Bildungsstandards aktuell: Französisch / Englisch in der Sekundarstufe II*. Eds. Bernd Tesch et al. Braunschweig: Westermann, 56-62.

3 Kultusministerkonferenz (2014). *Bildungsstandards für die fortgeführte Fremdsprache (Englisch / Französisch)*. Köln: Carl Link, 20.

4 Caspari, Daniela, and Ivo Steininger (2016). "Einfachheit in kinder- und jugendliterarischen Texten aus fremdsprachendidaktischer Sicht." *Einfachheit in der Kinder- und Jugendliteratur – ein Gewinn für den Fremdsprachenunterricht*. Eds. Eva Burwitz-Melzer and Emer O'Sullivan. Wien: Praesens Verlag, 38-41.

5 Vollmer, Helmut Johannes (2017). "Sprachbewusstheit." *Bildungsstandards aktuell: Französisch / Englisch in der Sekundarstufe II*. Eds. Bernd Tesch et al. Braunschweig: Westermann, 201-204.

6 Kultusministerkonferenz (2014), 21.

7 Faber, Michael (2000). *Under the Skin*. Edinburgh: Canongate Books, 174.

8 *Ibid*., 11, 14.

9 *Ibid*., 26.

10 Some examples from the first two chapters: *ibid*., 20, 24, 25, 28, 30.

11 Mensink, Gert B. M., Clarissa Lage Barbosa and Anna-Kristin Brettschneider (2016). "Verbreitung der vegetarischen Ernährungsweise in Deutschland." *Journal of Health Monitoring* 1.2: 8. Web. 13 June 2019.

12 Klafki, Wolfgang (1985). *Neue Studien zur Bildungstheorie und Didaktik: Beiträge zur kritisch-konstruktiven Didaktik*. Weinheim: Beltz.

13 Thaler, Engelbert (2008). *Teaching English Literature*. Paderborn: Schöningh, 105.

Bibliography

Primary Texts

Faber, Michael (2000). *Under the Skin*. Edinburgh: Canongate Books.

Ishiguro, Kazuo (2016). *Never Let Me Go*. Berlin: Cornelsen.

Le Guin, Ursula K. (2017[1969]). *The Left Hand of Darkness*. London. Gollancz.
Tiptree Jr., James (2018[1973]). "The Girl Who Was Plugged in." *Envisioning Other Worlds. Science Fiction and Dystopia*. Ed. Christian Ludwig. Berlin: Cornelsen, 31-75.

Secondary Literature

Burwitz-Melzer, Eva, and Daniela Caspari (2017). "Text und Medienkompetenz." *Bildungsstandards aktuell: Französisch/Englisch in der Sekundarstufe II*. Eds. Bernd Tesch et al. Braunschweig. Westermann, 56-83.
Caspari, Daniela, and Ivo Steininger (2016). "Einfachheit in kinder- und jugendliterarischen Texten aus fremdsprachendidaktischer Sicht." *Einfachheit in der Kinder- und Jugendliteratur – ein Gewinn für den Fremdsprachenunterricht.* Eds. Eva Burwitz-Melzer and Emer O'Sullivan. Wien: Praesens Verlag.
Klafki, Wolfgang (1985). *Neue Studien zur Bildungstheorie und Didaktik: Beiträge zur kritisch-konstruktiven Didaktik*. Weinheim: Beltz.
Kultusministerkonferenz (2014). *Bildungsstandards für die fortgeführte Fremdsprache (Englisch/Französisch).* Köln: Carl Link.
Mensink, Gert B. M., Clarissa Lage Barbosa and Anna-Kristin Brettschneider (2016). "Verbreitung der vegetarischen Ernährungsweise in Deutschland." *Journal of Health Monitoring* 1.2: 2-14. Web. 13 June 2019.
Thaler, Engelbert (2008). *Teaching English Literature*. Paderborn: Schöningh.
Vollmer, Helmut Johannes (2017). "Sprachbewusstheit." *Bildungsstandards aktuell: Französisch/Englisch in der Sekundarstufe II*. Eds. Bernd Tesch et al. Braunschweig. Westermann, 201-219.
Westphal, Gary (2005). *The Greenwood Encyclopedia of Science Fiction and Fantasy: Themes, Works, and Wonders. Volume 1.* Westport: Greenwood Press.

Claudia Deetjen (Würzburg)

Imagining Futures Beyond the Nation State: Mohsin Hamid's *Exit West* in the EFL Classroom

1. Introduction

Recent years have in many ways been characterised by a growing sense of global crisis in light of events and developments which challenge the powers of individual nation states, such as global financial instabilities, the effects of climate change, international terrorism or large-scale refugee movements. This sense of global crisis has also generated a growing awareness of the need to envision alternative forms of solidarity and responsibility beyond the nation state. It has increasingly been recognised, moreover, that education must play a key role in this context. Global education and Global Citizenship Education (GCE) have become influential approaches in foreign language teaching as well as in other subject disciplines, introducing global topics into school curricula and prompting discussions about the skills learners require who are growing up in an increasingly interconnected world.

In the following, I will explore how Mohsin Hamid's science-fiction novel *Exit West* (2017) may serve as a means of introducing a global perspective into the foreign language classroom by addressing global topics such as war, migration and national belonging and reflecting on possible future alternatives to the current international order. As a science-fiction novel, the text is of a "[s]peculative nature" and concerned with "philosophizing on 'what if?".[1] Science fiction was influentially defined by Suvin as "the literature of cognitive estrangement" generated by the introduction of a novum, as Suvin calls it, namely a possible difference from reality as we know it, whose consequences for individuals and for society at large are explored.[2] Hamid's novel reflects on what might happen if those who are affected by war, poverty or other adversities could simply escape their situation through magic doorways and travel somewhere else on the planet. How would this affect our current world order, the function of nation states and forms of national belonging? By posing questions such as these, I will argue in the following, the novel may serve to challenge students' perspectives on current developments such as the refugee crisis, prompt them to reflect on their own position in the contemporary world order and to conduct thought experiments about possible alternative futures, thereby acquiring key competencies in global citizenship. In the following sections, I will first outline central aims of global citizenship education approaches and then discuss ways in which Mohsin Hamid's novel may be used in the classroom to foster global citizenship competencies.

2. Global Citizenship Education

Approaches of Global Citizenship Education (GCE) are premised on the assumption that adolescents grow up as both citizens of nation states and as global citizens with certain rights and responsibilities towards a larger world community.[3] They aim at preparing them for this role by developing the necessary skills to responsibly function as world citizens. Depending on how global citizenship is conceived, GCE approaches may have a range of very different aims: they may serve the economic aim of preparing learners for a future global world of work (*qualification purpose*) by developing their linguistic skills as well as their knowledge of global structures. Moreover, GCE may also socialise learners in more idealistic ways (*socialisation purpose*) by developing skills and values necessary for students to function as responsible members of the wider global community (this includes human rights education, peace education or education for sustainable development). Finally, GCE may aim at turning learners into independent thinkers (*subjectification purpose*) by encouraging critical thinking skills and offering a space to develop their own interests and values.[4]

International organisations, national governments and educational institutions are increasingly including 'global education' and 'citizenship education' in their curricula and publishing educational frameworks as guidance for classroom practice. A global education agenda, for examples, is part of the UNESCO Sustainable Development Goals (SDGs) that make up the Agenda 2030 for sustainable development. The goals for global citizenship education as set forth by UNESCO focus on developing cognitive, socio-emotional and behavioural skills. Core competencies to be developed include

- an attitude supported by multiple levels of identity, and the potential for a collective identity that transcends individual cultural, religious, ethnic or other differences (for example, sense of belongingness to common humanity, respect for diversity);
- a deep knowledge of global issues and universal values such as justice, equality, dignity and respect (for example, understanding of the process of globalization, interdependence/interconnectedness, the global challenges which cannot be adequately or uniquely addressed by nation states, sustainability as the main concept of the future);
- cognitive skills to think critically, systemically and creatively, including a multi-perspective approach that recognizes different dimensions, perspectives and angles of an issue (for example, reasoning and problem-solving skills supported by a multi-perspective approach);
- non-cognitive skills, including social skills such as empathy and conflict resolution and communication skills and aptitudes for networking and interacting with people of different backgrounds, origins, cultures and perspectives (for example, global empathy, sense of solidarity);
- behavioural capacities to act collaboratively and responsibly to find global solutions to global challenges and to strive for the collective good (for example, sense of commitment, decision-making skills).[5]

The foreign language classroom may significantly contribute to Global Citizenship Education. When it comes to qualifying learners in an economic sense for mobile careers in a global world of work, foreign languages – in particular English as a lingua franca – are an essential tool for communication and interaction. Furthermore, beyond transmitting linguistic skills, the English in the Foreign Classroom (EFL) classroom also contributes to GCE by promoting cultural learning. It may raise students' awareness of the cultural dimensions of intercultural encounters and conflicts and enable them to competently manage such situations by fostering inter-/transcultural communicative competences. Moreover, the foreign language classroom is a place where learning about world cultures and global issues can take place – about diverse ways of life, (universal) values, topics of global relevance (such as neo-colonialism, globalisation, environmental issues, human rights). What is more, learners may become critical participants in global cultural discourses: when analysing and evaluating texts about international topics, learners may not only build up knowledge but also learn to examine and question discourses on global issues as well as become active, critical participants in these discourses by producing texts themselves.[6]

Finally, in important ways literary learning in the foreign language classroom may also play a key role in the development of global citizenship competencies. As Nussbaum has highlighted, the new social and political realities of a globalized world require that citizens develop attitudes and behaviours characterised by a "richness of human understanding and aspiration which cannot be supplied by economic connections alone".[7] In this context, literary texts are significant in developing a 'narrative imagination': "[c]itizens cannot think well on the basis of factual knowledge alone." They need to develop a "narrative imagination", an "ability to think what it might be like to be in the shoes of a person different from oneself, to […] understand the emotions and wishes and desires that someone so placed might have."[8] Literary texts, in their ability to represent the lives and problems of diverse sorts of people, allow readers to encounter and share a variety of perspectives and thereby develop their narrative imagination. This skill is an important prerequisite for becoming an informed and responsible member of the global community, since

> the first step of understanding the world from the point of view of the other is essential to any responsible act of judgement, since we do not know what we are judging until we see the meaning of an action as the person intends it.[9]

Next to promoting empathy and skills in changing perspectives, literary texts – and narratives more generally – may also play an important role in creating attachment to the world community, a sense of global identity. Stories, according to narrative approaches to identity construction,[10] constitute identity. Through telling and consuming stories of ourselves, of past and present experiences, we gain a sense of identity, of who we are, where we come from and where we are going.

Mohsin Hamid's science-fiction novel *Exit West*, I will argue in the following, holds great potential to foster competencies in global citizenship in the EFL classroom. The text may enhance learners' understanding of global topics like war, poverty and migration and promote an awareness of universal values like human rights. By reflecting on how instantaneous travel through magic doors may work as a solution to crisis, impact individual lives and identities and transform local and global communities, students may gain skills in creative, critical thinking about potential alternative futures and solutions to global problems. Exploring the story of the novel's protagonists Saeed and Nadia, students can develop their narrative imagination, gain key skills in changing perspectives and developing empathy. In the following section, I will focus on how and to what purposes *Exit West* may be used in the foreign language classroom and offer classroom suggestions for potential lesson designs.

3. Teaching Science Fiction: Mohsin Hamid's *Exit West*

Mohsin Hamid's novel *Exit West* addresses the refugee crisis which emerged during the second decade of the twenty-first century. According to the Office of the United Nations High Commissioner for Refugees, an estimated 1,008,616 refugees and migrants attempted to enter Europe by sea in 2015 alone, 49% of these being from Syria, 21% from Afghanistan and 9% from Iraq.[11] While the migration journey is often a perilous and traumatic one and integration into host countries difficult, the arrival of migrants in European countries has also caused organisational problems, from the provision of housing and management of the asylum process to schooling and an increasing nativist backlash. Hamid addresses the difficulties in his science-fiction novel and predicts possible future trajectories: what might happen if migration were commonplace and the entire planet were on the move? What problems would this cause and how might we handle it?

Hamid's *Exit West* was published in 2017 to great critical acclaim. It was selected as the New York Times Best Book of the Year, awarded the LA Times Book Prize for Fiction and shortlisted for the Man Booker Prize and the National Book Critics Circle Award. *Exit West* mainly follows the story of an unequal young couple, Saeed and Nadia, who fall in love in a city which is "still mostly at peace, or at least not yet openly at war".[12] The two meet in an evening class on corporate identity and product branding. Saeed, who is the son of a university professor and a teacher and works in an ad agency, is a conservative man believing in family values. Nadia is an independent and self-confident woman. She lives alone and works for an insurance company. Nadia wears a full black robe to ward off unwelcome male advances. She does not pray, rides a motorbike and enjoys the occasional psychedelic mushroom. Roughly the first half of the story is set in Saeed and Nadia's home city. Though it remains unnamed throughout the novel, critics have identified resemblances to the Syrian cities Aleppo[13] or Mosul.[14] Mohsin Hamid, on the other hand, has stated that he "modell[ed]" the city on his own birthplace:

> I wrote it thinking of Lahore, modelling it after the city of Lahore, where I live. And I just couldn't bring myself to fictionally ... cause to befall to Lahore the terrible events that happen to Saeed in Nadia's city. [...] But partly, I also wanted to open it up – to have people from other places imagine this as their city, so as to widen the entry point into the novel, for different types of [...] readers from different places.[15]

While their city is still at peace at the beginning of the novel, violence between government forces and fundamentalist militant groups soon escalates to civil war. Public life comes to a standstill, shops and businesses close; many people, among them also Saeed's mother, are killed. Those, like Saeed and Nadia, who have the means to do so, escape the violence and flee the city. Migrants in Hamid's *Exit West* travel through magical doors that have opened up all over the world. These doors defy the laws of physics; space-time compression allows instantaneous travel across vast distances – from war zones and refugee camps directly to Tokyo, London or Sydney:

> Rumours had begun to circulate of doors that could take you elsewhere, often to places far away, well removed from this death trap of a country. Some people claimed to know people who knew people who had been through such doors. A normal, they said, could become a special door, and it could happen without warning, to any door at all.[16]

In the course of the narrative, Saeed and Nadia migrate from their unnamed country in order to escape militant takeover of their city. Passing through magical doors, their journey takes them first to the Greek island Mykonos, where they live in a refugee camp, on to London, where they are first squatters in an unoccupied house and then become part of a workforce in the new "London Halo".[17] Finally, they move on to

California, where they help to build the city of Marin. Interspersed in the narrative of Saeed and Nadia, there are other travel accounts of people from diverse places, using the doors to travel great distances in all directions. It is not just refugees who are on the move in *Exit West*, but other alienated people as well. An accountant on the verge of suicide in London, for example, escapes his situation by stepping through a door to Namibia. An old Brazilian man steps through a door in an Amsterdam housing block and falls in love with an old Dutch man. When presenting the stories of these migrants, the novel uses shifting focalisation and thereby offers different angles on the issue of migration and different points of identification. Events are told from both the 'outsider perspective' of the migrants arriving in the host country or from the perspective of an 'insider', an inhabitant of the host country. In Sydney, for example, a man coming from "perilous circumstances" somewhere in Africa arrives. The reader is given access to his feelings of bewilderment and fear; he is aware of the "fragility of his body. He knew how little it took to make a man into meat: the wrong blow, the wrong gunshot, the wrong flick of a blade, turn of a car, presence of a microorganism in a handshake, a cough".[18] Another story presents the perspective of an observing bystander in Tokyo, reflecting on his dislike of the arriving migrants from the Philippines:

> Not the first time this week that he had seen a group of Filipinos who seemed oddly clueless in his bit of town. He disliked Filipinos. They had their place, but they had to know their place [...] He watched the girls walk. Considered. And slipped into a walk behind them, fingering the metal in his pocket as he went.[19]

Doors in *Exit West* grant transit mostly from poorer to richer places but also vice versa (destinations include Sydney, Tokyo, San Diego, Nadia and Saeed's city, Dubai, Namibia, Tijuana, Amsterdam, Marin, Palo Alto). While doors leading to richer countries are heavily guarded and travel is thus restricted, doors to poorer places are not. Much as the refugees do not know their destination when they step through a door, the authorities also do not know where or when the next door will appear. While the doors are a means of escape from war and poverty, they also create a growing sense of crisis and nativist backlash in the wealthy nations that are "building walls and fences and strengthening their borders, but seemingly to unsatisfactory effect".[20] Even though authorities in London attempt to secure the doors, the arrival of migrants is ultimately uncontrollable and the structure of the city is fundamentally transformed:

> All over London houses and parks and disused lots were being peopled [...] some said by a million migrants, some said by twice that. It was now said that between Westminster and Hammersmith legal residents were in the minority, and native-born ones vanishingly few, with local newspapers referring to the area as the worst of the black holes in the fabric of the nation.[21]

By making possible unchecked, free movement anywhere across the planet, the magical doors even out existing inequalities between the global North and the global South. Causing new forms of restriction and conflict, however, the doors are also a means of exacerbating these "unequal power dynamics", Lagji has pointed out, and giving rise to new forms of violence and nativist backlash.[22]

Exit West also explores the effects these doors have on larger society and on individuals. The house in London, where Saeed and Nadia first arrive, is inhabited by a diverse range of people – from countries such as Nigeria, Somalia, Guatemala or Indonesia. Nadia and Saeed respond differently to life in this hybrid, post-national community. Nadia easily adapts to the community of the house, realising that "they represented the birth of something new"[23] and becomes part of the house's governing council responsible for the management of the house's daily affairs. She even feels liberated by life in this new community, realising that "she had been stifled in the place of her birth for virtually her entire life [...] and a new time was here, and [...] she relished this like the wind in her face on a hot day".[24] Saeed, on the other hand, feels a sense of unease because he "is the only man from his country" in this house, a fact that "touched upon something basic, something tribal, and evoked tension and a sort of fear".[25] He longs to hear a familiar language, smell familiar foods and to be among countrymen. Saeed finds this familiarity in the "nearby house of his fellow countryfolk", a community that, as their leader suggests, represented "a banding together of migrants along religious principles, cutting across divisions of race or language or nation, for what did those divisions matter now in a world full of doors". Though these words remind him of the militants back home, Saeed is "moved" and even "strengthened by them".[26] When he eventually asks Nadia to move into the house of his countrymen, even though they would have to live in separate rooms divided along gender lines, the differences between the two become starkly apparent:

> 'Why would we want to move?' she said.
> 'To be among our own kind,' Saeed answered.
> 'What makes them our kind?'
> 'They're from our country.'
> 'From the country we used to be from.'
> 'Yes.' Saeed tried not to sound annoyed.
> 'We've left that place.'
> 'That doesn't mean we have no connection.'
> 'They're not like me. ' [27]

While post-national communities are thus emerging, nativist extremists across the globe react with violence and surveillance to the influx of migrants. As militants from Nadia and Saeed's country for example make their way to Vienna to stir up trouble, violence erupts –"the city had witnessed massacres in the streets, the militants shooting unarmed people and then disappearing"; some local people react by forming "a mob that was intending to attack the migrants"[28] while others try to prevent these riots. Also, in London police in full riot gear tries to evacuate the house where Nadia and Saeed first arrive. Moreover, migrants are attacked by nativist mobs "a strange and violent tribe, intent on their destruction, some armed with iron bars or knives"[29] and a campaign "to reclaim Britain for Britain" is started, supported by the army and the police.[30] There are even rumours of holding camps in London; migrants are kept in constant surveillance by drones and helicopters. Eventually, power is officially cut off in London's migrant district (Kensington and Chelsea), and a "dark London" is created where life is radically different from the rest of the city:

> From dark London, Saeed and Nadia wondered what life must be like in light London, where they imagined people dined in elegant restaurants and rode in shiny black cabs, or at least went to work in offices and shops and were free to journey as they pleased. In dark London, rubbish accrued, uncollected, and underground stations were sealed. The trains kept running, skipping stops near Saeed and Nadia but felt as a rumble beneath their feet and heard at a low, powerful frequency, almost subsonic, like thunder or the detonation of a massive, distant bomb. At night, in the

> darkness, as drones and helicopters and surveillance balloons prowled intermittently overhead, fights would break out, and there were murders and rapes and assaults as well.[31]

While Londoners react with xenophobia, there are others who greet migrants with compassion and solidarity, offering food and medicine. In the face of police and nativist violence, moreover, "a sort of camaraderie evolved [...] here they were being penned in together, and being penned in made them into a grouping, a group".[32] In the end, fighting abates in London, nativists back off perhaps because they have realised that the attempt to ward off migration is futile, perhaps because decency has won out.[33] Saeed and Nadia become part of a workforce to construct a new London Halo, new cities built to accommodate the arriving people, a development that occurs in similar ways throughout the world. As recompense for their work, the two are assigned land on which they might settle. Relations to native Londoners are appeased by a somewhat questionable "time tax", according to which a portion of migrants' income goes to the British.[34] Nonetheless conflict between nativists and migrants continues to simmer but a "tolerable safety"[35] has been achieved. Much as established social and political structures in the UK increasingly dissolve, news brings information about similar developments in other parts of the world. Migration has become commonplace, and the whole planet is on the move; mostly "the global south headed to the global north, but also southerners moving to other southern places and northerners moving to other northern places".[36] As a consequence, social and political structures everywhere are changing, and the contours of nation states are becoming blurred: regions are

> pulling away from nations, and cities pulling away from hinterlands [...] Without borders nations appeared to be becoming illusory, and people were questioning what role they had to play. Many were arguing that smaller units made more sense, but others argued that smaller units could not defend themselves.[37]

In the end, in the hope of leaving conflict behind, Saeed and Nadia move through a door to the new migrant city of Marin, close to San Francisco. The two live in a shanty with a view of the bay and the Golden Gate Bridge. Electricity is generated by solar panels, water is collected in buckets and sustenance is grown in a food cooperative for which Nadia comes to work. Though Marin is "overwhelmingly poor [...] there was nonetheless a spirit of at least intermittent optimism" perhaps because the place was less violent, perhaps because of the "mix of its people".[38] The novel ends on a positive note in a vision of new beginning. Nadia and Saeed, whose lives have grown apart, separate and each enter into new relationships. The city of Marin is undergoing an (economic) upturn. In Marin and

> in many other places too, places both near and far, the apocalypse appeared to have arrived and yet it was not apocalyptic, which is to say that while the changes were jarring they were not the end, and life went on and people found things to do and ways to be and people to be with, and plausible desirable futures began to emerge, unimaginable previously, but not unimaginable now, and the result was something not unlike relief.[39]

Hence, by presenting the story of Saeed and Nadia's journey from conflict to a new beginning, *Exit West* achieves empathy with two characters who become refugees. By offering snapshots of other stories of migration, the novel indicates that the experience of migration is shared by many living in situations of adversity and conflict; ultimately, it is shared by everyone. In a recent interview, Hamid points out that if "we can recognise the universality of the refugee experience – that those of us who have never moved are also migrants and refugees – then the space for empathy opens up".[40] Hence, in Mohsin Hamid's *Exit West* the SF device of the magic doors functions as a means of exploring the experience of migration from diverse perspectives and of imagining what it might be like to live in a post-national world where the borders of nation states may easily be traversed by everyone and no longer determine personal belonging and identity.

When using Mohsin Hamid's science-fiction novel with a focus on these issues in the classroom, students may acquire various global citizenship competencies. They may gain knowledge about the causes of displacement and about refugee experiences. Since the exact location of Saeed and Nadia's home country is left open, students are free to research a variety of global conflict scenarios. Moreover, they may acquire skills in changing perspectives, develop empathy as well as their "narrative imagination" because the experience of migration is explored from diverse perspectives in the novel. Finally, students may develop skills in creative critical thinking: discussing what might happen if instantaneous travel were possible, students may reflect on the significance of nation states, the necessity and the possibility of larger forms of identification (with other forms of community), solidarity and responsibility. These teaching aims may be achieved by classroom tasks presented in the table.

4. Teaching Mohsin Hamid's *Exit West*

Pre-reading tasks	*Do you identify yourself with a particular community or group?* *What is the nature of these groups/communities?* *Do you identify yourself as a German citizen? Why (not)?* *Do you think of yourself as a global citizen? Why (not)?* *Discuss whether it would be possible to imagine a world government. What (dis)advantages would this form of political organisation have?*
While-reading tasks	*Collect information on the SF device of the 'black doors' in the novel by creating a map that exhibits travel routes. Describe how the doors function and how travellers experience the journey. Comment on whether you believe the existence of such doors might scientifically be possible.* *When in Mykonos, Saeed has the chance to send an e-mail to his father. Write Saeed's e-mail in which he describes the camp and writes about his feelings upon arrival in the camp.* *When in the camp in Mykonos, there are rumours of doors opening up to Germany. Reflect on how Nadia and Saeed's story might have continued*

	had they travelled to Germany. Where might they have arrived and what might they have experienced there? Prepare a continuation of Nadia and Saeed's story in Germany. *Close-read chapter 7. Describe how Saeed and Nadia each manage the journey through the door and how they feel upon arrival. Analyse how their attitude towards their home country is changing. Comment on whose position you might share if you were in a similar situation.* *Analyse the depiction of dark London, located in Chelsea and Kensington. What divisions within London society does the novel outline here? Explore how this depiction of dark London corresponds to actual living conditions in that area of London by researching what happened during the Grenfell Tower fire on 14 June 2017 (North Kensington). Over half of the 72 victims had Arab names.* *Nadia comments on the outbreak of nativism in London: "I can understand it," she said. "Imagine if you lived here. And millions of people from all over the world suddenly arrived" (Hamid [2017], 162). Do you (dis)agree? Give reasons for your opinion.*
While-reading tasks	*Continue Saeed's or Nadia's story after they have separated. What happens in the years they do not see each other? Continue the story by writing a piece of fan fiction.*

	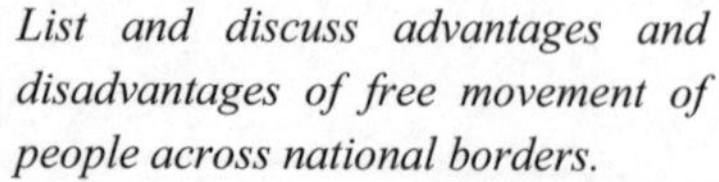 *List and discuss advantages and disadvantages of free movement of people across national borders.* *Read and discuss the article "Why there is no such thing as global citizenship" (Liu [2012]). Analyse the author's arguments. Do you agree or disagree with him? Explain why (not).* *Take the German citizenship test. Did you pass the test? Why (not)? How important do you think this test is?*

Table 1: Tasks for Teaching Mohsin Hamid's *Exit West*

5. Conclusion

Mohsin Hamid's first three novels – *Moth Smoke* (2000), *The Reluctant Fundamentalist* (2007) and *How to Get Filthy Rich in Rising Asia* (2013) – were all big commercial successes. His novel *The Reluctant Fundamentalist*, which was turned into a blockbuster in 2012, has also become an established text in the school canon. Hamid's earlier texts are all realist novels and focus on the experiences of characters from Pakistan; *Exit West* is his first attempt at science fiction. The novel combines elements of science fiction (or speculative fiction) with dystopia. Using the device of the magical doors, which function as space-time wormholes of sorts that make teleportation possible, the novel includes fantastic elements. The text, however, is not concerned with the nature of the doors (how exactly they operate remains a mystery) but rather with exploring the effects of this technology on individuals and the structure of society. The society Hamid envisions in his novel, while there are elements of dystopia in the depiction of nativist urban conflict, is ultimately positive and hopeful in character. As one reviewer points out, *Exit West*, as the title suggests, envisions an interconnected world, a new society, in which East and West meet, overcoming – though not without conflict – past divisions due to colonialism and globalization.[41]

By virtue of their "speculative nature" that makes reality appear 'strange' and opens up potential alternatives, science-fiction novels "ha[ve] the capacity to stimulate, to unsettle, to provoke the reader into an intellectual response".[42] Mohsin Hamid's *Exit West* may become a tool in the classroom that prompts students to question and re-consider their present national identities and their position in the global community and to engage in creative discussions about possible future societies, world orders and identities as global citizens. Because the text invites identification with Saeed and Nadia, who become refugees, and with countless other migrant experiences, students may develop empathy, a sense of solidarity with and responsibility for others in the world community – in particular, because they are made aware that the experience of these migrants might one day be their own.

Notes

1 Sawyer, Andy, and Peter Wright (2011). "Introduction." *Teaching Science Fiction*. Eds. Andy Sawyer and Peter Wright. New York: Palgrave, 1–20, 1.

2 Suvin, Darko (2016). *Metamorphoses of Science Fiction: On the Poetics and History of a Literary Genre*. Oxford: Peter Lang, 15.

3 GCE is a complex concept and difficult to fully define. The idea of global citizenship is an old one. Nigel Dower traces it back to Stoicism and the idea of cosmopolitanism, according to which all human beings are citizens (*polites*) of the world (*cosmos*) and hence belong a common moral realm (cf. Dower, Nigel [2002]. "Introduction." *Global Citizenship. A Critical Introduction.* Ed. Nigel Dower. New York: Routledge, 1–11.). GCE began to appear in the 1990s in the UK and the USA in the context of NGO and UN education material. It may be considered an umbrella term which encompasses many different approaches such as human rights and peace education as well as environmental education (cf. Sant, Edda, et al. [2018]. *Global Citizenship Education. A Critical Introduction to Key Concepts and Debates*. New York: Bloomsbury, 7).

4 *Ibid.*, 21-26.

5 UNESCO. *Global Citizenship Education. Preparing Learners for the Challenges of the Twenty-First Century,* 2014. Web. 7 February 2020 <http://unesdoc.unesco.org/images/0022/002277/227729e.pdf.>.

6 Sant et al. (2018), 201-202.

[7] Nussbaum, Martha (2002). "Education for Citizenship in an Era of Global Connection." *Studies in Philosophy and Education* 21, 289-303, 292.

[8] *Ibid.,* 299.

[9] *Ibid.*

[10] Ricoeur, Paul (1991). *From Text to Action: Essays in Hermeneutics II.* Thompson. Illinois: Northwestern University Press.

[11] Maley, William (2016). *What is a Refugee?* London: Hurst & Company, 68.

[12] Hamid, Mohsin (2017). *Exit West*. New York: Penguin, 1.

[13] Shriver, Lionel (2017). "Review of Exit West." *The Times* 4 March 2017: n. pag. Web. 4 February 2020 <https://www.thetimes.co.uk>.

[14] Giraldi, William (2017). "Review of Exit West." *The Washington Post* 23 February 2017: n. pag. Web. 1 Feb. 2020 <https://www.washingtonpost.com.>.

[15] Frostrup, Mariella, and Mohsin Hamid. *BBC Radio 4 Open Book*, 2017. Web. 4 February 2020 <https://learningonscreen.ac.uk>.

[16] Hamid (2017), 69-70.

[17] *Ibid.*, 167.

[18] *Ibid.*, 7.

[19] *Ibid.*, 28.

[20] *Ibid.*, 71.

[21] *Ibid.*, 126.

[22] Lagji, Amanda (2019). "Waiting in Motion: Mapping Postcolonial Fiction, New Mobilities, and Migration Through Mohsin Hamid's Exit West." *Mobilities* 14.2, 219-232, 219.

[23] Hamid (2017), 145.

[24] *Ibid.*, 156.

[25] *Ibid.*, 149-150.

[26] *Ibid.*, 152.

[27] *Ibid.*, 149.

[28] *Ibid.*, 104.

[29] *Ibid.*, 131.

[30] *Ibid.*, 132.

[31] *Ibid.*, 142.

[32] *Ibid.*, 124.

[33] *Ibid.*, 164

[34] *Ibid.*, 168.

[35] *Ibid.*

[36] *Ibid.*, 167.

37 *Ibid.,* 155.

38 *Ibid.*, 192-193.

39 *Ibid.*, 215-216.

40 Chandler, Caitlin L., and Mohsin Hamid (2017). "We Are All Refugees: A Conversation With Mohsin Hamid." *The Nation* 30 Oct. 2017: n. pag. Web. 20 January 2020 <https://www.thenation.com/article/we-are-all-refugees-a-conversation-with-mohsin-hamid/>. Critics have pointed out that Hamid here articulates a somewhat reductive view of refugee experiences, also adding that his science-fiction device of the doors negates the traumatic experience of flight.

41 Nguyen, Viet Than (2017). "Review of Exit West." *The New York Times* 10 March 2017: n. pag. Web. 10 January 2020 <https://www.nytimes.com/2017/03/10/books/review/exit-west-mohsin-hamid.html>.

42 Sawyer and Wright (2011), 1.

Bibliography

Primary Texts

Hamid, Mohsin (2000). *Moth Smoke*. New York: Penguin.

--- (2007). *The Reluctant Fundamentalist*. New York: Penguin.

--- (2013). *How to get Filthy Rich in Rising Asia. A Novel*. New York: Penguin.

--- (2017). *Exit West*. New York: Penguin.

Secondary Literature

Chandler, Caitlin L., and Mohsin Hamid (2017). "We Are All Refugees: A Conversation With Mohsin Hamid." *The Nation* 30 Oct. 2017: n. pag. Web. 20 January 2020 <https://www.thenation.com/article/we-are-all-refugees-a-conversation-with mohsin-hamid>.

Dower, Nigel (2002). "Introduction." *Global Citizenship. A Critical Introduction.* Ed. Nigel Dower. New York: Routledge, 1-11.

Frostrup, Mariella, and Mohsin Hamid. *BBC Radio 4 Open Book*, 2017. Web. 4 February 2020 <https://learningonscreen.ac.uk>.

Giraldi, William (2017). "Review of Exit West." *The Washington Post* 23 February 2017: n. pag. Web. 1 Feb. 2020 <https://www.washingtonpost.com>.

Lagji, Amanda (2019). "Waiting in Motion: Mapping Postcolonial Fiction, New Mobilities, and Migration Through Mohsin Hamid's Exit West." *Mobilities* 14.2, 219-232.

Liu, Eric (2012). "Why there is no such Thing as Global Citizenship." *The Atlantic* 14 Aug. 2012. Web. 14 February 2020 <https://www.theatlantic.com/national/archive/2012/08/why-theres-no-such-thing-as-global-citizenship/261128/>.

Maley, William (2016). *What is a Refugee?* London: Hurst & Company.

Nguyen, Viet Than (2017). "Review of Exit West." *The New York Times* 10 March 2017: n. pag. Web. 10 January 2020 <https://www.nytimes.com/2017/03/10/books/review/exit-west-mohsin-hamid.html>.

Nussbaum, Martha (2002). "Education for Citizenship in an Era of Global Connection." *Studies in Philosophy and Education* 21, 289-303.

Perfect, Michael (2019). "'Black Holes in the Fabric of the Nation': Refugees in Mohsin Hamid's Exit West." *Journal of Cultural Research* 23.2, 187-201.

Ricoeur, Paul (1991). *From Text to Action: Essays in Hermeneutics II.* Thompson. Illinois: Northwestern University Press.

Sant, Edda, et al. (2018). *Global Citizenship Education. A Critical Introduction to Key Concepts and Debates*. New York: Bloomsbury.

Sawyer, Andy, and Peter Wright (eds.) (2011). *Teaching Science Fiction*. New York: Palgrave.

Sawyer, Andy, and Peter Wright (2011). "Introduction." *Teaching Science Fiction*. Eds. Andy Sawyer and Peter Wright. New York: Palgrave, 1-20.

Shriver, Lionel (2017). "Review of Exit West." *The Times* 4 March 2017: n. pag. Web. 4 February 2020 <https://www.thetimes.co.uk>.

Suvin, Darko (2016). *Metamorphoses of Science Fiction: On the Poetics and History of a Literary Genre*. Oxford: Peter Lang.

UNESCO. *Global Citizenship Education. Preparing Learners for the Challenges of the Twenty-First Century,* 2014. Web. 7 February 2020 <http://unesdoc.unesco.org/images/0022/002277/227729e.pdf.>.

Liesel Hermes (Karlsruhe) and Christian Ludwig (Berlin)

John Marsden's *Tomorrow, When the War Began* – How War Can Change Young People's Lives

1. Introduction

Dystopian novels have experienced a rather unexpected revival since the turn of the millennium, resulting in a wealth of especially young adult dystopian novels currently on the market. This has also aroused the interest of educators who argue that the genre holds great potential for the English as a foreign language (EFL) classroom. While many of these novels are quite surprisingly read by more adults than teenagers, the great majority of them deal with archetypal adolescent themes such as love, growing up, and finding one's identity. Thus, they recapitulate many of the conventions of the classic *Bildungsroman*, using an apocalyptic event as a catalyst for both the development towards adulthood and of a dystopian society. The aim of the present article is to look at an Australian example of the genre in more detail: John Marsden's *Tomorrow, When the War Began* (1993), which became an instant success in Australia and was also adapted into both a film (2010) and television series (2016). The novel is the first in a series of seven books, telling the story of a group of teenagers who come back from a camping trip to discover that Australia has been invaded by an unknown hostile power, which forces them to hide in order to stay alive. While their families and friends are being held captive at the Showground – awaking vivid memories of the native reservations in Australian history – and the country's leaders have fled to the United States, from where they broadcast patriotic messages, the teenagers form an underground resistance group, using ambushes, raids, and hit-and-run tactics to free their beloved ones and return to their old lives.

The novel's content and enduring success and popularity should make reading the novel in the EFL classroom a rewarding experience. This article chooses a mostly post- and neo-colonial approach and explores some of the major themes of the novel, especially focusing on the teenagers' experiences of the hostile take-over and subsequent colonisation of their country while they are in the critical transition phase from adolescence to adulthood. Such an approach seems to be particularly fruitful not only with a view to Australia's colonisation history but also the increasing number of political, religious, and cultural conflicts which require or even force the individual to situate himself or herself in a constantly changing and globalising world. These characteristics illustrate the potential of the young adult dystopian genre for the contemporary classroom.

The first section of this article will provide a brief summary of the plot. The ensuing section will then discuss the genre of young adult dystopian fiction and its potential for the EFL classroom. The third section will concentrate on some of the novel's major themes, particularly on the teenage group's *rites de passage* and guerrilla warfare in the context of what could be considered Australia's 'second' or 'relived' colonisation. The article will conclude by providing some more practical suggestions for approaching the novel in the classroom.

2. *Tomorrow, When the War Began*

The 'war' series, *Tomorrow, When the War Began* by the highly acclaimed Australian young adult fiction author John Marsden, describes how the lives of a group of Australian teenagers change suddenly and unexpectedly when their country is invaded and subsequently colonised by an unnamed presumably Asian country.[1] While the motives for the invasion remain largely in the dark, the novel reveals some scattered information about the nature, level, and extent of the conflict, mostly revealed through the teenagers' observations and fragmentary information they gather as the following excerpt from a radio broadcast by the aggressor illustrates:

> It was a male voice, and all we could hear was this: '… warned America not to get involved. The General said that America would find herself in the longest, costliest and bloodiest war in her history if she tried to intervene. He said his forces have occupied several major coastal cities. Much of the inland has been taken already, and losses have been below

> expectations. […] 'The General repeated his claim that the invasion was aimed at "reducing imbalances within the region".[2]

Now entirely on their own, the teenagers, including the narrator, Ellie Linton, start a guerrilla war, harassing the largely unknown enemy to the best of their limited capabilities and causing as much damage to the invader's war machinery as possible.

Right at the beginning of the novel, the reader learns that both the world and the region are in a difficult political and economic situation, making the invasion of Australia more likely: a historical fact which will be discussed in more detail in section four. The country, however, is apparently in no position to defend itself; a fact which is emphasised by a reference to the former British Prime Minister Neville Chamberlain, who is still today remembered for his appeasement policy during the early years of the NAZI regime, allowing Hitler's annexation of the Sudetenland, purportedly to save peace. The ensuing quote from the novel illustrates the controversial opinions on the country's foreign policy and its ability to defend itself in case of an attack:

> I stopped and watched for a moment. 'We've got a wimp for a Foreign Minister,' the face was shouting. 'He's weak, he's gutless, he is the new Neville Chamberlain. He doesn't understand the people he's dealing with. They respect strength, not weakness!'
> 'Do you think defence is high on the government's agenda?' the interviewer asked.
> 'High? High? You must be joking! Do you know what they've cut from the defence budget?'[3]

Despite the sword of Damocles hanging over Australia, the novel, like other science-fiction classics such as *War of the Worlds*, starts rather unspectacularly in normal life: Ellie, the first person narrator, and her friends decide to go camping in the bush shortly before they leave school, ending up in a remote area called Hell. When the teenagers return home a few days later, however, they immediately notice that the entire town is devoid of people and that the pets and livestock are either missing or dying or dead. Quickly realising that their lives have changed irreversibly, they have to get used to a harsh and dangerous life underground. Suddenly, practical aspects of life (during war) such as food supplies, clothes, and cleanliness but also mere survival become some of the central concerns of the group as the ensuing quote, which exemplifies their gradual transition from normal teenagers to guerrillas, demonstrates:

> It suddenly seemed so obvious that if we had a future, it would be in Hell. And we began to realise that there might still be a life for us.
> 'We'll make lists,' Fi said. 'We need pens and paper, Corrie.'
> Our lists took nearly an hour to compile.
> […]
> Homer didn't comment on the family photos but when that encouraged other family treasures being added to the list he spoke up.
> […]
> 'Corrie, this isn't a picnic we're going on. We've got to start thinking of ourselves as guerrillas. We're already taking teddy bears and guitars. I think that's enough.'[4]

When their group is discovered by the alien forces, they manage to escape, knowing that two of their friends are left behind, one of them with a badly wounded leg. They succeed in freeing their injured friend, but also accidentally discover another teenager who had managed to hide from the soldiers while his parents had been arrested together with all the other inhabitants of their hometown. Living a life in hiding, romantic relationships develop and continue while the group tries to stay alive and gradually starts a guerrilla war. Eventually, destroying the main bridge of Wirrawee, the teenagers' hometown, becomes their main goal in the first book. Although the destruction of the bridge is successful, one of the female guerrillas is badly wounded and needs urgent medical attention. Her boyfriend sets out with her for the hospital in the occupied territory.

This brief summary of the first book already elucidates that armed conflict as well as life during the time of war feature strongly in the novel. However, the fact that teenagers are the main characters in *Tomorrow* also allows it to touch upon a plethora of themes, many of which are only loosely, if at all, connected to war itself.

In the ensuing section, it will be argued that the novel can be classified as a young adult dystopia, a genre which offers many advantages to L2 literature teaching.

Dystopian fiction can be considered one of the most influential genres of the twentieth century, mostly due "[to] the impact of two world wars and global conflicts of opposing political systems".[5] Only a few decades later, dystopias are once again extremely popular among adults and teenagers alike. However, in contrast to their twentieth century counterparts such as *1984* (1949) or *Fahrenheit 451* (1953), young adult dystopias now feature the struggles of young, mostly female, heroes, who become the (often involuntary) leaders of a seemingly futile resistance to the omnipotent (adult) state.[6]

Not least with the increasing incorporation of popular culture and small 'l' literature in foreign language learning, young adult dystopias' ongoing popularity naturally raises the question of whether they should also be read in the contemporary English classroom. In addition to the generally high popularity of speculative fiction among teenage and adult readers (and viewers!) alike, it is especially the teenage heroines (and less frequently heroes) who fight suffering and injustice in the totalitarian and (post-)apocalyptic world of young adult dystopias that appeal to teenagers, who often find themselves embarking on the inner and outer journey of becoming an adult. Closely related to this, the journey of the heroine and her companions often reminds young adults of their own typical problems such as friendship, family, loss, love, and sexual awakening. In other words, they go through exactly the same *rites de passage* as their fictional counterparts.

Despite the high topicality of young adult dystopias, there are also critical voices which argue that the dark and grim futures created in dystopian fiction should be deemed inappropriate for teenage readers, who grow up in a world that is in a bad and fragile state already. In contrast to this, Louis Lowry, the author of *The Giver* (1993), which is often referred to as the first young adult dystopia (*Tomorrow* was published in exactly the same year!), argues that this is the very reason for not keeping young adult dystopias away from today's teenage generation:

> 'Handle?' Young people handle dystopia every day: in their lives, their dysfunctional families, their violence-ridden schools. They watch dystopian television and movies about the real world where firearms bring about explosive conclusions to conflict.[7]

Similarly, Poladian also argues in favour of reading young adult dystopias in the classroom as

> [t]here is value in young adult readers finding violence in dystopian worlds. These books have often been banned because of adults who fear the violence will be too much for young readers. However, banning rather than finding a way to understand and treat violence is counterproductive.[8]

Their power to prepare students for the dystopian reality of the world, however, is not the only argument in favour of reading young adult dystopias in the classroom. By depicting a world that has gone or (far less frequently) is about to go awry, young adult dystopias particularly feature "those areas of technology, scientific progress, social developments etc. that have the potential to develop into problems and threaten to turn our world into a dystopian one".[9] What makes *Tomorrow* particularly worthwhile for the EFL classroom is its strong postcolonial connotation that concentrates on Australia's colonial past and fear of 'reverse neocolonialism' and allows students to share the postcolonial experience[10] as well as participate in the neo-/postcolonial discourse of the 21st century. In other words, young adult dystopias invite students to have a critical look at our contemporary world while, at the same time, distancing themselves from these global concerns through the alienness of the fictional dystopian world written about in the foreign language. As Basu, Broad, and Hintz argue:

> [t]heir narrative techniques often place us close to the action, with first-person narration, engaging dialogue, or even diary entries imparting accessible messages that may have the potential to motivate a generation on the cusp of adulthood.[11]

According to Hintz and Ostry, "dystopia can act as a powerful metaphor for adolescence".[12] In a similar vein, Krüger argues that one defining characteristic of young adult dystopias is the almost symbiotic relationship between adolescence and the dystopian society as both represent "permanent 'states of crisis' marked by conflict and anxiety".[13]

While the example which will be discussed in more detail in the remaining part of this article shows many typical dystopian characteristics, it can still be considered an 'unusual' example of young adult dystopia. The readers are not thrown into a distant post-apocalyptic world but find themselves in a world where economic, political, and most likely environmental problems are turning Australasia into a dystopian war zone. Thus, *Tomorrow* imagines a dystopia in becoming where a group of young adolescents fights a guerrilla war to avoid the permanent establishment of an oppressive occupation regime. Moreover, in contrast to most other young adult dystopias, Marsden's teenagers do not enter a conflict with "all (adult) authority"[14] but only with the adult members of the invading forces. Instead of seeking absolute independence, they frequently remember their teachers' and parents' advice when facing fundamental decisions. One poignantly illustrative example of this is the teenagers' initial focus on reconnaissance missions. When they arrive at the Mackenzies' house, Corrie discovers a last-minute warning message from her father, which he had faxed shortly before his imprisonment. Seeing her father's words makes her remember something her always cautious father used to say before the invasion: "[t]ime spent in reconnaissance is seldom wasted",[15] which becomes the group's motto for a while. Against this backdrop, the ensuing section discusses some of the major themes of the series, particularly focusing on the first novel.

4. Themes in *Tomorrow*

A variety of themes abound in Marsden's novel series, some of which will be discussed in more detail. While the novel is typically Australian in that the group, although they "commensurately maintain some stereotypical ethnic attributes",[16] are multicultural (Lee is of Thai-Vietnamese origin while Homer's background is Greek), it equally touches upon a variety of global issues ranging from social and economic division over human nature to migration.

The basic premise of the novel is a group of teenagers that find themselves in a series of existentialist situations that require life-and-death choices. By making these choices, they contribute to the destruction of their 'old' value system moving inexorably forward. Death quickly becomes daily routine and some members of the group lose their innocence by severely injuring or even killing people. Their 'violent' approach is, however, occasionally questioned in the novel series. For example, in the third book, a small number of enemy soldiers are killed in cold blood, an act of violence which horrifies some of the more pacifist members of the group. As Ellie, the protagonist and narrator, points out herself: "That's what war does to you. Either kills you in one go or destroys you bit by bit. One way or the other it gets you."[17] Existentialism, however, is not the novel's only philosophical notion. Right from the beginning of the series, Ellie's imagination is captured by the story of the alleged hermit murderer Bertram Christie, who languished in obscurity in exactly the same spot, eponymously referred to as Hell, where the teenagers camp a century later. Similar to Christie, the group uses Hell – by way of oxymoron referred to as a sanctuary – as a hiding spot. As the story goes, Christie decided to hide from the world as well as the gossip of the local community after he had been found innocent of murdering his wife and child, who had been badly burnt in a bushfire. Similar to the hermit, who has been forced to kill other humans, Ellie and her friends are also confronted with the fundamental decision of whether or not to kill:

> I too had blood on my hands, like the Hermit, and just as I couldn't tell whether his actions were good or bad, so too I couldn't tell what mine were. Had I killed out of love of my friends, as part of a noble crusade to rescue my friends and family and keep our land free? Or had I killed because I valued my life above that of others?[18]

Almost everything in the novel (series) happens against the backdrop of the country at war, evoking a fast-paced, sometimes violent action. The war topic is frequently reflected through intertextual references, including nineteenth and twentieth century German, US-American, and Australian war and apocalyptic fiction.[19] In addition to war, related issues such as colonisation, imperialism, racism, sin as well as guilt are also explored through references to other literary texts. To mention but one prominent example: on a lazy morning towards the end of the group's camping trip, Lee reads Erich Maria Remarque's *All Quiet on the Western Front* (1929),[20] that deals with the atrocities of the Great War from a front-line soldier's perspective, foreshadowing the teenager's impending doom. However, the two novels also share some central characteristics regarding their form and plot. Similar to *Tomorrow*, *All Quiet on the Western Front* – narrated by the nineteen-year-old soldier Paul Bäumer – is told from an adolescent perspective, which vividly illustrates how active combat changes people psychologically as it gradually strips them of their humaneness.[21] As Remarque writes in the epigraph to the novel:

> This book is to be neither an accusation nor a confession, and least of all an adventure, for death is not an adventure to those who stand face to face with it. It will try simply to tell of a generation of men who, even though they may have escaped (its) shells, were destroyed by the war.[22]

Remarque's account of the profound and compelling effect of war – which may be an adventure for the reader but not for those "who stand face to face with it" – closely resembles Ellie's vivid description of the psychological impact of war and how surviving is not the same as living:

> I began to think the damage to our country, to us even, went so deep now that it would never fully be repaired. I realised the worst damage wasn't the bombed buildings, the burnt-out cars, the shattered windows. It wasn't even the neglected farms and the holes in the fences and the crops gone to seed. It was the damage deep inside us. Words like spirit and soul started to mean more to me now. I felt closer than ever to Robyn, if that were possible. She understood that there are some things worse than physical injury and physical death. If your spirit and soul are damaged beyond repair, then what does it matter that you can still react to stimuli, respire and excrete, and do all the human functions of living creatures described in Chapter Four of our Year 9 Science textbook?[23]

It may be noted in passing that foreshadowing through dialogues, plot events, and a change in settings is one of the central narrative techniques especially in the first part of the novel. While it builds anticipation in the mind of the reader about what is going to come, it also emphasises to what extent the invasion and subsequent (guerrilla) war affects a group of normal teenagers. It forces them to grow up overnight, experience the harsh underground life in the bush, and damages their mental make-ups, moral norms, and, ultimately, humanity. Moreover, it connects two important junctures in the teenagers' lives: the symbolic juncture of becoming an adult; "a juncture that goes hand in hand with the dystopian aspect of the society"[24] Ellie lives in. The following statement by Ellie elucidates that the transition from one stage of growing up to the next is almost identical with how war has forced her to become an adult almost instantaneously:

> I realised to my disbelief that it had been only about 20 hours since we'd emerged from the bush into this new world. Lives can be changed that

> quickly. In some ways we should have been used to change. We'd seen a bit of it ourselves. This treehouse, for instance, Corrie and I had spent many hours under its shady roof, holding tea parties, organising our dolls' social lives, playing school, spying on the shearers, pretending we were prisoners trapped here. All our games were imitations of adult rituals and adult lives, although we didn't realise it then of course. Then the day came we stopped playing. We'd gone a couple of months without our usual games, but a few days into the school holidays I got my dolls out and tried to start up again. And it had all gone. The magic didn't work anymore.[25]

The fact that with the invasion maturity comes quickly to the teenagers is frequently alluded to throughout the novel, particularly by depicting them against the backdrop of the wild and harsh Australian outback, not least showcasing that, in contrast to the invaders, the teenagers are 'real' Australians. While before the invasion they fail to make choices about their food rations or are helpless when they find a snake in one of the sleeping bags, illustrating that the soon-to-come independence of their parents and life in hiding will pose a great challenge to the group. Or, as Nimon and Foster point out, the natural Australian landscape functions as a training ground, "as the settings for trials by ordeal which, if mastered, will admit them to maturity".[26] It may be worth noting that the nature theme features prominently throughout the novel, continuously emphasising the Australianess of Marsden's dystopia. Just to mention but one example, the outback's fauna functions as a metaphor for the anonymous invaders as Ellie convincingly describes it at the very beginning of the novel:

> There's constant little concentric ripples from insects touching it as they skim across the surface. I wonder where they sleep, and when. I wonder if they close their eyes when they sleep. I wonder what their names are. Busy, anonymous, sleepless insects.[27]

Closely related to this, references to Australia's colonial history can frequently be found in Marsden's series, highlighting the fact that imperialism and colonialism are still deeply engrained in Australian culture today. The novel can be read as a critical commentary on the Western colonisation of Australia, which seeks to understand the political, social, cultural, and psychological aspects of colonialist and anti-colonialist ideologies. Already in the first chapter, Ellie informs the reader about how Australia was colonised by her ancestors. Also, later on when the teenagers ponder upon how many humans might actually have seen Hell before them, Ellie suggests: "I mean, why would the kooris [aboriginals] have bothered? Why would the early explorers, or settlers, have bothered?"[28] In addition, the novel series also allows for a post- or neocolonial reading. Australia is being colonised by an alien invader just like the British colonised Australia in the late 18th century. It should be noted that the fact that Australia is invaded by an anonymous foreign power with the intention to colonise it and in the process to enslave or at least suppress the present inhabitants does not concern the indigenous population, but exclusively the former colonisers or settlers; which, according to Ross, "reveals a disturbing logic of effacement at work in his (Marsden's) texts".[29] Similarly to what their ancestors did, they are now the ones being colonised, facing the same destiny as the native population did at the beginning of the settlement through convicts in 1788, more than 200 years earlier.

It is important to point out here that while the invasion of Australia may seem highly improbable to readers who are not from the Asian and Pacific region, the novel's occupation scenario "reveals a national anxiety about invasion",[30] which, as Nimon and Foster point out, still "resonates through Australian popular culture" today.[31] While due to limits of space, an exhaustive discussion of the issue at hand is not possible, some distinct tendencies shall be noted. While the continent has come to understand itself as open and multicultural, xenophobic tendencies are still not entirely absent in Australian discourse as persistent concepts such as 'White Australia', 'the yellow peril', or 'Asiatic floods'[32] as well as the past and current refugee discussion illustrate. One of the very few publications on the Asian invasion threat in Marsden's novel series known to the authors of this article is Ross' seminal article "Prolonged Symptoms of Cultural Anxiety: The Persistence of Narratives of Asian Invasion within Multicultural Australia". She writes:

> In the latter half of the nineteenth century, in light of the Australian colonies' increasing awareness of their proximity to the relatively populous nations of Asia, fears began to be voiced concerning the possibility of Asian invasion. Paranoid predictions and warnings circulated in popular culture and an emphasis on the need to be ready for war was communicated through the writing of cautionary tales about what

> could happen should Australia be invaded. This initial, anxious, literary production was the beginning of what would become an enduring preoccupation of Australian popular fiction: the invasion narrative, a detailed set of discourses centring on Australian vulnerability and Asian menace.[33]

Even when Papua New Guinea (of all nations) and the United Nations later come to help,[34] Australia remains partly occupied, as a corollary of which the lives of all Australians are bound to change forever:

> Mum and I at least had something very specific to celebrate. Our property was confirmed as being in the returned territory. We were right on the edge, right on the border of the two new countries that now had to exist side by side, where over two hundred years there had been only one, but for now we were happy enough with that. We didn't want to think too much about the problems it would bring.[35]

As the brief overview of selected themes has shown, *Tomorrow* provides a cornucopia of opportunities for reading the novel with teenage students of English as a foreign language. In the following section, different approaches to working with the novel in class will be discussed. The more detailed lesson plan then concentrates on a postcolonial approach to the novel, particularly focusing on how the teenagers experience the oppression of the invasion and the beginning colonisation.

5. *Tomorrow* in the EFL Classroom

An increasing number of recent publications suggests making young adult dystopias part of the foreign language curriculum, especially because of "their social, political, and economic imaginings".[36] In depicting a world that is both imaginary and close to reality, they can help teenagers to understand critical developments and problems by magnifying them in a futuristic or alternative world. *Tomorrow*, which contains many warnings about society's current trajectory through both the invaders' and the teenagers' actions, may serve as an example here. As in other young adult dystopias, the teenagers are the liberators who try to free the world from the adult (in this case additionally alien) oppressors. The immediacy of young adult dystopias in general and *Tomorrow* in particular, however, does not merely lie in their topicality but also in their ability to illustrate the depiction of the heroine's (or hero's) adventurous journey. In the case of *Tomorrow*, the heroes are catapulted into a world of chaos and violence where they, at the same time, "like their teen readers, have to deal with recognisable concerns and problems, including friendship, family, betrayal, loss, love, death and sexual awakening".[37] As Basu, Broad, and Hintz argue:

> In emphasizing the trials of adolescents, YA dystopias recapitulate the conventions of the classic *Bildungsroman*, using political strife, environmental disaster, or other forms of turmoil as the catalyst for achieving adulthood. The novels detail how the conditions of the dystopian society force protagonists to fall from innocence and achieve maturity as they realize the dystopian realities in which they live.[38]

For Ellie, the immediacy of experiencing the invasion and subsequent colonisation of her country brings the concerns of the world risk society virtually to her doorstep, as the ensuing quote tangibly illustrates.

> I stumbled along, thinking of Mum and Dad. Our lives had always been so unaffected by the outside world. Oh, we'd watched the News on TV and felt bad when they showed pictures of wars and famines and floods. Occasionally, I'd tried to imagine being in the places of those people, but couldn't. Imagination has its limits. But the only real impact the outside world had on us was in wool and cattle prices. A couple of countries would sign an agriculture treaty thousands of k's away, on another continent, and a year later we'd have to lay off a worker.[39]

As far as the novel at hand is concerned, the immediacy of experiencing the world on the precipice of a new and dangerous world order is even more heightened by its (retrospective) journal form that gives a full 'factual' account of the group's fight for freedom,[40] not least with the desire to be remembered by future generations. Interestingly, Ellie, the female protagonist, is chosen to "write everything down".[41] Although she knows that she is "meant to be the best writer",[42] she does not feel comfortable with her role of recording the group's adventures: "I don't know if I will be able to do this. […] there is a bit more to it than just being able to write. There's a few little things can get in the way. Little things like feelings, emotions".[43]

As already mentioned, the novel lends itself to a discussion of colonial history as well as neocolonial tendencies in today's world. Ever since James Cook claimed possession of the east coast of Australia for the British Crown in 1770, Australia's past and present has been shaped by its colonial history. With regard to the foreign language classroom, postcolonial issues hold great potential for developing students' intercultural competence[44] and *Fremdverstehen*, especially as they allow students to learn about the postcolonial experience and actively participate in global postcolonial discourses. Ellie and her friends live in the Australia of the 1990s, shaped by increasing globalisation and the country's firm integration in the 'global North', while geographically connected with the 'global South'. Against the backdrop of the country's colonisation history, it is the 'second invasion' and colonisation of Ellie and her friends as 'native Australians' that concerns the teenagers. As Ross points out: "it is no longer Aboriginal Australians who belong, who see the land as their dreaming, but rather Ellie the white Australian who is positioned as native".[45] In the course of the series, Ellie comes to value her country and its way of life more highly while observing the degradation and increasing colonisation of the country by the new settlers. This ties in closely with the aim of transcultural learning in the classroom, which, according to Matz, Rogge, and Siepmann, emphasises the importance of local, regional, and national contexts as well as social and political interdependencies, also including factors such as power and inequality.[46]

With regard to working with the novel in the classroom, this dual colonial focus can encourage students to deal with both the early history of white colonisation, when the British sent the first convicts to Australia in 1788, including the fate of the Aboriginals, as well as the new colonisation experience of the descendants of the former settlers. Moreover, it allows students to discuss contemporary issues such as the rise of the new right or immigration and isolationist policies.

The following lesson plan is based on the idea that students keep a reading response journal while reading the novel. While reading journals can take many different forms, the overall objective is that they support students in better understanding the literary text and capturing their personal responses to the text. In addition to basic information about each chapter, such as setting, characters, and plot, further aspects can be added. Additional foci for journal entries for the novel could, for example, include:

- vocabulary lists, for example, focusing on Australian English or war related vocabulary
- aspects of Australian culture, for example, animals, plants, climate, nature, place names, traditions
- moral aspects of the group's actions
- life before and after the invasion
- character portraits
- list of intertexts and possibly their functions

In addition, students should be asked to write down their individual responses to the text or reactions to characters and their actions. Students should also be encouraged to comment on the settings, time, character development, or anything else that seems important to them.

Here, guiding questions for individual chapters could include:

- *What struck you most when reading the chapter?*
- *Were you reminded of anything that happened to you?*
- *Was there anything that you did not understand when reading the chapter? Is there anything you now understand better after having read the chapter?*
- *Speculate about what might happen in the next chapter.*
- *Which feelings did the chapter evoke in you?*
- *Which is your (least) favourite character? Why?*
- *Which questions would you like to ask a particular character?*
- *Which questions about the chapter would you like to ask the author?*
- *Write down your favourite lines/quotes.*
- *What aspects of the chapter would you like to discuss with your classmates/teacher?*

The lesson plan is based on the assumption that the reading journals motivate students to take a contrastive look at both the invaders'/colonisers' and invaded'/colonised' actions/experiences as well as other issues related to colonialism in the novel. Here, particular emphasis should be placed on the binary opposites of dominance and submission which are at play, particularly in the context of the long-standing Australian fear of being invaded by the 'Asian enemy'.

The students read chapters seven and eight at home, using a special set of guiding questions for their reading journal entries. In chapter seven, after visiting some of the group's homes and finding them deserted and animals dead, the group splits up on separate missions to reduce the hazard of being detected. Kevin, Corrie, and Ellie leave for the Showground, while the rest of the group visits more of the group's former homes that are still mainly intact. When Ellie and her group are discovered, they are pursued and shot at. At an abandoned house, Ellie lures the soldiers closer and directs a petrol-driven lawn mower to them that blows up; pursued by the screams of the injured soldiers, the teenagers escape. Chapter eight then focuses on the moral aspects of their guerrilla war and the central question of whether killing, under certain circumstances, is justified:

> It was hard for me to believe that I, plain old Ellie, nothing special about me, middle of the road in every way, had probably just killed three people. It was too big for me to get my mind around. When I thought of it baldly like that: killed three people, I was filled with horror. I felt that my life was permanently damaged, that I could never be normal again, that the rest of my life would just be a shell. Ellie might walk and talk and eat and drink but the inside Ellie, her feelings, was condemned to wither and die. I didn't think much about the three soldiers as people: I couldn't, because I had no real sense of them. I hadn't even seen their faces properly. […] So I tried to describe it all as though I were an outsider, a spectator, someone reading it from a book. […] I felt guilty and ashamed about what had happened.[47]

After she reports about what happened, Homer tries to console Ellie:

> This was it now, and normal rules don't apply. These people have invaded our land, locked up our families. […] The moment they left their country to come here they knew what they were doing. They're the ones who tore up the rule book, not us.[48]

In the classroom, the students use an adapted version of the Oxford Book Worms reading circle[49] for a close reading of chapters seven & eight. The method allows students to look at ethical questions from a number of different perspectives.

Introduction	Students train their critical thinking and discussion skills using the Reading Circle method. It allows for a structured and prepared discussion based on students' reading journal entries as well as research prior to the discussion.

Objectives	Raise awareness of the ethical issues related to 'justifiable killing' Develop students' discussion skills through preparing and doing an in-class discussion Develop oral fluency Develop higher level critical thinking skills Increase students' social skills through group work and collaborative learning Train students' close reading skills Develop students' writing skills through making a longer reading journal entry
Age	Advanced learners (year 11 or later)
Level	CEFR level B2 and above
Time	4 lessons (à 45 minutes), preferably two double lessons
Reading approach	Students have read the entire novel, keeping a reading journal through the whole reading. Close reading of chapters 7 & 8.
Materials/media	Novel, reading journals, role cards (discussion leader, summariser, connector, word master, culture collector), A2 paper for collecting ideas, empty note cards
Before lesson	Students read chapters 7 & 8 at home, using the following additional guiding questions for their reading journals: • *What happens in chapters 7 & 8?* • *How does Ellie injure/kill the soldiers?* • *Why does she do it?* • *In chapter 8, Ellie becomes aware of the consequences of her actions. How does she feel about the killing?* • *How does Homer attempt to console Ellie?* • *How did you feel about Ellie killing the soldiers?* • *Throughout the novel, it is insinuated that the soldiers are merely mercenaries. Does that change your attitude towards Ellie's act of killing?*
Double lesson	The content of the chapters is discussed with the whole class. For example, on the basis of the following questions: • *What are the most important events?* • *How is the plot structured?* • *Who is the narrator or speaker in the story?* • *What are the main conflicts of the two chapters?* • *What are the main themes?*

	• *Which figures of speech are used (for example, metaphors, similes)?*
Double lesson	Students are divided into five groups (or find themselves together in groups) of equal size, if possible. Each group is given five role cards, according to the Reading Circle method. The roles can be adapted according to the students' level, research skills, and time available. Students prepare their roles/arguments either in class or at home. The aim is to come up with a code of conduct for the guerrilla group whether killing may be justified during war or not. By doing so, the students reflect on the ethical concerns related to killing in war. Responsibilities of roles: Discussion leader: Prepares at least five general questions about the story and encourages the other group members to join the discussion, guides the discussion, and keeps it going. Summariser: Makes notes of the characters, events, and ideas, finds the key points, and retells the story in a short summary in his or her own words. Connector: Looks for connections between the story and world outside, makes possible connections to the group members' own experiences or to real life events and asks the group members if they can think of any connections themselves. Word master: Looks for words or short phrases that are new or difficult to understand and are important in the story and chooses five words that are important for the story and explains why or asks the group members what they think of the words Culture collector: Looks for both differences and similarities between the students' own cultures and the culture in the story.
Lesson 3	Students bring together their main arguments and ideas, according to their assigned roles. In a second step, they make notes of their main findings and agree on common outcomes.
Lesson 4	New groups are formed according to their roles. For example, all discussion leaders come together in a group, compare their findings and try to find common ground.

	The experts of each group (Big Brothers and Ministers) gather and find a common solution to the different proposals. They have 5' to discuss their correspondent topic (State Leadership, Justice, Economy, Equality, Education) and create something together. Once time is over, each expert group will have a spokesperson to briefly explain the conclusions they have reached. Unlike *1984*, this new world has been created upon a solid ground of unity in diversity, having a collage of voices in society.

Table 1: Lesson Sequence: *Heroes in Dystopia*

4. Conclusion

Gordin et al. are right when suggesting that "people perceive their environments as dystopic, and alas they do so with depressing frequency".[33] The twentieth century witnessed the despondency of the war generations, but it was also a period of transformation within these dystopian settings: from fear to bravery, from betrayal to martyrdom, from violence to peace. The Orwellian dissident has gradually taken new directions to fight against an oppressive dystopian regime without falling into failure. Similarly, utopianism has undergone a conceptual shift emphasising the importance of the transformative process. It originates on behalf of those dystopian rebels who ever felt despair in solitude and found the multitude as a new and more effective collectivising form of the utopian imagination[34] because "none of us [...] can become human at all, much less flourish, except in the company and conversation and caring of other human beings",[35] according to Chambers and Gregory.

Our educational environment can put the necessary materials at the pupils' disposal so that they can (de)construct their contemporary society, thanks to the use of dystopian fiction and the new technologies. Sampedro affirms that "when we teach, we touch the future. Everything we do today will have an impact tomorrow, so while teaching is indeed a big responsibility, it is also a fantastic opportunity".[36] The teaching of dystopias in the EFL classroom proves challenging for students of secondary level inasmuch as they are at a critical age. As teenagers, they can be indeed rebellious and sometimes outraged; the functioning of the world exceeds their comprehension and power, causing helplessness.

Notes

1 Ross claims that the unnamed enemy is clearly Indonesian. Ross, Catriona (2008). "Unsettled Imaginings: Australian Novels of Asian Invasion." PhD thesis. Web. 4 July 2019 <https://eprints.utas.edu.au/12396/>.

2 Marsden, John (1993). *Tomorrow, When the War Began*. London: Quercus, 168.

3 *Ibid.*, 9.

4 *Ibid.*, 111-112.

5 Heise, Ursula K. (2015). "What's the Matter with Dystopia?" *Public Books* 2 Jan. 2015. Web. 4 July 2019 <https://www.publicbooks.org/whats-the-matter-with-dystopia/>.

6 Heinze, Rüdiger (2018). "Through A Glass, Darkly: Contemporary Young Adult Dystopias." '*Tell Freedom I Said Hello*'. *Issues in Contemporary Young Adult Dystopian Fiction.* Eds. Christian Ludwig and Nicole Maruo-Schröder. Heidelberg: Winter, 27-46.

7 Lois Lowry as qtd. in Hintz, Carrie, and Elaine Ostry (2003). "Introduction." *Utopian and Dystopian. Writing for Children and Young Adults.* Eds. Carrie Hintz and Elaine Ostry. New York: Routledge, 1-20, 19.

8 Poladian, Laura (2016). "Narrating Trauma: The Value of Violence in YA Dystopian Fiction." *The Age of Dystopia. One Genre, Our Fears and Our Future.* Ed. Louisa MacKay Demerjian. Cambridge: Cambridge Scholars Publishing, 73-90, 87.

9 Ludwig, Christian, and Nicole Maruo-Schröder (2018). "'What, Indeed, Is the Matter With (Young Adult) Dystopia?' A Short Introduction." '*Tell Freedom I Said Hello*'. *Issues in Contemporary Young Adult Dystopian Fiction.* Eds. Christian Ludwig and Nicole Maruo-Schröder. Heidelberg: Winter, 11-26, 15.

10 Freitag, Britta, and Marion Gymnich (2007). "New English and Postcolonial Literature im Fremdsprachenunterricht." *Neue Ansätze und Konzepte der Literatur- und Kulturdidaktik.* Eds. Wolfgang Hallet and Ansgar Nünning. Trier: WTV, 258-276, 262.

11 Basu, Balaka, Katherine R.Broad and Carrie Hintz (2013). "Introduction." *Contemporary Dystopian Fiction for Young Adults. Brave New Teenagers.* Eds. Basu Balaka, Katherine R. Broad and Carrie Hintz. New York: Routledge, 1-15,1.

12 Hintz, Carrie, and Elaine Ostry (2003). "Introduction." *Utopian and Dystopian. Writing for Children and Young Adults.* Eds. Carrie Hintz and Elaine Ostry. New York: Routledge, 1-20, 9.

[13] Krüger, Nadine (2018). "'The Odds Are Never in Our Favor': Dystopia as Metaphor for Adolescence." *'Tell Freedom I Said Hello'. Issues in Contemporary Young Adult Dystopian Fiction.* Eds. Christian Ludwig and Nicole Maruo-Schröder. Heidelberg: Winter, 161-178.

[14] *Ibid.*, 161.

[15] Marsden (1993), 73. Hell is a pervading oxymoron throughout the novel series.

[16] Ross (2008), 93.

[17] Marsden, John (2012). *Darkness Be My Friend.* Kindle Ebook. London: Quercus Children's Books, pos. 2083.

[18] Marsden (1993), 216.

[19] Other intertexts in the first book include Robert C. O'Brien's *Z for Zachariah* (1974) and Walter D. Myers *Fallen Angels* (1988), a young adult novel about the Vietnam War. Nathaniel Hawthorne's *The Scarlet Letter* (1850) takes up the issue of sin and guilt. Moreover, Joseph Conrad's *Heart of Darkness* (1899) focuses on the topic of colonisation of Africa, imperialism, and racism.

[20] Remarque, Erich Maria (1987[1930]). *All Quiet on the Western Front.* New York: Ballantine Books.

[21] Today, symptoms of PTSD are increasingly recognised among war veterans.

[22] Remarque, Erich Maria (1987[1930]), epigraph, n. pag.

[23] Marsden, John (1997). *Burning for Revenge.* Sydney: Pan Macmillan Australia, 239.

[24] Heinze (2018), 32.

[25] Marsden (1993), 105-106.

[26] Nimon, Maureen, and John Foster (1997). *The Adolescent Novel. Australian Perspectives.* Wagga Wagga, N.S.W.: Centre for Information Studies, Charles Sturt University, 35.

[27] Marsden (1993), 2.

[28] *Ibid.*, 31. Here, the use of the word 'kooris' suggests that Robyn respects the cultures of the indigenous Australians.

[29] Ross, Catriona (2006). "Prolonged Symptoms of Cultural Anxiety: The Persistence of Narratives of Asian Invasion within Multicultural Australia." *JASAL* 5, 86-99, 91.

[30] Potter, Roy (2018). *Books for Boys. Manipulating Genre in Contemporary Australian Young Adult Fiction.* Trier: WVT, 118.

[31] Nimon and Foster (1997), 37.

[32] Cf. Ross (2006), 87.

[33] Ross (2008), 39.

34 The United States does not actively intervene in the conflict, presumably to avoid diplomatic or economic repercussions.

35 Marsden, John (1999). *The Other Side of Dawn*. Sydney: Pan Macmillan Australia, 287.

36 Heinze (2018), 27.

37 Young, Moira (2015). "Why Is Dystopia So Appealing to Young Adults?" *The Guardian* 23 Oct. 2011: n. pag. Web. 4 July 2019 <https://www.theguardian.com/books/2011/oct/23/dystopian-fiction>.

38 Basu, Broad, and Hintz (2013), 7.

39 Marsden (1993), 78.

40 While a single focaliser is problematic given the fact that the group frequently splits up for reconnaissance trips, this is overcome by a number of reports of subgroups which function as flashbacks, by which multiperspectivity is achieved.

41 Marsden (1993), 1.

42 *Ibid.*

43 *Ibid.*

44 For developing students' intercultural competence with Australian young adult literature see, for example, Hermes, Liesel (2012). "Australische Jugendliteratur und interkulturelles Lernen: James Moloneys Trilogie Dougy, Gracey und Angela." *Anglophone Literaturdidaktik: Zukunftsperspektiven für den Englischunterricht*. Eds. Julia Hammer, Maria Eisenmann and Rüdiger Ahrens. Heidelberg: Winter, 45-60.

45 Ross (2006), 94.

46 Matz, Frauke, Michael Rogge and Philipp Siepmann (2014). "Einleitung." *Transkulturelles Lernen im Fremdsprachenunterricht. Theorie und Praxis*. Eds. Frauke Matz, Michael Rogge and Philipp Siepmann. Frankfurt a.M.: Peter Lang, 8-17, 8.

47 Marsden (1993), 95-96.

48 *Ibid.*, 96-97.

49 Furr, Mark (2006). *Oxford Bookworms Club Reading Circles*. Oxford: University Press.

Bibliography

Primary Texts

Bradbury, Ray (2013[1953]). *Fahrenheit 451*. London: Harper Collins.
Conrad, Joseph (2016[1899]). *Heart of Darkness*. New York: W.W. Norton & Company.
Hawthorne, Nathaniel (2015[1859]). *The Scarlet Letter*. New York: Penguin.
Lowry, Lois (2014[1993]). *The Giver*. New York: Harper Collins Publishers.
Marsden, John (1993). *Tomorrow, When the War Began*. London: Quercus.
--- (1997). *Burning for Revenge*. Sydney: Pan Macmillan Australia.
--- (1999). *The Other Side of Dawn*. Sydney: Pan Macmillan Australia.
--- (2012). *Darkness Be My Friend*. Kindle Ebook. London: Quercus Children's Books.
Myers, Walter D. (2008[1988]). *Fallen Angels*. New York: Scholastic.
O'Brien, Robert C. (2016[1974]). *Z for Zachariah*. New York: Penguin.
Orwell, George (2008[1949]). *1984*. New York: Penguin.
Remarque, Erich Maria (1987)[1930]). *All Quiet on the Western Front*. New York: Ballantine Books.
Tomorrow, When the War Began. Dir. Stuart Beattie. 2010. Paramount Pictures.
Tomorrow, When the War Began. Dir. Brendan Maher. 2016. ABC3.
Wells, H.G. (2017[1898]). *The War of the Worlds*. Richmond, UK: Alma Books.

Secondary Literature

Basu, Balaka, Katherine R. Broad and Carrie Hintz (2013). "Introduction." *Contemporary Dystopian Fiction for Young Adults. Brave New Teenagers*. Eds. Basu Balaka, Katherine R. Broad and Carrie Hintz. New York: Routledge, 1-15.
Freitag, Britta, and Marion Gymnich (2007). "New English and Postcolonial Literature im Fremdsprachenunterricht." *Neue Ansätze und Konzepte der Literatur- und Kulturdidaktik*. Eds. Wolfgang Hallet and Ansgar Nünning. Trier: WTV, 258-276.
Furr, Mark (2006). *Oxford Bookworms Club Reading Circles*. Oxford: University Press.
Heinze, Rüdiger (2018). "Through A Glass, Darkly: Contemporary Young Adult Dystopias." *'Tell Freedom I Said Hello'. Issues in Contemporary Young Adult*

Dystopian Fiction. Eds. Christian Ludwig and Nicole Maruo-Schröder. Heidelberg: Winter, 27-46.

Heise, Ursula K. (2015). "What's the Matter with Dystopia?" *Public Books* 2 Jan. 2015: n. pag. Web. 4 July 2019 <https://www.publicbooks.org/whats-the-matter-with-dystopia/>.

Hermes, Liesel (2012). "Australische Jugendliteratur und interkulturelles Lernen: James Moloneys Trilogie Dougy, Gracey und Angela." *Anglophone Literaturdidaktik: Zukunftsperspektiven für den Englischunterricht.* Eds. Julia Hammer, Maria Eisenmann and Rüdiger Ahrens. Heidelberg: Winter, 45-60.

Hintz, Carrie, and Elaine Ostry (2003). "Introduction." *Utopian and Dystopian. Writing for Children and Young Adults*. Eds. Carrie Hintz and Elaine Ostry. New York: Routledge, 1-20.

Krüger, Nadine (2018). "'The Odds Are Never in Our Favor': Dystopia as Metaphor for Adolescence." *'Tell Freedom I Said Hello'. Issues in Contemporary Young Adult Dystopian Fiction*. Eds. Christian Ludwig and Nicole Maruo-Schröder. Heidelberg: Winter, 161-178.

Ludwig, Christian, and Nicole Maruo-Schröder (2018). "'What, Indeed, Is the Matter with (Young Adult) Dystopia?' A Short Introduction." *'Tell Freedom I Said Hello'. Issues in Contemporary Young Adult Dystopian Fiction.* Eds. Christian Ludwig and Nicole Maruo-Schröder. Heidelberg: Winter, 11-26.

Matz, Frauke, Michael Rogge and Philipp Siepmann (2014). "Einleitung." *Transkulturelles Lernen im Fremdsprachenunterricht. Theorie und Praxis.* Eds. Frauke Matz, Michael Rogge and Philipp Siepmann. Frankfurt a.M.: Peter Lang, 8-17.

Nimon, Maureen, and John Foster (1997). *The Adolescent Novel. Australian Perspectives*. Wagga Wagga, N.S.W.: Centre for Information Studies, Charles Sturt University.

Poladian, Laura (2016). "Narrating Trauma: The Value of Violence in YA Dystopian Fiction." *The Age of Dystopia. One Genre, Our Fears and Our Future.* Ed. Louisa MacKay Demerjian. Cambridge: Cambridge Scholars Publishing, 73-90.

Potter, Roy (2018). *Books for Boys. Manipulating Genre in Contemporary Australian Young Adult Fiction*. Trier: WVT.

Ross, Catriona (2006). "Prolonged Symptoms of Cultural Anxiety: The Persistence of Narratives of Asian Invasion within Multicultural Australia." *JASAL* 5, 86-99.

--- (2008). "Unsettled Imaginings: Australian Novels of Asian Invasion." PhD thesis. Web. 4 July 2019 <https://eprints.utas.edu.au/12396/>.

Young, Moira (2015). "Why Is Dystopia So Appealing to Young Adults?" *The Guardian* 23 Oct. 2011: n. pag. Web. 4 July 2019 <https://www.theguardian.com/books/2011/oct/23/dystopian-fiction>.

Almudena Machado-Jiménez (Jaén)

When Heroes Meet Orwell: From Dystopia to Utopia in the EFL Classroom

When it comes to the pinch, human beings are heroic.[1]

1. Introduction

Dystopias have undeniably become a blockbuster phenomenon in recent years. Despite its gruesome and dreadful setting, dystopian society hooks readers, who crave more of this misery while looking for better alternatives within the narrative. The appalling similarity between the real world and the dystopian scenario creates alliances between characters and readers, as both struggle in their quest for happiness. The longed-for utopia seems so unattainable that it can make one think that these notions of utopia and dystopia are incompatible. Thomas More's pun with the *u*-prefix – meaning both good (*eu*- ευ) and no (*ou*- οὐ) – entails that utopia is ideal as long as it is unreal. In contrast, the etymology of dystopia as 'bad place' does not specify if this social nightmare is fictional or not. Even the term anti-utopia, despite the fact that it is not an exact synonym of dystopia, actually denies the realization of utopia in society with the *anti*-prefix, suggesting that utopias inevitably end in dystopia.

Thus, it seems that our utopias are condemned to an eternal social unrealisation, since "the apparent realization of utopia implies the end of the utopian function and of the utopian spirit".[2] O'Brien observes that "this is the crux of the utopian imperative: how can an ideal become integrated into the real without becoming reified into another dogma, another doxa, another dystopia".[3] This implies a cycle of despair: as the individual utopia clashes with dissenting opinions, it inexorably turns into others' dystopia when introduced in society. Thus, these dissenters shelter in their own utopian desires, which may become dystopias if ever materialised.

History has witnessed countless attempts of establishing utopia and the failure of opposing ideas. Megalomaniac dreamers accomplished their dream in society and, in so doing, condemned their contemporaries to dystopia. However, the damnation of the utopian impulse results from the misconception of the very term utopia as a blueprint of perfectionism. Sargisson stresses this misinterpretation: "Perfection, I suggest, symbolizes death: the death of movement, the death of progress and process, development and change; the death, in other words, of politics."[4] Oppositely, she proposes an alternative view on utopia that advocates a dynamic and multidirectional model: transgressive utopianism. This approach aims to explore the possibilities that human beings can imagine, while it deconstructs the dualistic standards that have built traditional Western thinking. Likewise, transgressive utopianism embraces anarchic thought inasmuch as it dismantles social established truths though it does not offer alternative truths or desire a final solution.[5] Hence, even though at first dystopias might seem somehow gruesome as an education tool, they are the most effective, as their ambivalent nature and transformative potential "can still educate readers. [Dystopias] can still encourage us to resist ignorance and resignation".[6]

In particular, the concept of dystopia can be useful as a tool in the classroom, as students undertake a process of deconstruction and self-discovery in which they acknowledge their own potentialities. Dystopias can also be helpful to develop a global citizenship competence. Díaz-Pérez emphasises the importance of developing such a competence: "[t]here is a tendency to think that when a problem does not affect us directly as individuals it should not necessarily be a concern for us".[7] The view of fictional dystopias and their resemblance to the real world facilitates the global awareness that is needed in the mood of utopianism.

Not only do dystopias give us a wider vision in terms of space, but also of time. Gordin et al. remark that "utopias and dystopias are histories of the present",[8] where authors reflect their hopes and fears in the future as well as their nostalgia for the past. The analysis of past, present and future through the study of dystopias offers students a panorama of history in order not to fall again into the cycle of despair and in order to work towards a communal *eu*topia. This idea can only be achieved with an education for solidarity based on this new view on utopianism,[9] where students rewrite Orwell's dystopian ending together, enriching and valorising their differences as well as their mutual aspirations.

In this essay, I argue that dystopias can be used in the classroom – particularly as a tool for English as a foreign language (EFL) teaching – as a way to foster and encourage the positive qualities of utopianism, such as students' creativity, cooperation and critical thinking. The essay is divided into two main sections: first, I examine from a theoretical perspective the figure of the dissenter as a potential utopian leader. I begin by introducing the concept of Orwellian dystopia and its manifestations in the fiction and reality of the twentieth century. For this, I undertake a tri-temporal analysis of the dissident and the evolution of his/her characteristics and methods of rebellion. Past, present and future are examined in relation to a shift from violence to peaceful movements to fight against dystopia. The second section articulates a need for a methodology that promotes quotidian utopianism in students' lives and I present its possible didactic application with a lesson sequence, which has as its ultimate aim the realisation of *e*utopia in the classroom. The sequence will be divided in four lessons – introduction of the concepts of dystopia, past, present and future – plus a final project where the students reconstruct Orwell's model of dystopia as a *e*utopia. I conclude by claiming the importance of the transformative power of dystopias in education, especially at secondary level when students are at a critical age, not only to nurture utopianism in the EFL classroom but in a wider social context.

2. What to Study with Dystopias? Dissenters in a New Light

When George Orwell sympathised with socialist ideas and fought against fascism in the Spanish Civil War, he gave voice to the anonymous rebels of the resistance. Previously known as a great essayist and journalistic writer, he exposed the fragile resilience of the revolutionary spirit in miserable conditions in *Homage to Catalonia* (1938) and, in so doing, he chronicled the spirit of a century. He later criticised the communist doctrine in *Animal Farm* (1945), as it presented the failure of the utopian project of Animalism. This way, Orwell perfectly represented the cycle of despair of the modern era. Other post-war authors such as William Golding also disclosed the impossibility of utopian consensus in *The Lord of the Flies* (1954). However, unlike the Orwellian dystopia, Golding's social experiment revealed that the utopian failure was inherently human.

By choosing children, the author depicted a Hobbesian natural behaviour that unavoidably assumed the end of utopia.

Orwellian dystopia believes in the innocence and kindness of the individual and puts the blame on a totalitarian regime. The author presents the failed attempt of transgression but entrusts the reader to save humanity from this ongoing despair. Readers, who remain in the narrative as external dissidents, turn into potential heroes in their contemporary society. However, the figure of the rebel hero has undergone considerable changes throughout the 20th and 21st centuries. An overview of this evolution is necessary in order to make students understand the importance of believing in utopia.

2.1. Past and Wars: About Distortion and Extortion

The twentieth century was the quintessence of utopian failure and revival. Particularly during the first half, the world envisaged the near end of humankind under modern technological warfare, reaching the peak of wickedness in the Second World War. Apart from the game-changing scientific advances of the time, one of the most influential strategies of World War II was the use of propaganda to distort reality. The image and words of the political pamphlets were equally astonishing to the audience, causing the dehumanisation of the enemy through mockery or disgust.

Among the propagandistic techniques, animalisation was recurrently utilised by the Nazi anti-Semitic propaganda to downgrade the Jewish community to the category of rats. This is revisited decades later by Art Spiegelman in his graphic novel *Maus* (1996). Apart from the dehumanisation process, which is "just basic for the killing project",[10] the negative connotations that rats symbolise in Western tradition made the Nazi audience believe this slaughter was necessary and insignificant. However, by choosing mice, Spiegelman tries to make the reader sympathise with the victims. In addition, he does not dehumanise Nazis into cats in order to cause mockery, as the Allies' propaganda did, but because the atrocities committed caused them to convert into predators.

In contrast, the use of animalisation by Allies and later on by Orwell in *Animal Farm* causes the mockery of dictators, who were represented as cats, pigs, rats and even ducks,[11] while it praises the strength and loyalty of the Allies' powers with animals like the dog or the lion. Orwell was one of the most fervent followers of Socialism but also its most fearful caricaturist. The effectiveness of his social denouncement relies in the use of laughter as a weapon. [12] However, the novelist employs animalisation to upgrade animals to humans. Their innocence is a sign of honesty and goodwill, but at the end of the fable pigs are so similar to human beings that "it was impossible to say which was which". [13] The humanisation of animals means the loss of utopia due to corruption and the impossibility of escaping from the cycle of despair.

Linguistic distortion is the major tool of populist trickery in the dictator's personal utopia and Orwell was well aware of that. [14] He envisaged the influence of language upon thought in *Animal Farm,* when pigs breached the Seven Commandments of Animalism with success. Nevertheless, it is not until *1984* (1949) that his hypothesis of linguistic reduction and human involution is grounded with Newspeak: "[i]n the end we shall make thoughtcrime literally impossible, because there will be no words in which to express it." [15] Among its qualities, the notion of Doublethink is highlighted, as the inclusion of contradictory ideas under the same term makes manipulation of ideas more effective. This is perfectly illustrated with the names of the Ministries or with the motto "War is Peace, Freedom is Slavery, Ignorance is Strength." [16]

Language manipulation enables the sacralisation of the politics of Ingsoc under the almighty god-like figure of Big Brother. The ubiquity of Big Brother is also achieved by means of the anonymity of the actual political elite and a mass surveillance that ensures the fear and subjugation of citizens. For Orwell, technology was inherently damaging to humankind, while other authors such as Aldous Huxley defended the use of technology for social improvement despite acknowledging the risks of it falling into the wrong hands. Among the devices employed in *1984's* Airstrip One, the memory hole is crucial for the continuity of dystopia. Due to the manipulation of historical events, the population cannot scrutinise their past in order to find alternatives for the future: this is how the ill-use of the tri-temporal analysis ensures the cycle of despair.

Winston Smith, a worker at the ministry of Truth, knows the evil schemes of Ingsoc. His in-between position could be helpful to fight the system from within. And yet his solution to finish this nightmare is to escape from the system instead of confronting Big Brother. His dissidence can only be expressed in a confessionary notebook, but his transgressions are far from being heroic. His humanness leaves him alone, fragile and helpless, unable to realise a new utopia upon the established one. It is not until the modern superhero that new strategies of transgression start to be effective, even though this entails the explosion of the pillars of civilisation.

2.2. Present and Hopes: The Utopian Rebel

Twentieth century comics resume the classical tradition of the epic hero who faces the problems of contemporary society. But unlike the classical hero, superheroes can attain extraordinary attributes through other means than having a (semi-)divine nature. The twentieth century superhero presents the weaknesses of ordinary people, as s/he is another mortal with family, friends and problems. And yet the deeds of superheroes when fighting for a better world convert them into *utopian* rebels. Here, the qualifying term '*u*topian' maintains its original pun between 'good' and 'unreal', as comics explore the potentialities of human good nature as long as these characters undergo a process of supernatural transformation that transcends real human limitations. However, superheroes are intendedly imperfect in their nature and this is precisely the utopian transgression that envisages hopes for readers, who feel empathy towards superheroes while setting them up as role models. Superheroes' transgressive utopianism relies on the combination of special powers with human fragility and the appropriation of technology and anonymity as tools for resistance.

Regarding the former, their extraordinary nature leads them to a complicated relationship with authorities: sometimes allies – used as propagandistic tools, sometimes menacing forces – their mutant differences and strong individuality presented with awe as the Other. In order to cope with the pressure, superheroes have a split identity (private-public). Nonetheless, the case of the superhero V in Alan Moore and David Lloyd's *V for Vendetta* (1982-1988) "aggressively violate[s] the fundamental generic conventions of the superhero narrative",[17] because of his/her anarchic approach to dystopia. The Orwellian dystopia is revisited in this graphic novel. Oppositely to other superheroes, V does not intend to restore the system under a new utopian idea, but rather to smash it. And oppositely to Orwell's hero, V fights against the government from within instead of escaping. With anarchy, V fights against a justice compliant with fascism that dooms society to the cycle of despair: "justice is meaningless without freedom. [Anarchy] is honest. She makes no promises and breaks none."[18]

The society presented in *V for Vendetta* uses surveillance and other scientific methods of control. V, one of the victims of these experiments, makes use of her/his newly acquired special powers after an explosion to destabilise England's tyranny. Literature is even more important than science to achieve this goal, as it provides citizens the power to remember their history and conduct a tri-temporal analysis. After resurrecting from the flames, this character transforms his/her rage to stop being a victim of the system and uses his/her traumatic experience as a power. Unlike Winston Smith, s/he is not restrained by emotions, as "nobody is more free, more powerful and more dangerous than somebody who no longer fears death".[19] After the explosion, s/he is reborn under the identity of V, leaving behind his/her former identity in order to become the symbol of a utopian idea that cannot die.

The victory of V does not solely rely on science or literature, but most importantly on the appropriation of an anonymous identity. In a world under surveillance, the icon of Big Brother was the shield of the party. This correlation of privacy and freedom was exclusively possessed by the rulers of the country until superheroes created their split identities. The reader of comics is aware of their two faces, but this does not happen with V. V only shows his/her public identity throughout the narrative, therefore becoming another icon, able to embody the personality of all readers regardless age, gender, ethnicity or class. As an idea, s/he transcends human failure in the utopian project and, even though "V pointedly does not invite his audience to become his comrades",[20] the end of the novel shows the masses wearing V's mask too, ready to fight against injustices. *V for Vendetta* exposes the inner superhero within us. Still, to take heroism out of abstraction through violence endangers the idea of communal *eu*topia, hence other means of rebellion need to be explored and brought into action.

2.3. Future and Changes: Quotidian Utopianism

As has been aforementioned, transgressive utopianism lacks the ultimate truth to settle utopia on society. Rather, the utopian moment originates from its paradoxical hesitation: utopian thinkers question all social foundations but they do not stagnate in fear. In this ongoing questioning, change arises as the utopian solution as it opts for a dynamic conceptual space. Change becomes "a menace to stability",[21] since it exposes the idea of utopian perfectionism as the façade of dystopias' regime. However, the history and fiction of the twentieth century has witnessed some attempts of change which eventually failed when contaminated by perfectionism, causing this way society's deception. This era showed the worst of humankind, but also discerned a move towards a new conception of utopianism.

After the World Wars, armed conflicts continued around the world under the euphemism of 'The Long Peace'. This illustrates what Orwell states about linguistic distortion: "defenceless villages are bombarded from the air […] this is called pacification".[22] However, Orwell also justifies violent means to fight against social injustices: "I don't, however, agree with the pacifist attitude […]. I still think one must fight for Socialism, and against Fascism, I mean physically with weapons".[23] His attitude has the activism his characters lack due to fear, but history has proved that fighting violence with violence is a direct cause to end in a cycle of despair.

V smashes the government without proposing an alternative in social organization, hence the anarchic utopian transgression. However, this bombastic rebellion again results in a recurrence of violence and seems unattainable to the average reader. This way, a new approach in this transgressive utopianism arises, which I label as quotidian utopianism. This utopian movement comes from non-violent resistance in the fight for social rights. Their leaders confront unjust laws of their governments, protesting with ordinary acts, like Rosa Parks refusing to give up her seat in a bus, Marsha P. Johnson wearing make-up or Malala Yousafzai going to school. These techniques of social disobedience cause the population to understand divergence in a positive sense and the dangers of a single view.

These social rebels prove to be the most successful form of the *eu*topian hero. They trespass with words of protest and show publicly their dissidence. Despite lacking the armour of anonymity, their bodies become the shield and icon of liberation and their humanity changes from being a weakness to their best line of defence. Moreover, quotidian utopianism leads by example and its solidarity serves as an eye-opening strategy. Orwell saw the potentiality of joining the intellect of the rebel with the lower classes to break social hierarchies, but, moved by the solitude of the modern individual, he never joined forces:

> If Orwell (or Winston) could see the 'proles' as people, living, working and thinking, whole human beings, rather than merely an obtuse, inert mass […] perhaps the tyranny of *Nineteen Eighteen-Four* would not seem so complete, so irresistible.[24]

The quotidian utopians enable this union inasmuch as they occasionally are members of the oppressed collectives. Their life experiences are joined with an education towards communal *eu*topia – based on equality in multiplicity – in which all members learn from each other. These paths to arrive at communal *eu*topia are uncertain, not bound to happen. They are not predetermined, as we forge them to fluctuate. Those destinations are not properly a place and never reach an end, as this supposes the end of utopia too. Utopianism's adaptability and resilience inhabit within us, becoming a "necessary mode of being for anyone who challenges the now"[25] and seeks better futures every day.

3. How to Study Dystopias? An Approach to Utopian Learning

Among the social leaders mentioned in the essay, Malala Yousafzai stands out for this didactic proposal due to her youth, history and resolution to face dystopia. As a teenager, she confronted a dystopian reality through quotidian utopianism. At her speech for the United Nations, she emphasised the need of education as the means to change the world:

> [I]f we want to achieve our goal, then let us empower ourselves with the weapon of knowledge and let us shield ourselves with unity and togetherness. […] Let us wage a global struggle against illiteracy, poverty and terrorism and let us pick up our books and pens. They are our most powerful weapons.[26]

She equates the strength of education with the weapons of the terrorists who attacked her. Thus, she uses empathy as a method of rebellion and escapes from the vengeance and violence in order to break the cycle of despair. Moreover, she defends a *eu*topian education, which

> promotes and encourages a critical take on things, an education to train us to think for ourselves as part of a global community we can shape according to a set of universal values, like generosity, solidarity, responsibility, caring, peace, tolerance and justice.[27]

Hence, likewise the demands of totalitarian regimes' orthodoxies and the imposition of a given methodology upon students without attending to their personal needs and interests result in what Orwell called the "gramophone mind".[28] The communal *eu*topia in the classroom shows solidarity with a kaleidoscopic arrangement of methodologies that enrich the multiple intelligences of students, together with their motivation and cooperation, achieving the aforementioned union in the multitude. Moreover, utopianism ensures the transformative power in the student, since Wells states that

> learning is an active and constructive process that involves a triple transformation: of the learner's repertoire for action; of the tools and practices involved, as the learner constructs his or her unique version of them; and of his or her relationship with others and thus of his or her identity.[29]

He continues displaying how this transformative process can only be achieved with a relationship based on interdependence and co-construction.[30] The subject of English as a Foreign Language can act as the link between all subjects and students, teaching towards a transdisciplinary education. Particularly, the use of dystopian literature as macro-theme is highly beneficial to strengthen links between subjects and beyond them, with our contemporary society. Chambers and Gregory claim that "literature is always at the heart of things, but from there we try to move 'out' to make fruitful connections to current educational thinking".[31] Likewise, Brøgger affirms that we construct our world "in the very act of trying to understand it",[32] and dystopias enact our utopian impulse to continue working for a better world.

The ensuing lesson sequence encapsulates the theoretical background previously expounded about the cycle of despair between utopia and dystopia as well as the analysis of past, present and future. However, thanks to cooperative methodologies students will use this knowledge in order to avoid dystopia and reach *eu*topia.

Introduction	In this sequence, students acquire knowledge through cyclical learning. The sequence consists of four lessons plus a final task: • the first lesson serves as an introduction to dystopias, as well as presenting the objectives of the final task, • the second deals with the past and science fiction during the two World Wars, • the third is about the present and hopes put in heroic figures, • the fourth focuses on the future and the possibility of empowering students to bring change themselves, • the final task explores on the potentiality of the Orwellian dystopia to create utopian projects cooperatively. All lessons are operated cyclically, with a reflection brainstorming at the beginning of the lesson which is revisited at the end to confront students with their previous ideas and prejudices. This time journey culminates in the final task where students become protagonists and their critical thinking is put to the test to show empathy, understanding, solidarity and utopianism in the classroom.
Topic	Heroes in Dystopia: From Orwell's Nightmare to Bright Futures
Objectives	WRITING, SPEAKING AND INTERACTING Exchanging information about comics and superheroes; participating in debates about dystopias; expressing complaints and desires; writing original fictional narratives about future societies; negotiating with partners to find agreement. READING AND LISTENING Analysing the characters of comics and novels; translating from Newspeak to English; skimming and scanning; comprehension of different types of media: cartoons, informational videos, songs, etc.; understanding facts about the World War II and other historical events. LINGUISTIC KNOWLEDGE *Functions* Past events and beliefs; desires and hypotheses; discussing a topic and giving personal opinions; making predictions about the future; giving advice and expressing obligation.

	Vocabulary Superpowers; euphemisms; science fiction and technology; Newspeak; binary opposites; literary terms; political terms. *Grammar* Second Conditional; use of 'will' for future predictions; modal verbs 'can', 'could' and 'be able'; differences between the modal verbs 'should', 'must', 'have to'. *Pronunciation* To practice the pronunciation of modal verbs 'would' /wud/, 'should' /ʃud/ and 'could' /kud/ REFLECTION UPON THE LANGUAGE Reflecting on the use and meaning of grammar and vocabulary; using language following cooperative principles and positive values like respect of otherness; taking part in self- and peer-corrections; accepting errors as an integral part of the learning process, and yet showing interest to overcome deficiencies. SOCIOCULTURAL ASPECTS AND MULTICULTURAL AWARENESS Appreciation of the foreign language as a tool to expand our vision of reality, as well as to reflect, communicate and express ideas; interest in and positive attitude towards other cultural manifestations; intercultural awareness by means of the language; empathy with other peoples and their difficulties.
Age	Secondary level students (around 15 years old)
Level	CEFR level B1
Time	4 lessons of 60 minutes, plus a final task
Materials/ media	Classroom material: whiteboard, computer, overhead projector and the Internet. Students' material: special clothes for costumes, etc. Other material: realia (a seashell, official documents and photographs), comics, books, videos, dictionaries, cards. *Heroes in Dystopia* Portfolio: lesson sequence exercises, self-assessment and extra space for students' creativity Web tools: RealTimeBoard, Google Drive, WebQuest
1st lesson: "Utopias and Dystopias"	*Presentation of the lesson sequence and explanation of the final task* (5', Teacher) The teacher explains the organization of the sequence and how students must prepare the final task, by arranging them in groups and assigning them a role. Following the model of Airstrip One in George Orwell's *1984*, students will create a

	name for their society and a slogan. All groups will have a president (Big Brother), a Minister of Justice (Minipax), a Minister of Economy (Miniplenty), a Minister of Equality (Miniluv) and a Minister of Education (Minitrue). This activity will be part of the homework, as students have to prepare a presentation about the society they have created and show it to their classmates the day of the final task. *Reflection Brainstorming #1* (3', Teacher-Whole Class) Ask students questions like *What do utopia and dystopia mean? What's power? Is there a perfect society? What elements must a perfect society have?* The teacher can also show them book covers or film posters of famous dystopias and ask them if they are familiar with them. *Warm-up: Making Opposite Worlds* (5', Individual Work) Ask students to match opposite terms (e.g. utopia/dystopia, love/hate, peace/war, etc.) *Reading: Guess the Title* (20', Pair Work) Give each pair Mustapha Mond's final speech from Aldous Huxley's *Brave New World* and O'Brien's final speech from George Orwell's *1984*. Without the novel titles, each student reads one of the texts and answers some comprehension questions. After this, students interact with their partners, summarising the most important ideas from their text, so that they can answer the following questions: *Can you tell the differences and similarities between these two texts? What's wrong with these fictional societies? Are they similar to our contemporary society? How will it end, in your opinion? Can you think of a title for these novels?* *Listening and Speaking: The Lords VS the Flies* (20', Big Group Work) As a pre-listening activity, the teacher introduces the topic by asking questions like *Would you like to live on a desert island?* or *Do you think life with adults is better?* Then comes the listening activity, with a trailer of Harry Hook's adaptation of *The Lord of the Flies*. Students watch the video twice to answer some comprehension questions. As a post-listening activity, students participate in a debate. The teacher divides the class in two teams, "The Lords" (children who want to go back home) and "The Flies" (children who want to stay on the island). Each group has to write reasons to support their view and then discuss together which is the best option. After the debate, they watch the film to know which team is the winner.

	Revisiting of Brainstorming #1 (2' Teacher-Whole Class) After the activities of the lesson, the class goes back to their initial answers at the brainstorming. As a cyclical learning process, they may have changed their previous prejudices and ideas, expanding this way their critical thinking and their knowledge about the world.
2nd lesson: "Past and Wars"	*Reflection Brainstorming #2* (3', Teacher-Whole Class) Ask students questions like *Why are there wars? Who wins in a war? Do you think it is possible to have a Third World War in the future?* or *How did WWII society think the future would be?* The teacher can also show them photos from the Second World War. *Warm-up: Revisiting Wartoons* (5', Individual Work and Whole Class) The teacher shows students the Looney Toones' sketch "The Ducktators". Students try to guess the historical characters and whose side they think made the sketch: the Axis or the Allies. After this, they listen to the sketch to answer further comprehension questions. As a post-listening activity, students are asked to choose animals that best represented historical characters in WWII. *Speaking and Reading: What am I in Animal Farm?* (15', Small Group Work) The teacher gives a summary of Orwell's *Animal Farm* and its relation with the communist regime. Students are divided in seven groups and each of the members receives one card with two sides: one with the historical character and the other with the matching animal. They cannot see the latter, but their peers can, so students need to ask yes/no questions round after round to guess the animal. Once the first part is finished, students are reassembled by making new groups according to their animal. All groups are given brief extracts from the novel to guess which of the characters correspond to their animal (e.g. sheep, Old Benjamin, Boxer, the dogs, Napoleon, Mollie, etc.) *Vocabulary: Auctioning Newspeak* (15', Teacher-Whole Class) The teacher explains Newspeak and gives students terms from this language. Students guess their English equivalents. After this, the teacher shows the similarity between Newspeak vocabulary and the use of euphemisms in society. For this game, students are in pairs and each pair is given 100 points that can be used in the auction of terms. The teacher shows euphemisms on the board with a definition that may be true or

	false. Students have to bid wisely how to use their points by thinking if the definitions are correct or not. At the end of the game, the teacher shows the solutions: pairs that bid for a correct definition double their points and pairs that bid for an incorrect definition lose all their points. *Grammar, Vocabulary and Speaking: Real Science Fiction* (15', Individual Work and Teacher-Whole Class) The teacher provides historical background about the technological devices invented during the 20th c. in reality and science fiction (e.g. radar, spaceflight, human teleportation, lightsaber, etc.). Students put these devices in the correct column (depending on whether they existed during WWII, they were created after or they have not yet been created). The teacher and the students correct this together. Then, students practice the use of 'could', 'can' and 'will be able to' by creating sentences with those devices. *Revisiting of Brainstorming #2* (2' Teacher-Whole Class) HOMEWORK *Reading and Writing: Holocaust in Maus* Students are given two extracts of Art Spiegelman's comic *Maus*, one dealing with the time before WWII and the other during WWII. They have to answer some comprehension questions and imagine a possible ending for the protagonist or ask how they would feel in this situation.
3rd lesson: "Present and Hopes"	*Reflection Brainstorming #3* (3', Teacher-Whole Class) Ask students questions like *If you could change the world, what would you do? What is a hero? Who's a hero for you? What is the difference between a hero and a superhero?* *Warm-up: "If Today Was Your Last Day", by Nickelback* 10' (Individual Work) To revise the second conditional, the teacher plays the song and asks students to fill the gaps with the modal verbs missing. Students are asked to say the grammatical structure. Finally, students have to complete the sentence "If today were my last day, ..." according to their own wishes. *Grammar and Vocabulary: Hero ingredients* (10', Individual Work and Whole Class) Students are asked first what is necessary to become a hero. Then a list of elements (e.g. courage, weapons, scientific modifications, studying, etc.) are given to students and they have to place them in the most appropriate place in the table according to their criteria (the columns are classified according

	to modal verbs: 'must', 'should', 'do not have to', 'should not' and 'must not'). When their choices are shared with their classmates, students should make a sentence using the corresponding modal verb. *Grammar and Speaking: If I were a Superhero…* (15', Small Group Work) Students are required to work in groups of three or four and fill with their personal opinion a table with the following features: their superhero's name, their superpower, their costume design and the villain they would fight against. Students will ask each other and write their answers, imagining they are superheroes. After that, students will go around the class looking for people who share their superpower in order to create a team. *Reading, Writing and Speaking: V for Vindications!* (20', Small Group Work) With the teams of the previous activity, students now read the extract when V appears on TV in Alan Moore's comic no. 5 of *V for Vendetta.* After this, the teacher asks the teams to think about a problem they would like to solve in their society. For this, students also have to create a name for their organization and a logo. Finally, they will share their ideas with their classmates and ask them for other possible solutions. *Revisiting of Brainstorming #3* (2', Teacher-Whole Class)
4th lesson: "Future and Changes"	*Reflection Brainstorming #4* (3', Teacher-Whole Class) Ask students questions like *Do you think wars are a solution for the problems in the world? What do you want to be in the future? Do you know a person that made history? Do you admire her/him? Is violence necessary? What is the most powerful weapon to change the world?* *Warm-up: Erasing Dumb Laws* (10', Individual Work and Teacher-Whole Class) The teacher gives students a list of laws from many countries in the world, some of them being currently repealed but many others still valid, although they are unjust or absurd. Students circle the ones which are believed to be still valid. Then, they correct the exercise together and the teacher explains that all these laws were valid once in history, although some of them were finally repealed. Finally, a short debate about these laws will be held. *Reading (and Listening), Writing and Speaking: Treasure Hunt "Leaders for Change"* (30', Small Group Work and Teacher-Whole Class)

	For this activity, laptops are necessary. Students form five groups and each group is in charge of answering some questions about an important social leader in history (e.g. Mahatma Gandhi, Nelson Mandela, Marsha P. Johnson, Emmeline Pankhurst and Rosa Parks). Individually, they will write down their answers, having previously looked for information from the web resources provided. Once they have written down the information, a couple of minutes can be used for sharing ideas and resolving doubts in the group. After this, students proceed to the second part of the activity, in which they are redistributed in new groups, with one member of each of the former groups in each of the new groups. This part of the activity is devoted to a meeting of leaders based on role-play, in which each student imagines they are the character from the former group and explains the struggles and challenges of their situation to the rest of the new group members. Then, a whole class debate will be arranged. *Listening: Malala Yousafzai's Speech at the UN* (10' Individual Work and Whole Class) The teacher asks students if teenagers can change the world or if they are too young. After this debate, they listen to the last part of Malala Yousafzai's speech at the UN. Students answer some comprehension questions. Then a discussion is raised by the teacher about the problems of war and the power of education to change the world for better. *Revisiting of Brainstorming #4* (2' Teacher-Whole class) HOMEWORK *Writing: Time Capsule* Students have to write a short commentary (100-150 words) about how the world and they themselves will be in 2050, but as it is a time capsule, they are invited to attach more items, like photographs, personal objects, etc. The day of the Final Task students will bring their letters and realia and these will be collected in a box.
Final Task: "Our Ideal World"	The groups created at the beginning of the unit hold their presentations about the society they have designed. Each group will devote 5' to explain their project. Once the presentations have finished, students will vote for their favourite one. However, the points obtained do not determine the winner. Students will go one step further in this democratic representation, creating a common utopia in the next part of the activity.

	The experts of each group (Big Brothers and Ministers) gather and find a common solution to the different proposals. They have 5' to discuss their correspondent topic (State Leadership, Justice, Economy, Equality, Education) and create something together. Once time is over, each expert group will have a spokesperson to briefly explain the conclusions they have reached. Unlike *1984*, this new world has been created upon a solid ground of unity in diversity, having a collage of voices in society.

Table 1: Lesson Sequence: *Heroes in Dystopia*

4. Conclusion

Gordin et al. are right when suggesting that "people perceive their environments as dystopic, and alas they do so with depressing frequency".[33] The twentieth century witnessed the despondency of the war generations, but it was also a period of transformation within these dystopian settings: from fear to bravery, from betrayal to martyrdom, from violence to peace. The Orwellian dissident has gradually taken new directions to fight against an oppressive dystopian regime without falling into failure. Similarly, utopianism has undergone a conceptual shift emphasising the importance of the transformative process. It originates on behalf of those dystopian rebels who ever felt despair in solitude and found the multitude as a new and more effective collectivising form of the utopian imagination[34] because "none of us [...] can become human at all, much less flourish, except in the company and conversation and caring of other human beings",[35] according to Chambers and Gregory.

Our educational environment can put the necessary materials at the pupils' disposal so that they can (de)construct their contemporary society, thanks to the use of dystopian fiction and the new technologies. Sampedro affirms that "when we teach, we touch the future. Everything we do today will have an impact tomorrow, so while teaching is indeed a big responsibility, it is also a fantastic opportunity". [36] The teaching of dystopias in the EFL classroom proves challenging for students of secondary level inasmuch as they are at a critical age. As teenagers, they can be indeed rebellious and sometimes outraged; the functioning of the world exceeds their comprehension and power, causing helplessness.

However, the teaching *of* and *through* dystopias is highly rewarding: the understanding of and critical stance on their reading may channel the students' emotions into a positive attitude that helps them build hopeful prospects. It is precisely during this attempt of trying their best that utopianism is finally born.

Notes

1 Orwell, George (2002 [1941]). "The Art of Donald McGill." *Essays*. Ed. John Carey. New York: Everyman's Library, 383.

2 Dias de Carvalho, Adalberto (2005). "From Contemporary Utopias to Contemporaneity as a Utopia." *Utopia Matters: Theory Politics, Literature and the Arts*. Eds. Fatima Vieira and Marinela Freitas. Porto: Universidade do Porto, 65.

3 O'Brien, Eugene (2008). "'Towards Justice to Come': Derrida and Utopian Justice." *Exploring the Utopian Impulse: Essays on Utopian Thought and Practice*. Ed. Tom Moylan. Oxford: Peter Lang, 43.

4 Sargisson, Lucy (1996). *Contemporary Feminist Utopianism*. London: Routledge, 37.

5 *Ibid.,* 127.

6 Baccolini, Raffaella (2013). "Living in Dystopia." *Dystopia(n) Matters. On the Page, on Screen, on Stage.* Ed. Fátima Vieira. Newcastle upon Tyne: Cambridge Scholars Publishing, 45.

7 Díaz-Pérez, Francisco Javier (2013). "Introduction to Global Issues in the Teaching of Language, Literature and Linguistics." *Mehrsprachigkeit in Europa/Multilingualism in Europe, Volume 7: Global Issues in the Teaching of Language, Literature and Linguistics*. Eds. Francisco Javier Díaz-Pérez et al. Bern: Peter Lang, 8.

8 Gordin, Michael. D., et al. (2010). "Introduction: Utopia and Dystopia beyond Space and Time." *Utopia/Dystopia: Conditions of Historical Possibility*. Eds. Michael D. Gordin et al. Princeton: Princeton University Press, 1.

9 Dias de Carvalho (2005), 73.

10 Spiegelman, Art (2011). *MetaMaus: A Look Inside a Modern Classic*. New York: Pantheon Books, 115.

11 In 1942, a Looney Tunes sketch called "The Ducktators" was released, where the Axis leaders Hitler, Mussolini and Tojo are caricatured as ducks. *The Ducktators*. Dir. Norm McCabe. 1942. Leon Schlesinger.

[12] See Lázaro Lafuente, Luis Alberto (1987). *Pensamiento y obra de George Orwell: Estudio de* Animal Farm *como síntesis de toda su producción literaria.* Valladolid: Secretariado de Publicaciones Universidad de Valladolid.

[13] Orwell, George (2008[1945a]). *Animal Farm. A Fairy Story*. London: Penguin Books, 95.

[14] See Orwell, George (2002[1945b]). "Politics and the English Language." *Essays* (2002). Ed. John Carey. New York: Everyman's Library, 954-967.

[15] Orwell (2000[1949]), 60.

[16] *Ibid.*, 6.

[17] Paik, Peter Y. (2010). *From Utopia to Apocalypse: Science Fiction and the Politics of Catastrophe.* Minneapolis: University of Minnesota Press, 11.

[18] Moore, Alan, and David Lloyd (2005). *V for Vendetta*. New York: DC Comics, 41.

[19] *Ibid.*, 155.

[20] *Ibid.*, 165.

[21] Huxley, Aldous (1994[1931]). *Brave New World.* London: Vintage Classics, 198.

[22] Orwell, George (2002[1945b]), 963.

[23] Rai, Alok. (1988). *Orwell and the Politics of Despair: A Critical Study of the Writings of George Orwell*. Cambridge: Cambridge University Press, 89.

[24] *Ibid.*, 144.

[25] Sargisson, Lucy (2012). *Fool's Gold? Utopianism in the Twenty-First Century*. New York: Palgrave Macmillan, 242.

[26] Yousafzai, Malala (2013). "Malala Yousafzai: 16th Birthday Speech at the United Nations." *Malala Fund* 12 July 2013. Web. 1 March 2020 <https://malala.org/newsroom/archive/malala-un-speech>.

[27] Sampedro, Rick (2013). "We Teach, We Touch the Future – Global Issues in ELT." *Mehrsprachigkeit in Europa/Multilingualism in Europe, Volume 7: Global Issues in the Teaching of Language, Literature and Linguistics.* Eds. Francisco Javier Díaz-Pérez et al. Bern: Peter Lang, 41.

[28] Orwell, George. (2002[1945c]). "The Freedom of the Press." *Essays*. Ed. John Carey. New York: Everyman's Library, 896.

[29] Wells, Gordon (2008). "Dialogue, Inquiry and the Construction of Learning." *Transforming Learning in Schools and Communities: The Remaking of Education for a Cosmopolitan Society.* Eds. Bob Lingard, Jon Nixon and Stewart Ranson. London: Continuum International Publishing, 237.

[30] *Ibid.*, 238.

[31] Chambers, Ellie, and Marshall Gregory (2006). *Teaching and Learning English Literature.* London: SAGE, 2.

[32] Brøgger, Fredrik Christian (1992). *Culture, Language, Text: Culture Studies within the Study of English as a Foreign Language*. Oslo: Scandinavian University Press, 86.

[33] Gordin et al. (2010), 2.

[34] Skrimshire, Stefan. (2008). *Politics of Fear, Practices of Hope: Depoliticisation and Resistance in a Time of Terror*. London: Continuum International Publishing, 176.

[35] Chambers and Gregory (2006), 21.

[36] Sampedro, Rick (2013), 41.

Bibliography

Primary Texts

The Ducktators. Dir. Norm McCabe. 1942. Leon Schlesinger.

Golding, William (1954). *Lord of the Flies.* London: Faber and Faber.

Huxley, Aldous (1994[1931]). *Brave New World.* London: Vintage Classics.

Lord of the Flies. Dir. Harry Hook. 1990. Columbia Pictures.

Moore, Alan, and David Lloyd (2005). *V for Vendetta.* New York: DC Comics.

Orwell, George (2002[1941]). "The Art of Donald McGill." *Essays*. Ed. John Carey. New York: Everyman's Library, 373-384.

--- (2008[1945a]). *Animal Farm. A Fairy Story*. London: Penguin Books.

--- (2002[1945b]). "Politics and the English Language." *Essays*. Ed. John Carey. New York: Everyman's Library, 954-967.

--- (2002[1945c]). "The Freedom of the Press." *Essays*. Ed. John Carey. New York: Everyman's Library, 888-897.

--- (2000[1949]). *Nineteen Eighty-Four.* London: Penguin Classics.

Spiegelman, Art (1996). *The Complete Maus.* London: Penguin Books. .

Secondary Literature

Baccolini, Raffaella (2013). "Living in Dystopia." *Dystopia(n) Matters. On the Page, on Screen, on Stage.* Ed. Fátima Vieira. Newcastle upon Tyne: Cambridge Scholars Publishing, 44-45.

Brøgger, Fredrik Christian (1992). *Culture, Language, Text: Culture Studies within the Study of English as a Foreign Language*. Oslo: Scandinavian University Press.

Chambers, Ellie, and Marshall Gregory (2006). *Teaching and Learning English Literature.* London: SAGE.

Dias de Carvalho, Adalberto (2005). "From Contemporary Utopias to Contemporaneity as a Utopia." *Utopia Matters: Theory Politics, Literature and the Arts.* Eds. Fatima Vieira and Marinela Freitas. Porto: Universidade do Porto, 63-80.

Díaz-Pérez, Francisco Javier (2013). "Introduction to Global Issues in the Teaching of Language, Literature and Linguistics." *Mehrsprachigkeit in Europa/Multilingualism in Europe, Volume 7: Global Issues in the Teaching of Language, Literature and Linguistics.* Eds. Francisco Javier Díaz-Pérez et al. Bern: Peter Lang, 7-14.

Gordin, Michael. D., et al. (2010). "Introduction: Utopia and Dystopia beyond Space and Time." *Utopia/Dystopia: Conditions of Historical Possibility.* Eds. Michael D. Gordin et al. Princeton: Princeton University Press, 1-17.

Lázaro Lafuente, Luis Alberto (1987). *Pensamiento y obra de George Orwell: Estudio de* Animal Farm *como síntesis de toda su producción literaria.* Valladolid: Secretariad de Publicaciones Universidad de Valladolid.

O'Brien, Eugene (2008). "'Towards Justice to Come': Derrida and Utopian Justice." *Exploring the Utopian Impulse: Essays on Utopian Thought and Practice*. Ed. Tom Moylan. Oxford: Peter Lang, 11-46.

Paik, Peter Y. (2010). *From Utopia to Apocalypse: Science Fiction and the Politics of Catastrophe.* Minneapolis: University of Minnesota Press.

Rai, Alok. (1988). *Orwell and the Politics of Despair: A Critical Study of the Writings of George Orwell.* Cambridge: Cambridge University Press, 89.

Sampedro, Rick (2013). "We Teach, we Touch the Future – Global Issues in ELT." *Mehrsprachigkeit in Europa/Multilingualism in Europe, Volume 7: Global Issues in the Teaching of Language, Literature and Linguistics.* Eds. Francisco Javier Díaz-Pérez et al. Bern: Peter Lang, 39-48.

Sargisson, Lucy (1996). *Contemporary Feminist Utopianism.* London: Routledge.

--- (2012). *Fool's Gold? Utopianism in the Twenty-First Century*. New York: Palgrave Macmillan.

Skrimshire, Stefan. (2008). *Politics of Fear, Practices of Hope: Depoliticisation and Resistance in a Time of Terror.* London: Continuum International Publishing.

Spiegelman, Art (2011). *MetaMaus: A Look Inside a Modern Classic*. New York: Pantheon Books.

Wells, Gordon (2008). "Dialogue, Inquiry and the Construction of Learning." *Transforming Learning in Schools and Communities: The Remaking of Education for a Cosmopolitan Society.* Eds. Bob Lingard, Jon Nixon and Stewart Ranson. London: Continuum International Publishing, 236-256.

Yousafzai, Malala (12 July 2013). "Malala Yousafzai: 16th Birthday Speech at the United Nations." *Malala Fund.* Web. 1 March 2020 <https://malala.org/newsroom/archive/malala-un-speech>.

Martin Štefl (Prague)

The Human/Machine: Science Fiction as a Primer for Critical Thinking in ESL Teaching for Secondary Students

1. Introduction

The aim of the pedagogical approach to science fiction proposed in the present chapter is to show the potential of the genre for developing students' literacy, analytical and critical thinking skills through exploring the relationship between humanity and technology. More specifically, science fiction can raise students' awareness of the fact that seemingly unproblematic and taken-for-granted concepts like human nature are open to interpretation through assessing how (modern) technologies shape our daily lives, and that what it means to be human is closely related to the use of technologies.

Consequently, the suggested sequence questions implicit and/or automatically accepted essentialist, normative and/or materialist interpretations of what it means to be human, and raises awareness of the fact that categories and constructs commonly used in our everyday life and language, such as the duality of human and machine, man and woman, human and environment, individual and society, us and others, etc., are more fluid and/or problematic than they might seem.

The first part of this paper gives a general introduction to the lesson sequence while the second part introduces the primary texts and contextualises each of them. The third part discusses the theoretical background and links it to the primary texts. Finally, the description of the lesson sequence sums up the tasks, materials and activities used.

2. Primary Texts for the Course

The lesson reading is comprised of texts which juxtapose humanity and technology or human and machine. It is generally believed that

> [b]y distorting and exaggerating human situations, the utopian text acts as a criticism of life, and by offering a possible, alternative model of social organisation, whether positive or negative; it also acts as an implicit and explicit proposal for a substitutive organisation.[1]

In line with this assumption, two out of three primary texts, namely, Ayn Rand's *Anthem* (1938) and E. M. Forster's "The Machine Stops" (1909), classify as dystopian science fiction. Both texts have become classic examples of early and very early twentieth century science-fiction literature and rank among now iconic texts of authors like G. H. Wells' *The Time Machine* (1895), *The Sleeper Awakes* (1910), *The First Man on the Moon* (1901) – or perhaps Jack London's *The Iron Heel* (1908) – and later flagship dystopias such as Aldous Huxley's *Brave New World* (1932), George Orwell's *1984* (1948), Karel Čapek's *Rossum's Universal Robots* (1921), Kurt Vonnegut's *Player Piano* (1952) or Ray Bradbury's *Fahrenheit 451* (1953).

The third text used in the sequence is A. C. Clarke's *2001: Space Odyssey*, namely the first chapter entitled "Primeval Night". Perhaps also thanks to the now legendary film version of the novel directed by Stanley Kubrick, *2001: Space Odyssey* (1968) established Clarke among legendary science fiction authors like Isaac Asimov, Ray Bradbury, E. E. Smith or later Philip K. Dick. The novel represents one of the key examples of space exploration and artificial intelligence narratives, although its philosophical and theological dimensions should not be underestimated. The status of *2001: Space Odyssey* as a utopian and/or dystopian novel is open to discussion. On the one hand, the novel shows positive advancements of the human species; however, at the same time, it pictures risks, perils and doomsday anxieties connected with humanity's advanced technologies, a recurrent topic in A. C. Clarke's fiction. Perhaps the most fitting description of the novel in this respect might be "mostly utopian".[2] Taken as an independent text, "Primeval Night" is on the verge of alien invasion/intervention and belongs to the genre of philosophical science fiction.

3. Theoretical Background

The theoretical linchpin uniting all selected texts is post-human philosophy, which addresses the complex and dynamic relationship between humankind and technology. This relationship was theorised by thinkers such as Bernard Stiegler in his seminal *Time and Technics 1: The Fault of Epimetheus* (1998), work of scientists/thinkers such as Kevin Warvick, Darren Tofts, Arthur Bradley or Donna Haraway, and practically explored by artists/performers such as Neil Harbisson, Moon Ribas, Havve Fjell or, perhaps most famously, Stelarc.

The following section provides a brief account of selected post-human theories, which should give practitioners just an idea of the theoretical framework important for this sequence, and explain how these theories relate to the texts at hand. The aim is to show that the primary texts selected are suitable for discussing the multiple facets of the relationship between mankind and technology within the theoretical framework provided by post-human philosophies.

Post-human philosophies argue that "contemporary technology has radically transformed our understanding of what it is to be human".[3] Expanding on this statement, Clarke's "Primeval Night" introduces a number of important post-human issues as it "presents an imagined future and *past* to help us understand the present".[4] "Primeval Night" combines two stories: first, the story of a crystal monolith installed on our planet to educate the man-apes, and, second, the introduction of primitive technology such as stones, animal horns or branches and the resulting development. Commenting on the change triggered by the use of these tools, the narrator notes that

> [t]heir [man-apes'] bone clubs had increased their reach and multiplied their strength; they were no longer defenseless against the predators with whom they had to compete. The smaller carnivores they could drive away from their own kills; the larger ones they could at least discourage, and sometimes put to flight.[5]

This short extract shows that, first, technology does not mean only 'modern' (say 20th and 21st century) technology. Second, the change in man-apes' minds made possible by the use of prehistoric tools suggests that their 'nature' lies in their capacity to use but also to be changed by these tools, i.e. to be conditioned by technology. In line with this key idea, post-human theorists such as Stiegler or Clark uncompromisingly speak about humans as "human-technology symbionts: thinking and reasoning systems whose minds and selves are spread across biological brain and nonbiological circuitry".[6] Thanks to this circuitry,

> [t]heir [man-apes'] massive teeth were growing smaller, for they were no longer essential. The sharp-edged stones that could be used to dig out roots, or to cut and saw through tough flesh or fiber, had begun to replace them, with immeasurable consequences. No longer were the man-apes faced with starvation when their teeth became damaged or worn; even the crudest tools could add many years to their lives. [...] And then the world began to change.[7]

"Primeval Night" thus showcases the evolutionary dependency between technology and humanity, illustrating Stiegler's argument that "there never was a pre-technological human being in the first place [...] because we were always already post-human".[8] Thus, a human being ought to be described as a "being [...] characterized in its forms of life by the nonliving – or by its traces that life leaves in the nonliving." [9] Consequently, a species which was "on the road to extinction", i.e. into non-existence, was set on a completely different, successful evolutionary path thanks to its pairing with technology.

Interestingly enough, "Primeval Night" touches upon a motif which plays a crucial role in Stiegler's argument as well as in a number of science-fiction stories, namely, the Promethean myth of external intervention which triggers the human (man-ape) capacity to evolve by exposing technology. Stiegler ingeniously uses Plato's version of the myth of Epimetheus (*Protagoras* 320c – 328d) to argue that humanity is "constituted by an originary lack of defining qualities" that must be supplied from outside by "technical artefacts".[10] According to this myth, the Titans Prometheus and Epimetheus were charged by the gods with equipping newly created creatures with 'natural' qualities. Epimetheus hastily distributed all qualities among various animals but forgot to equip humans. With no qualities left, Epimetheus called for his smarter brother's help. Prometheus, finding other animals "suitably furnished", but humans alone "naked and shoeless" with "neither bed nor arms of defence" had no other choice but to steal "the mechanical arts of Hephaestus and Athene, and fire with them (they could neither have been acquired nor used without fire), and gave them to man." Only thanks to these gifts humans "had the wisdom necessary to the support of life".[11]

Plato's myth lends Stiegler a metaphor to argue that humans are nothing without their technology, or, more specifically, that their being takes place through technology. "Primeval Night" reflects Stiegler's interpretation of Plato's myth by elucidating that before the advent of technology, the man-apes had (unlike other animals) no 'natural' qualities, or 'natural weapons':

> The nearest worthwhile grazing was now more than a mile from the caves, and they [man-apes] had to share it with a herd of large, antelope-like beasts who barely tolerated their presence. They could not be driven away, for they were armed with ferocious daggers on their foreheads – *the natural weapons which the man-apes did not possess* (my emphasis). So Moon-Watcher and his companions chewed berries and fruit and leaves and fought off the pangs of hunger – while all around them, competing for the same fodder, was a potential source of more food than they could ever hope to eat.[12]

As both Stiegler and Clarke show, the formative relationship between human and machine has played a role from the very beginning of human evolution, and has become more pronounced thanks to modern technologies. Consequently, in Stiegler's own words, technology "becomes the interface through which the human qua living matter enters into relation with the milieu".[13]

Importantly, for both Stiegler and Stelarc, an artist/thinker known for experimenting with body/technology merging, technology stands for a neutral phenomenon that is without inherent risks. The complex status of technology and normative value it is ascribed can be further followed in Rand's *Anthem*.

If it is true that dystopias "fuse two fears, the fear of utopia and the fear of technology",[14] Rand's vision in *Anthem* seems to embrace only one half of the definition. Promoting her philosophy of objectivism, Rand does not share Clarke's cautious treatment of technology nor Stiegler's complex post-human approach and instead opts for a straightforwardly anthropocentric, optimistic creation myth "which conflates technological creation with the liberation of the individual",[15] once again, framed within the story of Promethean myth; it is not a coincidence that Rand's version drops Epimetheus, since in her account there is no room for technology to fail.

Anthem presents a totalitarian dystopia from which (modern) technology has been removed after the so-called 'Great Rebirth'. The resulting equalitarian society, a mockery of Communist/Collectivist social engineering experiments, is one in which its citizens have "no cause to exist save in toiling for other man".[16] Regarding the anthropocentric role of technology in Rand's stories, it has been correctly observed that:

> Rand's belief system is marked at its core by an intellectual investment in technology, an assertion that man's progress is indicated by technological development; moreover, that technological progression is at the heart of humanity's worth.[17]

Rand thus works with a rather black-and-white interpretation of technology and its relation to humanity, which reminds us of Heidegger's critique of modern technology as a 'standing reserve':[18] an instrumental, anthropocentric interpretation of technology which disregards the post-human assumption that in the human-technology relationship "the main [organizing] tendency does not derive from an organizing force – the human".[19] *Anthem* nevertheless teaches us a valuable lesson. Like other dystopian classics such as Orwell's *1984* or Huxley's *Brave New World*, Rand describes technology (or rather its absence) as an instrument in the hands of the totalitarian regime, but also as capable of changing the social and political life of man. Notably, Rand's treatment of the matter seems devoid of the "Faustean and Frankensteinean"[20] fear of the destructive potential of technology – one can simply think of Mary Shelley's version of the Promethean story. In a happy, technophiliac narrative of human progress, Equality 7-2521/Prometheus uses his re-discovery of electricity/light as a principle of human individuation, and a tool to deconstruct the dystopian system. Unlike in, for example, Kurt Vonnegut's "Harrison Bergeron" and other dystopias where technology dehumanises, in *Anthem* technology humanises: to be human means to use technology. Once again, Rand's story, unlike Clarke's, does not seem to accentuate any potential dangers: the rediscovery of technology simply brings an end to one socio-political construct of humanity:

> Everything which comes from the many is good. Everything which comes from one is evil. Thus we have been taught with our first breath. We have

> broken the law, but we have never doubted it. [...] There is no life for man save in useful toil for the good of our brothers. But we lived not, when we toiled for our brothers, we were only weary. There is no joy for men, save the joy shared with all their brothers. But the only things which taught us joy were the power created in our wires, and the Golden One.[21]

Through the emancipating role of technology, Rand's *Anthem* partly reveals that human existence is constructed through narratives which attempt to maintain the status quo through preserving the borders between human/technology, collective/individual, man/woman, good/evil, natural/unnatural, and comes closer to the idea of human qua constructed cyborg, famously championed by Haraway in her "A Cyborg Manifesto".[22] Using the concept of cyborg to illustrate her point, Haraway's political post-humanism argues that:

> A cyborg is a cybernetic organism, a hybrid of machine and organism, a creature of social reality as well as a creature of fiction. Social reality is lived social relations, our most important political construction, a world-changing fiction.[23]

The aim of Rand's capitalist mission is of course completely different from Haraway's, yet their dialogue seems highly productive. Rand, "a true Priestess of competitive capitalism",[24] deconstructs a totalitarian dystopia only to replace it with what Haraway calls the "the tradition of racist, male-dominant capitalism; the tradition of progress; the tradition of the appropriation of nature as resource for the productions of culture".[25] Consequently, instead of offering a post-human "multiplicity of contestable futures",[26] Rand champions (yet) another "territory of production, reproduction, and imagination", which ends with the famous re-invention of the pronoun 'I' standing for pure individuality. As if responding to Rand's story, it is Stelarc who from his post-humanist perspective states that

> [o]f course, language makes it difficult to speak without referring to an 'I'. But when this body speaks as an 'I', it understands that the notion 'I' in the English language is a simplification of a much more complex relationship between bodies, between the body and its culture and its institutions, between the body and its technologies.[27]

It is precisely this "complex relationship" which Rand's story only hints at without giving it the attention it deserves and thus usefully exposes it to critical analysis.

Similarly to Clarke and Rand, Forster's "The Machine Stops" uses its dystopian setting to complicate the assumed unity of the 'I'. Discussing Forster's story, Zimmerman and Morgan used Merleau-Ponty's phenomenology of perception to argue that "perception [...] does not come from the world or from our intimate elaboration of it [but rather] from our experience of participation in the world".[28]

If our perception is determined by our experience of the world which is conditioned or indeed supplanted by the Machine as Forster's story seems to suggest, the Machine becomes a giant invisible interface which brackets out the "horror of direct experience"[29] of the outside world and replaces it with its machine-representation. With modern interface theories showing that "[p]erception is not reconstruction, [but] construction of a niche-specific, problem-specific, fitness enhancing interface",[30] "The Machine Stops" can be argued to picture a dystopia in which (almost) all bodily and human functions (including perception) are replaced by the machine. Hence the value of Forster's text for today's readers is not only in that "[i]t is suggestive of today's Facebook and Twitter trends with their superficial attraction as contemporary forms of human contact",[31] but also in painting an exaggerated picture of the post-human condition humans already find and have always found themselves in.

4. Lesson Sequence

The aim of the sequence is to raise students' awareness of the humankind/machine relationships, encouraging them to take a critical, reflective perspective on modern life. The texts are meant to be read at home and later discussed in class using secondary texts and resources.

The purpose of the initial lesson is to prepare students for the upcoming discussion and reading. It introduces different instances of unexpected interactions between humans and technology, including works by artist and performer Stelarc, whose technological experiments are highly provocative and open to many interpretations. Short quotes from Stelarc's texts,[32] together with quotes from Haraway's *Cyborg*

Manifesto,[33] articles on body hacking and selected references to relevant science-fiction concepts serve as provocative lead-ins into a critical analysis of the primary texts.

The second lesson is based on the discussion of Clarke's "Primeval Night", showing that being human entails a close interaction with different technologies. After discussing suggested lead-in questions, including the reference to the Promethean myth, students are encouraged to prepare a more detailed interpretation using selected quotes from "Primeval Night".[34]

Rand's *Anthem* is the focus of this lesson. Setting aside prevailingly political and/or sociological interpretations, the discussion again focuses on the relationship between humans and technology. The discussion focuses on Rand's optimistic – perhaps naïve – liberating interpretation of the role of technology. This interpretation is often the subject of students' criticism. The material offers topics for general in-class discussions as well as more detailed research topics suitable for team work and presentation.

The fourth lesson relies on Forster's "The Machine Stops", which provides yet another, more skeptical perspective of the relationship between man and technology in which technology functions as an interface disabling any direct experience. After a lead-in, a general discussion and analysis of key concepts, students are provided with materials which facilitate their interpretations.[35]

During the lessons, students should become aware that technologies are not only next to us, but all around us and inside us and that human interaction between humans and machines is more complex than meets the eye.

Introduction	In this sequence, students will explore a series of iconic science fiction texts and interpret these, using extracts from literary texts, theory and articles to critically assess the relationship between the human and machine and re-consider how technology shapes our everyday existence. The sequence works with three primary texts which deal with different forms of the relationship between human and technology.
Topic	Humanity and/vs. Technology

Objectives	To develop students' literacy, analytical and critical thinking skills through exploring the relationship between humanity and technology; to raise students' awareness of the fact that concepts like 'human nature' are open to interpretation through assessing that/how (modern) technologies shape our daily lives. To develop and practice: • understanding/interpreting literary texts • critical thinking • discussion and presentation skills
Age	Secondary students (15-19)
Level	CEFR level B2 and above
Time	4 lessons (90 mins.) + 1 lesson for final discussion (60 mins.); the length of the individual lesson depends on pupils' levels and use of additional materials. Motivated students of B2+ levels are usually able to finish lesson activities in the given time. For B2 and below be ready to add up to 50% of the expected time.
Materials/media	See bibliography for full reference. Primary Texts: 1. *2001: A Space Odyssey* (Chapter I: "Primeval Night"; approx. 30 pages of text) 2. *Anthem* (full text; approx. 40 pages of text) 3. "The Machine Stops" (full text; approx. 25 pages of text) Extracts used in discussions: *Extended-Body: Interview with Stelarc* "A Cyborg Manifesto" *Protagoras.* "Body-Hackers: People Who Turn Themselves into Cyborgs" Suggested additional reading: "Silly Asses" *Frankenstein, Or the New Prometheus.* *YouTube* Videos: *2001: A Space Odyssey – The Dawn of Man*

1st lesson: Introduction to the sequence 1) Brainstorming modern technologies 2) Skimming through/discussing a short article in teams 3) Interpreting the notion of technology-based work of art/performance 4) Brainstorming man/machine bonding in art 5) Discussing 'Faustean fears and Anxieties' in relation to technology 6) Discussing the cyborg as a socio-political construct in. 7) Introducing new text: HW lead-in	1) Ask students to brainstorm about the way modern technologies shape the way of life in their region/city and, more specifically, the relationship between being human and using technologies; ask students to create a list of technological innovations which changed human behavior. 2) Ask students to skim through an article on body hacking by Oliver Wainwright (see bibliography) and decide about the most useful and useless technological modifications. Encourage in-class discussion. 3) Read the short excerpt from an interview with 'cyborg artist' Stelarc (from "How can the body function" up to "appendage of the body", Atzori and Woolford); stimulate the discussion by exploring images available on Stelarc's official web. Ask students if Stelarc's text and his work challenge the meaning of technology and its relation to what it means to be human. 4) Encourage students to mention more examples of man/machine bonding, including cyborgs, prosthetics, etc. Ask how these seeming unnatural constructs and Stelarc's performances challenge what it means to be human in the age of modern technologies. Raise students' awareness of typical arguments used in this context: argumentum ad *naturam* and ad *populum*. 5) In the above mentioned interview, Stelarc mentions "Frankensteinian fear of incorporating technology into the body" and the fact that according to him we "shouldn't consider our relationship to technology in a Faustian way". Ask students about emotions/feelings Stelarc's work provokes and encourage them to give different explanations of these phrases referring to the story of Goethe's *Faust* and Mary Shelley's *Frankenstein*.

	6) The distinction between the human and the machine has important socio-political consequences. Donna Haraway famously called the cyborg an important element of a "border war" and suggested making the borders more fluid. This would affect other seemingly fixed borders such as gender, racial or social divisions and show them as artificially/politically constructed. Ask students to read the extract from Haraway's "A Cyborg Manifesto" and answer the following questions: *a) What is Haraway's definition of a cyborg?* *b) What do you think Haraway means by the "Western tradition?"* *c) What does she mean by a "border war?" What borders or boundaries does she have in mind? How can the concept of a Cyborg be used in this "war?"* *d) What does Haraway mean by "taking pleasure in confusing these boundaries?"* 7) Introduce A. C. Clarke's *2001: A Space Odyssey*. Ask students to read the first chapter of the book called "Primeval Night" and tell them that it is going to introduce an interesting yet challenging interpretation of the relationship between man and technology. Homework: Read A. C. Clarke's *2001: A Space Odyssey*, Chapter I: Primeval Night.
2nd lesson: A. C. Clarke's *2001: A Space Odyssey*, Chapter I: Primeval Night 1) Introducing the discussion 2) Brainstorming creation myths and in-class discussion 3) Teamwork: micro-presentations 4) Interpreting text using theory 5) Optional task: Text comparison	1) Watch the section entitled "The Dawn of Man" from Stanley Kubrick's movie *2001: A Space Odyssey* (1968) to refresh the content and trigger an in-class discussion. 2) Explain why "Primeval Night" might be understood as a 'creation myth'. Ask students to briefly brainstorm other creation myths they know and encourage them to compare. Focus on the role technology plays in the creation of mankind – first as an alien intervention, second, in the 'technology-related' evolution of mankind. Mention

6) Introducing new text: HW lead-in	similar concepts appearing in science fiction, e.g. Ridley Scott's *Prometheus* (2012). Remind the students that the full name of Shelley's novel discussed in their 1st lesson is *Frankenstein, or The New Prometheus* and ask them to think of reasons for mentioning Prometheus in the title. During the in-class discussion, the teacher might ask questions like: *a) Where does the crystal monolith come from and what is its role?* *b) Who is the main hero of the story?* *c) What is the main moral of the story (if there is one)?* *d) What is the outcome of the story?* *e) What does the story tell us about mankind and its relation to technologies?* *f) What are some of the most important events of the story (besides the appearance of the crystal)?* *g) In what sense can the text be seen as a sci-fi story? Is it a typical one?* 3) Split students into smaller groups and ask them to prepare micro-presentations responding to extracts (a–f), paying special attention to the underlined sections (emphasis added). Each group chooses the topic they find the most interesting. 4) Ask students to read an extract from Plato's dialogue *Protagoras* dealing with the myth of Prometheus and Epimetheus. Challenge students to discuss the relevance of the Promethean myth to "Primeval Night" and/or to write a short essay on the topic: The Relationship between Technology and Humanity in A. C. Clarke's "Primeval Night" and the Promethean Myth. 5) Optional task: Ask students to read Isaac Asimov's sci-fi vignette "Silly Asses" and consider its moral message against the 'moral' of "Primeval Night".

	6) Introduce Ayn Rand's *Anthem*. Give student's brief background information, feel free to mention that the Promethean myth plays an important role in the text. Homework: Read Ayn Rand's *Anthem*.
3rd lesson: Ayn Rand's *Anthem* 1) Lead-in: General discussion 2) Teamwork: Discussing key terms 3) Teamwork: Micro-presentations 4) Introducing new text: HW lead-in	1) Lead-in: General Discussion Suggested lead-in questions might include: *a) What is the role of technology in Rand's story?* *b) Who is the main hero of the story?* *c) What is the main moral of the story (if there is one)? Do you agree with it?* *d) Imagine you were a feminist critic. What would you have to say about Rand's text?* *e) Can you find some similar points shared by both Clarke's and Rand's texts?* *f) What are some of the most important events of the story?* *g) In what sense can the text be seen as a sci-fi story? Is it a typical one?* 2) In teams, distribute cards with the following key terms (see below) from the text and ask them to be able to define these terms using quotations from the text. Council of Eugenics; Council of Vocations; Golden One; Great Rebirth; Home of the Peasants; Home of the Scholars; Home of the Useless; Palace of Corrective Detention; Palace of Mating; The Great Rebirth; The Transgression of Preference; Uncharted Forest; Unmentionable Times; Unspeakable Word; World Council 3) In teams, ask students to prepare short presentations on the following topic areas related with the text: *a)* "We are alone under the earth". Rand's text works not only with the idea of individuality but also with the closely connected notion of 'privacy', which all characters in the story are deprived of. It has been claimed that the idea of privacy is one of the greatest (technological) achievements

	of the modern (western) society. Research the internet for the 'history of privacy' and prepare a short presentation which describes the (lack of) privacy in Rand's text in a socio-cultural context. *b)* Collective vs. Individual Besides being an author of books, Rand was also a philosopher. Here is a brief summary of her philosophical position: • Follow reason, not whims or faith. • Work hard to achieve a life of purpose and productiveness. • Earn genuine self-esteem. • Pursue your own happiness as your highest moral aim. • Prosper by treating others as individuals, trading value for value. (Bullet point summary adapted from: *AynRand.org*. Web. 12 January 2019 <https://www.aynrand.org/ideas/overview>.) Explain how these principles translate into *Anthem*. Think about the role technology plays in the struggle between living as an individual and living as part of a collective. *c)* The language and memory in *Anthem* What is the role of language in the text? Why is it such a sin to write (and read) and why is it considered so dangerous? How does language and the way things/concepts are referred to in the text reveal the nature of the regime described in *Anthem*? *d) Anthem* as a Promethean Myth Equality 7-2521 becomes a true 'Promethean character'. Based on your knowledge of the myth and your own research, explain the importance of this myth in relation to the role of knowledge and technology in the story. 4) As an introduction to the next home reading assignment, Forster's "The Machine Stops", watch the opening sequence of Fritz Lang's *Metropolis*. Explain that it is a critique of mechanisation and life of people in the age

	of machine production; ask students to compare the setting with Rand's book, focusing on the role or work/labor and technology and the so-called 'human condition'. Homework: Read E. M. Forster's "The Machine Stops".
4th Lesson: "The Machine Stops" 1) Lead-in: General discussion 2) Teamwork: Discussing key terms 3) Teamwork: Discussing quotes in relation to the text. 4) Teamwork: Comparing the text to life with modern technologies/social media using	1) Lead-in: General Discussion Suggested lead-in questions might include: *a) What is the role of technology in Forster's story?* *b) Who is the main hero of the story?* *c) What is the main moral of the story (if there is one)? Do you agree with it?* *d) Why does Kuno want to see his mother 'in person'? Why is she reluctant to do this?* *e) Can you find some similar points shared by both Clarke's, Rand's and Forster's texts?* *f) How would you describe the functioning of the Machine and its impact on human life?* *g) Do you agree that the Machine represents advancement in human condition as suggested by the air ship attendant?* (Forster [1909], 9.) *h) Kuno complains that the Machine deprived him of the "sense of space" – what does he mean by his complaint?* (*Ibid.*, 11.) *i) The story works with motion as an important symbol – explain how and why?* 2) Distribute the following keywords and ask students to explain their meaning: *(terrors of) direct experience – Central Committee – exchange of ideas – homelessness – direct speech – Committee of the Machine – first hand ideas – the Book of the Machine* 3) Ask students which of the following quotes best describes Forster's story. Allow them to work in pairs and encourage them to do a quick research on the quotes. 4) Forster's text seems to imply some of the phenomena which appeared with the advent

	of modern communication technologies and social media. Ask students to brainstorm/find online the following 'conditions' connected to the (over)use of social media. *a)* Online interaction substitution for offline interaction *b)* Distraction and procrastination *c)* Sedentary lifestyle habits *d)* Fear of missing out *e)* Status anxiety *f)* Information overwhelm
5th Lesson: Conclusion & Suggestions for further discussion/essays 1) Lead-in: General discussion 2) Critical reflection on texts read in the sequence using a quote	1) As an introduction to the final discussion, ask students to consider how each of the stories/materials read in the sequence contribute to the discussion of human nature as seen through human interaction with (modern) technologies. 2) Based on students' reading and in-class discussions, ask students to critically reflect on the following quote: "[We] have always been augmented by our instruments, our technologies. Technology is what constructs our humanity; the trajectory of technology is what had propelled human developments." (Zylinska and Hall [2002], 114.)

Table 1: Teaching Science-Fiction Texts

5. Conclusion

Exposing multiple facets of the relationship between humankind and technology and showing that we humans have "always been augmented by our instruments, our technologies",[36] it is possible to conclude that all discussed primary texts offer a picture of human-technology relationship with a different level of complexity and different agenda. Forster's text provides a technophobic critique of a world in which the human-technology complex becomes increasingly usurped by the Machine, imaginatively playing out numerous dystopian scenarios, and suggests an escape. Analogically, Rand's text opts for an escape towards individuality through technology, however, without questioning the human-technology relationship beyond its instrumental (political) dimension, failing to transcend the anthropocentric understanding of technology. Clarke's "Primeval Night", although not playing the Faustian complex card as ostentatiously as Forster, comes closest to portraying the full complexity of the human-technology relationship as theorised by post-human philosophies such as Stiegler's. Closing with Stelarc's line, which echoes both Stiegler's and Haraway's post-human approach, we may conclude that

> what's interesting about the arts is that they generate a multiplicity of contestable futures, the multiplicity of the future scenarios. It's about challenging the status quo.[37]

Despite or perhaps thanks to the variety of approaches these texts offer, they may serve as a useful starting point of a discussion concerning the supposed 'status quo' of our human condition at the beginning of the 21st century. As such they might be expected to help students reflect on social and philosophical phenomena that otherwise would have remained covered under the routines of their everyday lives and open them up to the multiplicity of unexpected interpretations.

Notes

1 Caporaletti, Silvana (1997). "Science as Nightmare: 'The Machine Stops' by E.M. Forster." *Utopian Studies* 8.2: 32-47. Web. 25 July 2019 <https://www.jstor.org/stable/20719683>.

2 Cirucci, Angela M., and Barry Vacker (eds.) (2018). *Black Mirror and Critical Media Theory.* New York: Lexington Books, 211.

3 Bradley, Arthur, and Louis Armand (2006). "Introduction: Thinking Technicity." *Technicity*. Eds. Arthur Bradley and Louis Armand. Prague: Litteraria Pragensia, 3.

4 Sims, Christopher A. (2013). *Tech Anxiety: Artificial Intelligence and Ontological Awakening in Four Science Fiction Novels*. Jefferson: McFarland & Co., 11.

5 Clarke, Arthur C. (1968). *2001: Space* Odyssey. Web. 15 June 2019 <https://archive.org/details/SpaceOdyssey_819/page/n1>.

6 Clark, Andy (2000). *Natural-Born Cyborgs: Minds, Technologies, and the Future of Human Intelligence.* Web. 1 August 2019 <https://www.edge.org/conversation/natural-born-cyborgs>.

7 Clarke (1968), 12.

8 Arthur Bradley (2007), "No Future? Bernard Stiegler's Politics of Memory." *Mapping Liminalities: Thresholds in Cultural and Literary Texts*. Eds. Lucy Kay et al. Bern: Peter Lang, 188.

9 Stiegler, Bernard (1998). *Time and Technics 1: The Fault of Epimetheus*. Trans. Richard Beardsworth and George Collins. Stanford: Stanford University Press, 50.

10 Bradley, Arthur (2011). *Originary Technicity*. London: Palgrave Macmillan, 122.

11 Plato (1891) "Protagoras." *The Dialogues of Plato (428/27 - 348/47 BCE),* 1214. Trans. Benjamin Jowett. Web. 12 June 2019 <https://webs.ucm.es /info/diciex/gente/agf/plato/The_Dialogues_of_Plato_v0.1.pdf>.

12 Clarke (1968), 3.

13 Stiegler (1998), 48.

14 Beauchamp, Gorman (1986). "Technology in the Dystopian Novel." *Modern Fiction Studies* (*Special Issue: Science and Fantasy Fiction*) 32.1, 53-63.

15 Murnane, Ben (2018). *Ayn Rand and the Posthuman The Mind-Made Future.* London: Palgrave, 7.

16 Rand, Ayn (1938). *Anthem*, 27. Web. 15 January 2019 <https://www.anderson5.net/cms/lib02/SC01001931/Centricity/Domain/222 /Anthem%20by%20Ayn%20Rand.pdf>.

17 Murnane (2018), 7.

18 Heidegger, Martin (2012). "Positionality." *Bremen and Freiburg Lectures*. Trans. Andrew J. Mitchell. Indianapolis: Indiana University Press.

19 Stiegler (1998), 49.

20 Atzori, Paolo, and Kirk Woolford (n.d.). "Extended-Body: Interview with Stelarc." Web. 2 January 2018 <http://web.stanford.edu/dept/HPS/stelarc/a29-extended_body.html>.

21 Rand (1938), 32.

22 Haraway, Donna J. (2016[1985]). "A Cyborg Manifesto." Web. 5 November 2018 <https://warwick.ac.uk/fac/arts/english/currentstudents/undergraduate /modules/fictionnownarrativemediaandtheoryinthe21stcentury/manifestly_h

araway_----_a_cyborg_manifesto_science_technology_and_socialist-feminism_in_the_....pdf>.

23 *Ibid.*, 5-6.

24 Beauchamp (1986), 57.

25 Haraway (2016[1985]), 6-7.

26 Stelarc (2013). "Phantom Flesh: Extreme Performance Artist Stelarc Interviewed." *The Quietus* 6 March 2013. Web. 5 June 2019. <http://thequietus.com/articles/11469-stelarc-interview>.

27 Zylinska, Joanna, and Gary Hall (2002). "Probings: An Interview with Stelarc." *The Cyborg Experiments: The Extensions of the Body in the Media Age*. Ed. Joanna Zylinska. London: Continuum, 121.

28 Zimmermann, Ana Cristina, and W. John Morgan (2017). "E. M. Forster's 'The Machine Stops': Humans, Technology and Dialogue." *AI and Society* 34.1: 37-45, 41. Web. 2 August 2019 <DOI: 10.1007/s00146-017-0698-3>.

29 Forster, E.M. (1909). "The Machine Stops." Web. 22 January 2019 <https://www.ele.uri.edu/faculty/vetter/Other-stuff/The-Machine-Stops.pdf>, 7.

30 Hoffman, Donald (2009). "The Interface Theory of Perception: Natural Selection Drives True Perception to Swift Extinction." *Object Categorization: Computer and Human Vision Perspectives*. Eds. Sven J. Dickinson et al. Cambridge: Cambridge University Press, 148-166, 159.

31 Zimmermann and Morgan (2017), 3.

32 This is the excerpt from Stelarc used in lesson one: "How can the body function within this landscape of machines? Technology has speeded up the body. […] We can't continue designing technology for the body because that technology begins to usurp and outperform the body. Perhaps it's now time to design the body to match its machines. We somehow have to turbo-drive the body-implant and augment the brain. We have to provide ways of connecting it to the cyber-network. At the moment this is not easily done, and it's done indirectly via keyboards and other devices. […] Mind you, I'm not talking here in terms of sci-fi speculation. For me, these possibilities are already apparent. […] New technologies tend to generate new perceptions and paradigms of the world, and in turn, allow us to take further steps. If we consider technologies as intermediaries to the world, then, of course, we never have direct experiences. […] Technology has always been coupled with the evolutionary development of the body. Technology is what defines being human. It's not an antagonistic alien sort of object, it's part of our human nature. It constructs our human nature. We shouldn't have a Frankensteinian

fear of incorporating technology into the body, and we shouldn't consider our relationship to technology in a Faustian way – that we're somehow selling our soul because we're using these forbidden energies. My attitude is that technology is, and always has been, an appendage of the body." Atzori and Woolford (n.d.).

33 This is the excerpt from Haraway: "A cyborg is a cybernetic organism, a hybrid of machine and organism, a creature of social reality as well as a creature of fiction. Social reality is lived social relations, our most important political construction, a world-changing fiction. [...] Contemporary science fiction is full of cyborgs – creatures simultaneously animal and machine, who populate worlds ambiguously natural and crafted. [...] By the late twentieth century, our time, a mythic time, we are all chimeras, theorized and fabricated hybrids of machine and organism – in short, cyborgs. [...] In the traditions of "Western" science and politics – the tradition of racist, male-dominant capitalism; the tradition of progress; the tradition of the appropriation of nature as resource for the productions of culture; the tradition of reproduction of the self from the reflections of the other – the relation between organism and machine has been a border war. The stakes in the border war have been the territories of production, reproduction, and imagination. This essay is an argument for *pleasure* in the confusion of boundaries and for *responsibility* in their construction. It is also an effort to contribute to [...] the utopian tradition of imagining a world without gender, which is perhaps a world without genesis, but maybe also a world without end." Haraway (2016[1985]), 6-7.

34 These are the excerpts from "Primeval Night": (a) "In the hundred thousand years" to "sometimes put to flight"; (b) "And then the world began" to "toolmakers had been remade by their own tools"; (c) "And somewhere in the shadowy centuries" to "and he was beginning to grope toward a future."; (d) "The stone club" to "very literally, in their own hands"; (e) "As his body became more and more defenseless" to "he was living on borrowed time." (f) "For a long time, intoxicated by victory" to "and they did no hunting that day." Clarke (1968).

35 Here are the quotes for the discussion of Forster's story: (a) "A house is a machine for living in." Le Corbusier (1986). *Towards a New Architecture.* New York: Dover Publication. (b) "To live means to leave traces. In the interior, these are accentuated." Benjamin, Walter (1999). *The Arcades Project.* Trans. Howard Eiland and Kevin McLaughlin. London: Belknap Press, 9. (c) "Consider, if you will, Me + +I consist of a biological core surrounded by extended, constructed systems of boundaries and networks.

[…] The boundaries define a space of containers and places (the traditional domain of architecture), while the networks establish a space of links and flows. Walls, fences, and skins divide; paths, pipes, and wires connect." Mitchell, William J. (2003). *Me++: The Cyborg Self and the Networked City*. Cambridge, Ma: MIT Press, 18. d) "Instead of a cyborg resulting from some kind of medical/military idea of a traumatised body, a body whose organs have been replaced by technology, we can simply think of amplifying or extending the body with its internet connectivity." Stelarc (2013). "Phantom Flesh: Extreme Performance Artist Stelarc Interviewed." *The Quietus* 6 March 2013. Web. 5 June 2019 <http://thequietus.com/articles/11469-stelarc-interview>. (e) "The city is also a machine for living. I want to make sure it is beneficial for the human body." Fend, Peter, and Jerome Sans (1994). "The City as a Machine for Living in." *Grand Street No. 50, Models*: Autumn 1994. Web. 12 May 2019 <https://s3.amazonaws.com/contemporaryartgroup /files/documents_file_469.pdf >.)

[36] Zylinska and Hall (2002), 114.

[37] Stelarc (2013).

Bibliography

Primary Texts

Asimov, Isaac (1958). "Silly Asses." Supernova Condensate. Web. 15 June 2019 <https://supernovacondensate.net/2012/06/23/isaac-asimov-silly-asses/>.

The Ayn Rand Institute. *AynRand.org*. Web. 12 January 2019 < https://www.aynrand.org/ideas/overview>.

Bradbury, Ray (1993). *Fahrenheit 451*. New York: HarperCollins Publishers.

Čapek, Karel (2011). *RUR & War with the Newts (S.F. MASTERWORKS).* Trans. Adam Roberts. London: Orion Publishing Group.

Clarke, Arthur C. (1968). *2001: Space Odyssey*. Web. 15 June 2019 <https://archive.org/details/SpaceOdyssey_819/page/n1>.

Forster, E.M. (1909). "The Machine Stops." Web. 22 January 2019 <https://www.ele.uri.edu/faculty/vetter/Other-stuff/The-Machine-Stops.pdf>.

Huxley, Aldous (2011[1932]). *Brave New World.* London: Random House.

London, Jack (2005). *The Iron Heel and other Stories.* London: Jack Leonaur.

"Metropolis (opening scenes) with Score by Zack Kline." Producer Zack Kline. 2015. *Youtube*. Web. 12 June 2019 <https://www.youtube.com/watch?v=0mK46KprASM>.

Orwell, George (2000[1949]). *1984*. London: Penguin Books Ltd.

Plato (1891) "Protagoras." *The Dialogues of Plato (428/27 - 348/47 BCE),* 1214. Trans. Benjamin Jowett. Web. 12 June 2019 <https://webs.ucm.es/info/diciex/gente/agf/plato/The_Dialogues_of_Plato_v0.1.pdf>.

Prometheus. Dir. Ridley Scott. 2012. 20th Century Fox.

Rand, Ayn (1938). *Anthem*. Web. 15 January 2019 <https://www.anderson5.net/cms/lib02/SC01001931/Centricity/Domain/222/Anthem%20by%20Ayn%20Rand.pdf>.

Shelley, Mary (1993[1818]). *Frankenstein*. Hertfordshire: Wordsworth Classics.

2001: A Space Odyssey – The Dawn of Man. Dir. Stanley Kubrick. 1968. *Youtube*. Web. 12 April 2019 <https://www.youtube.com/watch?v=ypEaGQb6dJk>.

Vonnegut, Kurt (1961). "Harrison Bergeron." Web. 2 March 2020 <https://archive.org/stream/HarrisonBergeron/Harrison%20Bergeron_djvu.txt>.

--- (1999[1952]). *Player Piano*. New York: Bantam.

Wells, George Herbert (2018). *Complete Novels of H. G. Wells*. E-book. MyBooks Classics.

Secondary Literature

Atzori, Paolo, and Kirk Woolford (n.d.). "Extended-Body: Interview with Stelarc." Web. 2 January 2018 <http://web.stanford.edu/dept/HPS/stelarc/a29-extended_body.html>.

Beauchamp, Gorman (1986). "Technology in the Dystopian Novel." *Modern Fiction Studies* (*Special Issue: Science and Fantasy Fiction*) 32.1, 53-63.

Benjamin, Walter (1999). *The Arcades Project*. Trans. Howard Eiland and Kevin McLaughlin. London: Belknap Press.

Blackman, Lisa (2008). *The Body: The Key Concepts*. Oxford, New York: Berg.

Bradley, Arthur, and Louis Armand (2006). "Introduction: Thinking Technicity." *Technicity*. Eds. Arthur Bradley and Louis Armand. Prague: Litteraria Pragensia.

Bradley, Arthur (2007), "No Future? Bernard Stiegler's Politics of Memory-" *Mapping Liminalities: Thresholds in Cultural and Literary Texts*. Eds. Lucy Kay et. al. Bern: Peter Lang.

--- (2011). *Originary Technicity*. London: Palgrave Macmillan, 122.

Caporaletti, Silvana (1997). "Science as Nightmare: 'The Machine Stops' by E.M. Forster." *Utopian Studies* 8.2: 32-47. Web. 2 25 July 2019 <https://www.jstor.org/stable/20719683>.

Cirucci, Angela M., and Barry Vacker (eds.) (2018). *Black Mirror and Critical Media Theory.* New York: Lexington Books.

Clark, Andy (2000). *Natural-Born Cyborgs: Minds, Technologies, and the Future of Human Intelligence.* Web. 1 August 2019 <https://www.edge.org /conversation/natural-born-cyborgs>.

Fend, Peter, and Jerome Sans (1994). "The City as a Machine for Living in." *Grand Street No. 50, Models* (Autumn, 1994). Web. 12 May 2019 <https://s3. amazonaws.com/contemporaryartgroup/files/documents_file_469.pdf >.

Haraway, Donna J (2016[1985]). "A Cyborg Manifesto." Web. 5 November 2018 <https://warwick.ac.uk/fac/arts/english/currentstudents/undergraduate/modules/fictionnownarrativemediaandtheoryinthe21stcentury/manifestly_haraway_----_a_cyborg_manifesto_science_technology_and_socialist-feminism_in_the_....pdf>.

Heidegger, Martin (2012). "Positionality." *Bremen and Freiburg Lectures*. Trans. Andrew J. Mitchell. Bloomington and Indianapolis: Indiana University Press.

Hoffman, Donald (2009). "The Interface Theory of Perception: Natural Selection Drives True Perception to Swift Extinction." *Object Categorization: Computer and Human Vision Perspectives*. Cambridge: Cambridge University Press.

Le Corbusier (1986). *Towards a new architecture.* New York: Dover Publication.

Mitchell, William J. (2003). *Me++: The Cyborg Self and the Networked City*. MIT Press.

Murnane, Ben (2018). *Ayn Rand and the Posthuman The Mind-Made Future.* London: Palgrave.

Sims, Christopher A. (2013). *Tech Anxiety: Artificial Intelligence and Ontological Awakening in Four Science Fiction Novels*. Jefferson: McFarland & Co.

Stelarc (2013). "Phantom Flesh: Extreme Performance Artist Stelarc Interviewed." *The Quietus* 6 March. Web. 5 June 2019 <http://thequietus.com /articles/11469-stelarc-interview>.

Stiegler, Bernard (1998). *Time and Technics 1: The Fault of Epimetheus*. Trans. Richard Beardsworth and George Collins. Stanford: Stanford University Press.

Wainwright, Oliver (2015). "Body-Hackers: People Who Turn Themselves into Cyborgs." *The Guardian* 14 August 2015. Web. 20 May 2019

<https://www.theguardian.com/artanddesign/architecture-design-blog/2015/aug/14/body-hackers-the-people-who-turn-themselves-into-cyborgs>.

Zimmermann, Ana Cristina, and W. John Morgan (2017). "E.M. Forster's 'The Machine Stops': Humans, Technology and Dialogue. " *AI and Society*. Web. 2 August 2019 <DOI: 10.1007/s00146-017-0698-3>.

Zylinska, Joanna, and Gary Hall (2002). "Probings: An Interview with Stelarc." *The Cyborg Experiments: The Extensions of the Body in the Media Age*. Ed. Joanna Zylinska. London: Continuum.

Katalin Schober (Potsdam)

Performing Possible Worlds – How to Foster Empathy with Fantastic Literature

1. Introduction

Fostering empathy with fantastic literature may seem a fruitless, if not impossible, endeavour at first sight, the more so as literary texts termed 'fantastic' incorporate elements that do not bear any resemblance to the 'real' world. Imaginary settings, fabulous creatures, and miraculous powers obviously do not mimetically represent the world of our sensory experience. These stock features of fantastic texts are rather said to distort our knowledge of the world that we as human beings have access to.

If we agree with these general insights into the characteristics of fantastic texts and the corresponding readers' responses they elicit, how can we thus feel with supernatural characters or empathise with fanciful storyworlds, which do not exist in reality? What is more, why should we include them in our schools' curricula, in particular in the English as a Foreign Language (EFL) classroom?

The above-sketched contradiction operates along the well-known lines of the epistemic precariousness of literature, a debate that can be traced back to antiquity. The aim of this paper, however, is neither to retrace the manifold transformations of this controversy nor to argue against those who proclaim the untruth of literary, especially of fantastic, texts, and accordingly their unworthiness in ethical terms.

By contrast, the aim is to show to what extent learners' empathy may be activated and advanced by fantastic texts. The focus of this paper, hence, is not placed on the epistemic conditions of fantastic literature, but on pupils' learning processes in terms of their reading experiences. It builds on the assumption that children and young adults are well-acquainted with the general setup of fantastic texts, a circumstance which, in turn, adds to their willingness to playfully engage with the possible worlds these texts bring forth.[1] The sheer pleasure children and young adults display when they are absorbed by their reading experiences constitutes, one may even say, an argument in its own right for the use of fantasy in schools, in particular in the EFL classroom. Yet this aspect will merely be taken as the starting point for a broader argument that combines notions of empathy and possible worlds with drama pedagogy approaches recently re-employed by foreign language didactics. The goal is to ultimately develop and devise lessons within this framework.

2. Empathy, Possible Worlds, and Drama Pedagogy Approaches

There has been a revived interest in questions pertaining to empathetic readings of literature, the poetics of affect, and readers' moral understanding in recent literary theory.[2] Indeed, as Keen shows, notions of empathy are decidedly not an innovation of the twenty-first century.[3] She pinpoints the Scottish Enlightenment as the era in which the concept of sympathy started to be regarded as a specifically interpersonal capability enabling a partaking in the thoughts and feelings of one's fellow humans as well as of fictional characters. The precondition for sympathy is the human imagination, which allows us to picture the joys and sorrows of others, to be moved by them, to relate them to our own experiences, and thus to gain new insights into our own lives.[4] Keen retraces the famous stances of philosophers such as David Hume, Adam Smith, or Lord Kames and situates them within the debates of the long eighteenth century surrounding the emergence of a then-new genre, the novel, whose naissance triggered countless debates around the alleged risks and seeming potential of its readings.[5]

This sketch of the idea of sympathy indicates that the groundwork for our today's concept of empathy was originally broader, since it did not reduce a heightened partaking to a mere identification, but it allowed for an inner distancing and hence, a deeper reflection upon the storyworlds of one's readings. It is this recurring cognitive motion which should serve as a guiding concept for the following didactic reflections aiming at a connection of more extensive reading-for-pleasure processes with closer analyses.

Before discussing a suitable approach to this goal, however, we need to enquire into the aesthetic qualities of literary, including fantastic, texts, in particular into the poetic patterns which elicit specific responses. Here, the concept of possible worlds, originally borrowed from philosophical logic and then transferred to literary theory, proves fruitful. According to Lobsien,[6] possible worlds as brought forth by literature offer coherent alternatives to the world of our sensory experience. Even if they might play with impossibilities, such as fantastic texts do, they still produce possible worlds, i.e. storyworlds that are consistent with their own poetic properties. Consequently, narrative structures, the aesthetic makeup of fictional time, place, and characters, as well as poetic descriptions need to be judged by their own standards. If recurrent distortions or reversals are an integral part of storyworlds, then they are in line with the notion of possible worlds. Readers may, as a result, accommodate their viewpoint to them so that they are able to understand their manifold levels step by step.

At this point, drama pedagogy, or performative, approaches come into play. They are a highly productive way of fostering not only linguistic, but also literary competences and ultimately, they allow for a deeper sense-making in terms of the learners' exploration of literary (possible) worlds as well as of the world of their daily experience. EFL scholars have repeatedly noted the benefits of drama activities:[7] they enable learners to feel with fictional characters, to identify with them, but also to critically engage with them. By means of enacting a character's thoughts and emotions, learners express their underlying motives. Consequently, they begin to understand the enacted storyworlds better, and as a result, they may start to reflect upon their own motivations in greater detail. Finally, this deep understanding of literary depictions may be used as a starting point for further productive ways of engaging with possible worlds, such as creative writing tasks. Hence, drama activities are useful tools of cultivating multiple competences, all of which necessitate a minimum of sympathising with the storyworlds in question. In this context, drama activities may, as Crumpler and Wedwick note,

> help teachers of […] young readers step into fictional worlds that they have created with students, and engage in interpretations of literature that are social, innovative, critical and could transform classrooms into spaces where imagination fuels learning.[8]

Drawing on the above-sketched notions of empathy and possible worlds as well as on drama pedagogy approaches, the following reflections will develop classroom designs from the lower to the middle secondary levels.

They are arranged according to the anticipated pupils' responses to three fantastic texts and the respective goals of the lessons.

3. Performing Familiarity

Roald Dahl's *Matilda*[9] may well be termed a classic of children's literature. Readers delight in this story of empowerment as they follow young Matilda teaching herself how to read, write, and calculate, and above all, how to take care of herself. She is thus able to navigate her way through the world of adults, in particular of her parents, who ignore her brilliant mind, her sentiments, and her wishes. Neither are her feelings validated by them nor her most basic needs of establishing and maintaining caring and nurturing relationships with others. Luckily, Matilda is able to connect to other people who show a sincere interest in her: the librarian, to start with, later on her teacher in elementary school, Miss Honey, or fellow pupils, and of course, the characters that people the fictional worlds of her literary imagination. In this sense, one might be tempted to call her habit of becoming fully consumed by books escapism. But it is definitely more than escapist reading what she displays. In a way, she certainly finds a safe place in her own imagination, which allows for a sort of mirroring she cannot find in the world of her daily experience. However, it is this specific form of validation that later enables her to approach the 'real' world without hesitation and fear. It is thus escapism in a fuller sense that this children's novel puts forth.[10]

Generally speaking, this novel may be termed a hybrid genre, which combines realistic and fantastic elements. The storyworld of *Matilda* is realistically depicted to a certain degree, and it thus parallels the everyday world of its readers at the time. There are, however, several instances in which the marvellous reveals itself. When the protagonist discovers her supernatural powers, she first of all uses them for her own amusement in daily life. Later on, her ability to move things without touching them enables her to punish those who were cruel to her and her friends, such as Ms. Trunchbull, the nasty headmistress. In this respect, fantastic elements indicate an extended allegory as they embody (and help to accomplish) young Matilda's yearning for justice, mutual kindness, and caring relationships, which are eventually established when Matilda and Miss Honey create a home for themselves at the end of the story.

With this hopeful message, the novel lends itself to readings for empowerment.[11] Furthermore, as it negotiates a young child's initial sense of alienation, it parallels a feeling that is highly familiar to young adults juggling the manifold expectations of growing up, a complex task that includes sentiments of loneliness and confusion at times. The novel is consequently well suited for explorations within the lower secondary classroom of EFL education as well, since pupils will find it easy to feel with the protagonist, even if they are older than Matilda.

The following lesson plan builds on this moment of familiarity, that is on the shared sense of alienation between the protagonist and the audience. Its aim is to encourage a deeper engagement with the pupils' personal experiences and feelings as mirrored back to them through a performative-critical reading of the novel. Therefore, after a first discussion of the novel's setting and its main characters, the pupils are asked to perform a dramatic reading of one scene. Here Matilda's father introduces his son to some of his business calculations. It is, however, Matilda who is the one to correctly answer his questions, and not her elder brother, a fact that clearly upsets her father.

Having read the scene once for a general understanding, the pupils are then asked to practise variations of dramatic readings, in which they experiment with prosodic features, such as the pitch and volume of their voices.[12] In a consecutive task, the question can be discussed how varied prosodic features correspond with different emotional expressions. For example, when Matilda's father gets angry, he might even be shouting at his daughter, whereas she (and her voice) will probably remain calm and collected. The combination of a dramatic reading with critical book talk in class requires that the pupils sympathise with the characters before they can then engage in more complex reflections upon the character's emotions.

What is more, the teacher may ask the pupils what they actually felt while expressing the characters' thoughts and feelings. They may be surprised to note that their dramatic readings triggered them to really feel with the characters, a fact which can be used for further reflections in class. Here, for example, the pupils can ask themselves if they know similar situations, in which they felt nervous, upset, or calm and collected, in comparison to the characters from *Matilda*.

In a follow-up task, the pupils may finally try to fill in the gaps by posing questions to the novel's characters and answering them. Miss

Honey, whose unhappy childhood is paralleled by Matilda's rather unloving family, might be used as an example in this context. Possible questions include, among others, as to how she might assert herself and talk to her aunt, Ms. Trunchbull, in a more self-confident manner so to set healthy boundaries for herself. These questions may lead to a general discussion of what the pupils can do if they are ever faced by bullies. With its multilayered themes, Roald Dahl's *Matilda* is thus highly useful for empowerment readings that build on initial moments of familiarity. The table below summarises the lesson plan for this section.

Introduction	In this sequence, pupils will be introduced to critical terminology on science fiction, while starting to read *The Hunger Games*. The critical terminology they learn in this sequence can then be used in the further discussion of the novel.
Objectives	To develop and practise: • vocabulary connected with feelings and sentiments • the ability to read and understand a fictional text • pupils' speaking skills, in particular prosodic features • the ability to empathise with a fictional character
Age	Lower secondary level, 11 to 13 years of age
Level	A2/B1
Time	Five lessons (à 45 minutes)
Materials/media	Excerpts from the novel: Dahl (1988), 12-13 (1st lesson) *Ibid.*, 51-55 (2nd and 3rd lesson) Film version: *Matilda* (1996)
1st lesson	Ask pupils to … • briefly outline the story's setting, Matilda's family situation, her wish to read books, and her first walk to the library

	• describe Matilda's thoughts and feelings • guess how the story might go on
2nd and 3rd lesson	Ask pupils to ... • briefly sum up the speaking situation between Matilda's father, her brother, and herself • describe the feelings of the father and Matilda as expressed by their way of speaking • practise various dramatic readings of the scene present it to one another and reflect upon the feelings of the characters
4th and 5th lesson	Ask pupils to ... • reflect upon their actual feelings they experienced during their dramatic readings • describe everyday situations in which they experienced feelings similar to the novel's characters • discuss personal resources the pupils may resort to in times of difficulty
Follow-up lessons	Ask pupils to... • watch the film and to outline the other characters' status as well as their personal stories, e.g. of Ms. Trunchbull and Miss Honey • pose questions to Miss Honey and ask her how she might assert herself, e.g. with regard to Ms. Trunchbull • take over Miss Honey's point of view and answer these questions

Table 1: Reading for Empowerment: Roald Dahl's *Matilda*

4. Performing Alterity

Neil Gaiman's young heroine Coraline shares the sense of alienation with the character of Matilda, since from the protagonist's viewpoint, her parents do not show enough interest in their daughter.[13] Yet, whereas *Matilda* presents a more clear-cut version of positive, nurturing vs. negative, malicious characters, the parent-child-relationship depicted in Neil Gaiman's graphic novel adaptation is more complex. As typical of this genre, it makes use of intricate text-image-relationships, which necessitate a multimodal approach to its storyworld and characters.

In this novel, two versions of love are presented, which are entwined with two different worlds: one is similar to the readers' world of their sensory experience, the other is nightmarish. Whereas the former belongs to 'real' characters, and thus to Coraline's 'real' parents, who unconditionally love her, the latter is a world seemingly mirroring the 'real' one with Coraline's 'other' mother luring her into this 'other' place. The highly possessive style of love this 'other' mother shows is in fact aimed at the fulfilment of her personal needs. Correspondingly, the 'other' world is characterised by ever-changing distortions, being figments of the 'other' mother's imagination, which make any orientation impossible.

It is the inconclusiveness of this place which seems to be insurmountable in itself. While Coraline is able to enter it through a magical passageway in her new home at the beginning, she quickly has to realise that she is trapped. In order to find a way back into the 'real' world and to block any passages between the two places, she needs to rely on her innermost virtues of wisdom and courage. Therefore, she has got some help, for example, in form of a cat that can shift between the worlds as she pleases, and a magic stone which allows Coraline to see more and helps her to free three enslaved children souls, her 'real' parents, and herself.

But first of all, she needs to understand who really loves her and whom she loves in return, that is to say where she truly belongs. Unsurprisingly, she refuses to have her eyes blinded by her 'other' mother, a symbolic decision that shows her insight that she is not made for the 'other' world. Having reached this understanding, she is then able to tackle the 'other' world's challenges, which are actually made up of Coraline's innermost fears of being trapped and powerless.

The graphic novel thus presents at least two forms of alterity – of aesthetic and ethical quality – that are deeply intertwined. The aesthetic form of this graphic novel constitutes one central theme as the protagonist needs to identify the fantastic elements as figments of the 'other' mother's imagination. Only then is she able to see possible ways of overcoming the hurdles of this 'other' place. Another form of alterity is of ethical quality as the novel raises complex questions of character formation and defies easy answers. The protagonist's emotional evolution follows a spiral movement combining more and more subtle observations of the worlds she moves in with closer self-reflections. As a result, Coraline is more aware of her own needs and feelings, she can express them more clearly, and she is able to step back from momentary sensations. In the end, she is also able to reconcile herself with her 'real' parents, even if she reproached them for being inattentive beforehand.

The aim of the lessons is accordingly to enable the pupils to understand aesthetic as well as ethical forms of alterity in order to finally encourage them to ponder the manifold resources they can resort to in times of difficulty. In this respect, the lessons aim at a broader character formation of secondary pupils, who find themselves in a crucial transition period of identity construction.[14] Therefore, it is suggested to combine drama pedagogy approaches with critical reflections.

First of all, the teacher may ask the pupils to describe the initial panel of the graphic novel so as to outline the general situation, the setting, and to activate intelligent guessing where the door or the passageway may lead to.[15] As a second step, the pupils may visualise Coraline's feelings at various stages of the storyline by performing freeze frames, which may then be used as a starting point to discuss her inner state of mind, in particular her initial sense of separation from the adults' world, her subsequent terror in face of the 'other' mother's power games, and finally her courage and resolution to tackle the challenges. In a following activity the pupils may be asked to perform a hot seat, which requires them to swap perspectives in order to pose questions to the protagonist and to answer them. Here, the teacher may integrate the hot-seat activity into a broader role play between Coraline's 'real' parents and herself, focusing on the question of their respective expectations, feelings, and needs. This activity necessitates a deeper understanding, which avoids the blaming game by going beyond the dichotomy of the other and self, and replacing it instead by a fuller awareness of the universality of human feelings.

The teacher may eventually use the negotiation of the story's manifold meanings, especially its allegorical setup, as a starting point for a general reflection upon possible resources the pupils can resort to if they ever feel overwhelmed by their emotions or powerless when facing (seemingly) overpowering challenges. What can the pupils, for example, do in order to feel grounded in life, to maintain a healthy balance between the manifold expectations they are facing? What do they specifically do when they are confronted with a challenge at school or at home which seems all too tricky? Where can they seek help? A discussion of these questions may finally lead to a more comprehensive appreciation of the fact that everyone's reactions result from complex emotions and thoughts, which are unfamiliar usually only at first sight. When compared to one's own experiences, one may start to realise how central they are to human life in general.

5. Beyond Dichotomies: Performing the Ethics of Fantasy

The last example takes the idea of universal human experiences further by suggesting a performative reading of the film adaptation of *The Hunger Games*.[16] Essentially speaking, the focus of the film (and of the lessons) is on ethical questions which are negotiated throughout the story around Katniss Everdeen. The female protagonist of this highly popular, dystopian piece of fiction manages to overcome the deep inhumanity of the Capitol by means of dissimulation, thus bringing the merciless game to perfection. But before the underlying power system can be turned upside down, Katniss encounters various predicaments which obviously do not have easy answers. She is, however, able to survive them without compromising her innermost values of humanity, compassion, and courage, all of which manifest themselves in her actions.

Generally speaking, the fantastic elements of this dystopian story consist of its unspecified time and place of action as well as its imaginary characters. They may, however, be seen as a part of an extended allegory, which operates on two levels of meaning, the literal and another one alluded to. In this respect, the storyworld as brought forth by *The Hunger Games* constantly evokes further literary and historical worlds, which, in turn, are deeply imbued with utopian, revolutionary, or science fiction constructs. If a teacher wanted to employ the text for higher secondary levels, readings for intertextual references might be recommended. In this case, however, the focus is on a younger age group, in particular on pupils on the brink of their GCSEs. Therefore, the focus will be shifted from a deeper textual analysis to the ethics of the text in order to encourage the pupils to think about general questions of the good life. Such a reading is also in line with Crumpler and Wedwick's observations on young adult fiction, who note that young adult literature negotiates wide-ranging ethical issues by raising questions about power struggles and social injustice.[17]

Whereas the original book version lends itself to performative approaches focusing on those characters who have only little to say as compared to Katniss's extended first-person-narrative, [18] the film adaptation may concentrate on the protagonist instead. Here, in the film, the protagonist's thoughts and feelings are revealed, above all, by her actions and body language, rather than by deeper first-person-reflections, which, in turn, constitute a large part of the book. In this respect, the film allows for deeper interpretations of Katniss's actions as well as her preceding decision-making processes.

Accordingly, the main goal is to enable the pupils to negotiate some of the story's dilemmas such as the recurring life-or-death situations Katniss finds herself in. After a general introduction to the story's setting, its situation, and the main conflicts, the teacher may ask the pupils to adopt the protagonist's role in a hot-seat session, to feel with the character, and to answer questions as to whether or not Katniss should save the life of others (e.g. Primrose, Peeta) and thereby risk her own life.

As a final step the pupils can be asked to take on various roles, to prepare short statements of what is important to their characters, and then to join in a general discussion about the Capitol's injustice as presented in the film. At this point, the pupils may ask themselves to what extent they would personally compromise their values when faced with life-threatening decisions. The session can then be concluded by creative writing tasks, aiming at a continuation of the story, or by further philosophical reflections about the storyworld's ethical setup.

6. Conclusion

Fantastic texts are well suited for lower to middle secondary levels, since they are usually highly popular within this age group. What is more, they are easily accessible as more and more texts of this genre are published and read (or viewed) by a larger audience today.[19] The most important reason for the use of these texts, however, needs to be seen in relation to the pupils' reading experiences and the corresponding goals in class. As suggested earlier, these texts lend themselves to readings focusing on the pupils' empathy and consequently on a deeper understanding of the possible worlds as evoked by fantastic literature.

As fantastic texts usually operate on several levels, they may well be used to initiate an understanding of the complexity of literature. Consequently, pupils may begin to grasp a sense of literary alterity, a fact which, in turn, may lead them to develop their ability to empathise with other characters, their thoughts and feelings, more profoundly.[20] Those stories, like *Matilda*, which present characters with rather familiar conflicts, can be used as a starting point to cultivate the skill of empathy. Step by step, teachers may then rely on more intricate stories, such as *Coraline* or *The Hunger Games*, so that the pupils' abilities are taken to a level beyond their everyday knowledge. Ultimately, the pupils may begin to cultivate a better understanding, not only of literature, but of themselves.

Notes

1 For a discussion of the genre's popularity among young adults, cf. Hallet, Wolfgang, and Juliane Witzenberger (2018). "Fantasy: Fiction, Films, Fans. Fantastische Welten in der Fremdsprache erkunden." *Der Fremdsprachliche Unterricht Englisch* 151, 2.

2 For an overview of the manifold relationships between literature and emotions, cf. Hogan, Patrick Colm (2018). *Literature and Emotion*. New York: Routledge.

3 Cf. Keen, Suzanne (2007). *Empathy and the Novel*. Oxford: Oxford University Press, 42.

4 Cf. Lobsien, Eckhard (2016). *Englische Poetik 1650 bis 1950. Feldstruktur und Transformation*. Würzburg: Könighausen & Neumann, 21.

5 Cf. Keen (2007), 42-45. For a more detailed discussion of the concept of the imagination (and its derivatives) in the long eighteenth century in terms of philosophy, aesthetics, and poetics, cf. Engell, James (1981). *The Creative Imagination. Enlightenment to Romanticism.* Harvard: Harvard University Press.

6 Cf. Lobsien (2016), 19.

7 Cf. Beach, Richard, et al. (2016). *Teaching Literature to Adolescents*. 3rd ed. New York: Routledge, 202-228.

8 Crumpler, Thomas P., and Linda Wedwick (2011). "Readers, Texts, and Context in the Middle. Re-imagining Literature Education for Young Adolescents." *Handbook of Research on Children's and Young Adult Literature*. Eds. Shelby A. Wolf et al. New York: Routledge, 73.

9 Cf. Dahl, Roald (1988). *Matilda*. New York: Puffin.

10 With this plotline, Roald Dahl's *Matilda* is well-suited for the lower secondary classrooms according to the criteria as put forth by Crumpler and Wedwick (2011), 67.

11 For questions of readings for empowerment, cf. Bland, Janice (2013). *Children's Literature and Learner Empowerment. Children and Teenagers in English Language Education*. London: Bloomsbury Academic.

12 For a general discussion of the uses of drama pedagogy approaches to train phonetic and prosodic features in the EFL classroom, cf. Elis, Franziska (2015). "Mit dramapädagogischen Methoden sprachliche und kommunikative Kompetenzen fördern." *Handbuch Dramendidaktik und Dramapädagogik im Fremdsprachenunterricht*. Eds. Wolfgang Hallet and Carola Surkamp. Trier: WVT, 89-115. For a discussion of such approaches to Roald Dahl's *Matilda*, cf. Schober, Katalin (2018). "Roald Dahls *Matilda*. Mit szenischem Lesen zur Selbstreflexion." *Praxis Englisch* 5, 15-19.

13 Cf. Gaiman, Neil (2008). *Coraline*. The Graphic Novel Adaptation by P. Craig Russel. New York: Harper Collins.

14 For a discussion of questions pertaining to identity construction within EFL education, cf. Lewis, Cynthia, and Jessica Dockter (2011). "Reading Literature in Secondary School. Disciplinary Discourses in Global Times." *Handbook of Research on Children's and Young Adult Literature*. Eds. Shelby A. Wolf et al. New York: Routledge, 82-84.

15 Cf. Gaiman, *Coraline*, 1.

[16] Cf. *The Hunger Games*. Dir. Gary Ross. 2012. DVD. Lions Gate Home Entertainment UK Ltd., 2013.

[17] Cf. Crumpler and Wedwick (2011), 67.

[18] For an introduction to performative approaches to the book version, cf. Bland, Janice, and Anne Strotmann (2014). "*The Hunger Games*: An Ecocritical Reading." *CLELE Journal: Children's Literature in English Language Education* 2.1, 39-40.

[19] In this respect, fantastic texts fulfil the criteria of accessibility and popularity, as suggested by Bland and Strotmann. Cf. Bland and Strotmann (2014).

[20] The link between intercultural empathy and an understanding of literary alterity was noted most prominently by Bredella and Burwitz-Melzer within the German EFL research tradition. Cf. Bredella, Lothar, and Eva Burwitz-Melzer (2004). *Rezeptionsästhetische Literaturdidaktik. Mit Beispielen aus dem Fremdsprachenunterricht Englisch*. Tübingen: Narr Francke, 141.

Bibliography

Primary Texts

Dahl, Roald (1988). *Matilda*. New York: Puffin.

Gaiman, Neil (2008). *Coraline*. The Graphic Novel Adaptation by P. Craig Russel. New York: Harper Collins.

The Hunger Games. Dir. Gary Ross. 2012. DVD. Lions Gate Home Entertainment UK Ltd., 2013.

Matilda. Dir. Danny DeVito. (1996). Sony Pictures Home Entertainment, 1998.

Secondary Literature

Beach, Richard, et al. (2016). *Teaching Literature to Adolescents*. 3rd ed. New York: Routledge.

Bland, Janice (2013). *Children's Literature and Learner Empowerment. Children and Teenagers in English Language Education*. London: Bloomsbury Academic.

Bland, Janice, and Anne Strotmann (2014). "*The Hunger Games*: An Ecocritical Reading." *CLELE Journal: Children's Literature in English Language Education* 2.1, 22-43.

Bredella, Lothar, and Eva Burwitz-Melzer (2004). *Rezeptionsästhetische Literaturdidaktik. Mit Beispielen aus dem Fremdsprachenunterricht Englisch*. Tübingen: Narr Francke.

Crumpler, Thomas P., and Linda Wedwick (2011). "Readers, Texts, and Context in the Middle. Re-imagining Literature Education for Young Adolescents." *Handbook of Research on Children's and Young Adult Literature*. Eds. Shelby A. Wolf et al. New York: Routledge, 63-75.

Elis, Franziska (2015). "Mit dramapädagogischen Methoden sprachliche und kommunikative Kompetenzen fördern." *Handbuch Dramendidaktik und Dramapädagogik im Fremdsprachenunterricht*. Eds. Wolfgang Hallet and Carola Surkamp. Trier: WVT, 89-115.

Engell, James (1981). *The Creative Imagination. Enlightenment to Romanticism.* Harvard: Harvard University Press.

Hallet, Wolfgang, and Juliane Witzenberger (2018). "Fantasy: Fiction, Films, Fans. Fantastische Welten in der Fremdsprache erkunden." *Der Fremdsprachliche Unterricht Englisch* 151, 2-7.

Hogan, Patrick Colm (2018). *Literature and Emotion*. New York: Routledge.

Keen, Suzanne (2007). *Empathy and the Novel*. Oxford: Oxford University Press.

Lewis, Cynthia, and Jessica Dockter (2011). "Reading Literature in Secondary School. Disciplinary Discourses in Global Times." *Handbook of Research on Children's and Young Adult Literature*. Eds. Shelby A. Wolf et al. New York: Routledge, 76-91.

Lobsien, Eckhard (2016). *Englische Poetik 1650 bis 1950. Feldstruktur und Transformation*. Würzburg: Könighausen & Neumann.

Schober, Katalin (2018). "Roald Dahls *Matilda*. Mit szenischem Lesen zur Selbstreflexion." *Praxis Englisch* 5, 15-19.

Klara Stephanie Szlezák (Passau)

From Androids to Alternate Histories: Integrating Philip K. Dick's Fiction into the EFL Classroom

1. Introduction

"In a metaphorical sense," James E. Gunn writes in *Inside Science Fiction*, "science fiction might be considered letters from the future, from our children, urging us to be careful with their world."[1] At no earlier point in time may this have rung truer than in the present moment, when Fridays for Future and all that they entail remind us of the precarious state in which we will leave this planet to future generations. In addition, at no previous point may Gunn's metaphorical take on the genre of science fiction have made a stronger case for the contemporaneity of the genre and its inclusion into the classroom, English as a foreign language (EFL) and otherwise. In the face of the havoc that humankind is wreaking on the globe and the all but ubiquitous global political tensions and instabilities, post-apocalyptic scenarios – brought about by both environmental collapse and global nuclear warfare – appear exceedingly pertinent to the lifeworlds of today's students.

In times of such troubling, interconnected developments as vast deforestation, global warming, and the rapid extinction of species, a scenario like the one described in the following does not seem inconceivable:

> For a long time he stood gazing at the owl, who dozed in its perch. A thousand thoughts came into his mind, thoughts about [...] the days when owls had fallen from the sky; he remembered how in his childhood it had been discovered that species upon species had become extinct and how the 'papes had reported it each day – foxes one morning, badgers the next, until people had stopped reading the perpetual animal obits.[2]

Similarly, in times of all but failing diplomacy and multilateral threats of nuclear (re-)armament, a scenario like the one described below appears hauntingly prophetic:

> [N]o one today remembered why the war had come about or who, if anyone, had won. The dust which had contaminated most of the planet's surface had originated in no country and no one, even the wartime enemy, had planned on it. First, strangely, the owls had died. […] Medieval plagues had manifested themselves in a similar way, in the form of many dead rats. This plague, however, had descended from above. […] the sun had ceased to shine on Earth […].[3]

These two passages reflect the state of our planet after World War Terminus, a global war ending in a radioactive fallout, which leaves the planet nearly uninhabitable to humans and animals and necessitates both the colonization of other planets and the expansion of android technology. Both scenarios are depicted in the 1968 novel *Do Androids Dream of Electric Sheep?* by the American science-fiction author Philip K. Dick.

Needless to say, Dick's fiction is as topical as ever. Visions of a world wrecked by warfare and the ensuing ecological catastrophe and hypothetical scenarios of how humans cope with such wreckage are central both to *Do Androids Dream of Electric Sheep?* (and *Blade Runner*) and to the future generations who will have to find a way to deal with an exploited and lastingly damaged planet.

Widely acclaimed and characterized as a "([…] highly prolific) exponent" of "the fiction of the paranoid vision in science fiction",[4] Philip K. Dick (1928-1982) has written a considerable number of well-known novels and short stories, including "The Minority Report" (1956), *The Man in the High Castle* (1962), "We Can Remember It for You Wholesale" (1966), *Do Androids Dream of Electric Sheep?* (1968), and *A Scanner Darkly* (1977). Dick's fiction does not only have a wide circle of avid readers, it has also proven a prolific source for filmmakers producing works for the small and the big screen. Popular cinematic works such as *Blade Runner* (1982), *Total Recall* (1990; 2012), *Minority Report* (2002), or *A Scanner Darkly* (2006), as well as the recent Amazon TV series *The Man in the High Castle* (2015-2019) are based on works by Dick. Thus, the potential of Dick's works for the EFL classroom is significantly, albeit not exclusively, grounded in the wealth of available film adaptations.

As such, Dick's works provide fruitful ground for the students' exploration of intermedial differences and similarities. While the comparative study of literature and film (in the form of adaptations) in the EFL classroom is by no means limited to the science fiction genre, this chapter will argue that the genre in general, and Dick's fiction in particular, encourage students to use their imagination and to think beyond the limitations of historical knowledge or facts. Science fiction allows them to also draw connections to their increasingly technologized and digitized realities. Dick's works, as this chapter will demonstrate, can be used to enrich the EFL classroom via creative writing tasks or transcultural learning projects, which both can be triggered by intermedial considerations.

2. Philip K. Dick in the EFL Classroom

Among the various literary genres, science fiction is a comparatively 'young' genre. While science fiction reaches back well into the nineteenth century, it was not "recognized as a distinct literary genre"[5] until the mid-twentieth century. Although possibly "fatally stained from its pulp past",[6] science fiction has since entered not only academe, where it is submitted to stringent critical analysis, but has also been included in school and university syllabi. In this context, this chapter presents one approach to the inclusion of science fiction in the classroom, with a focus on the English as a foreign language classroom and on one author's works in particular.

Science fiction as a genre – and as a genre which is inherently fluid –[7] could not be any more topical in the age of the 'IT revolution', which has substantially changed both the 21st-century workplace and humans' private lives through innovations and trends such as digitization and the ubiquity of (personal) electronic devices, or Artificial Intelligences and automation, to name just some examples. Describing the particular appeal of science fiction literature in our time, Vint observes that

> [s]cience fiction participates in both promoting [the] myth of technological mastery and transcendence, and deflating it. It provides the language, images, and concepts that celebrate our cultural preoccupation

with science and technology, and that express our anxieties and fears regarding how they are changing our world and our selves.[8]

The idea that technoscience advances humankind and opens up new horizons (both quite literally with regard to travel into outer space and metaphorically with regard to experimentation with artificial intelligence, genetic manipulation, or mind expansion) runs alongside the notion that technoscience harbors the ever looming danger that humans' technological accomplishments could get out of hand at any moment and subjugate humankind in turn. The blessing and curse of science and technologization, so to speak, are inseparable, and it is this fundamental ambivalence that lends science fiction its lasting appeal and that turns it into a rewarding subject for the classroom – EFL and beyond.

Several of the central features of science fiction make this dynamic genre particularly apt for its inclusion in a teaching context. Jacobsen thus claims that

> pedagogical studies are integral to, rather than tangential to, the scholarship of science fiction. Understanding science fiction requires more than just being able to dissect a story or a novel, or apply a theoretical viewpoint to a film. A profound understanding of science fiction means realizing what science fiction can be made to reveal about the world.[9]

This asset of science fiction that Jacobson mentions, namely to provoke revelations about the world we live in, is what ultimately makes it so valuable for teaching younger generations. Not only does this pedagogical value extend to other areas of teaching; the reach of science fiction into other subject areas, besides (foreign language) literature, in turn enhances its pedagogical value. As the genre designation indicates, science fiction crosses conventional borders between various disciplines: teaching science fiction is characterized by the subject matter's

> all-inclusiveness. The kinds of subjects that can be taught through science fiction involve all the social and physical sciences, history, ideas, futurology, religion, morality, ecology, reading skills, and many others.[10]

Not only, then, does science fiction enrich English language teaching via the foreign-language texts it provides; it also lends itself to cooperation across the established boundaries between school subjects as the historical, scientific and technical, and ethical questions it raises are best discussed across the disciplines.

Not surprisingly, then, several widely known science fiction writers' professional or lay interests lie beyond the realm of literature. Isaac Asimov, for instance, taught biochemistry, Stanisław Lem received medical training; similarly, though not professionally, Philip K. Dick thoroughly engaged in metaphysics. In this regard, Parrinder, for instance, observes that in Dick's fiction

> the disintegration of the scientific vision is reflected in the partial disintegration of the imagined world. [...] The elements of parody and satire in these novels testify to their genetic descent from earlier science fiction. The fiction of [...] Dick [...] is a response to the changing nature of scientific thought and of our notions of 'reality' itself.[11]

As the "nature of scientific thought" as well as "our notions of 'reality' itself" are constantly shifting, Dick's works become all the more enticing and can serve as a mediator for students' responses, not least thanks to its parody and satire. Dick's writings are no doubt dark but at the same time not devoid of a certain humor. While some of the stylistic nuances in his writings might or might not be perceivable to younger learners of English, his plots and characters provide ample ground for the exploration of central themes in science-fiction literature. Two aspects within the broad spectrum offered by science-fiction literature that are also central in Dick's writings appear particularly pertinent to the EFL as well as the interdisciplinary school curriculum: the projected coexistence of human beings and androids in a highly technologized world and the projection of a different course of events due to an alternate course of history. While both conjecture a possible future for this planet and its inhabitants, the former starts from the present state of affairs whereas the latter looks back first and rewrites history to look ahead into a corresponding hypothetical present and future.

Whereas the former constellation is the one on which the focus will lie in the following, the latter will briefly be addressed at this point. Apart from the extension of their language skills, Dick's novel *The Man in the High Castle* provides students with ample opportunities for intercultural learning by asking them to activate and expand their geographical and historical knowledge about the United States as well as transatlantic, or even global relations. In a hypothetical future ruled by the victorious Axis powers, the United States as part of the defeated Allies no longer exists as we know it today. Not unlike post-war Germany, it is split up between Japan and the Third Reich, which, not unlike the winning powers after World War II, find themselves in a struggle for power. Such a scenario provides fruitful ground for students' hypotheses about the progression of the story, about how this alternative history unravels, and, in addition, invites students to reflect on and debate such enduringly crucial questions as the ethics of warfare and its aftermath, the vagaries of human life, and the power dynamics inherent in historiography.

With the fourth and final season released in late 2019, the TV series based on the novel can be used in the EFL classroom as an addition to (excerpts of) Dick's text. The more recent production date, its availability through Amazon streaming, and the shorter duration of a TV series episode as compared to a full-length feature film may enhance its general appeal to a teenage audience.

3. Teaching Philip K. Dick on the Page and on Screen

As mentioned above, *The Man in the High Castle* is not the only work by Dick that has been adapted for the screen. Ridley Scott's blockbuster *Blade Runner*, based on his novel *Do Androids Dream of Electric Sheep?*, is widely regarded as a classic of the science-fiction genre in cinema history and has for the most part received positive reviews. Less action-loaded than the bulk of more recent science-fiction movies, *Blade Runner* is a fascinating take on the *film noir* and captivates its audiences primarily through its atmosphere and its poignant characters. While the 2017 sequel *Blade Runner 2049*,[12] starring Harrison Ford and Ryan Gosling, may be more widely known among younger audiences, it is the 1982 film that lends itself to the exploration of intermedial differences and similarities between book and film in the EFL classroom.

While the adaptation considerably changes the book's plot and partly its themes, it largely succeeds in capturing its mood and manages to translate into the filmic medium some of the central questions and concerns that the book raises. In *Do Androids Dream of Electric Sheep?*, as Vint rightly observes, the inquiry into the relationship between humans and robots is answered by the conclusion that "their difference rests on the question of empathy, a capacity androids are said to lack, a reversal of the typical preference for reason." In addition, "[the] rights, or lack thereof, held by artificial beings are explored".[13] Both issues are central to the lesson sequence proposed in the following.

How fruitfully science fiction, and science-fiction films in particular, can be employed in the EFL classroom was demonstrated a few years ago by Peter Bruck, who presented several approaches to various science-fiction films in his didactic handbook *Future Worlds* (2012). Among the films he included were also two films based on works by Philip K. Dick: *Minority Report* and *Blade Runner*. In his introduction, Bruck states that one premise of science-fiction films is that the fictionalized future they present is plausible in the sense that the scientific and technological developments they depict are conceivable as the further development of present science and technology.[14] This is a crucial aspect when it comes to affectively engaging students in the exploration of science fiction: if the fictionalized future results from the advancement of the current state of affairs, then this future, or aspects of it, might possibly be (aspects of) the future they will live in, in decades to come. Bruck goes on to identify "inquiries into human identity and self-assertion in the face of cloned replicants"[15] as a central theme in *Blade Runner* – this theme, which is so striking in the film, will also play a vital role in the lesson sequence outlined in the following.

In the proposed lesson sequence, the goal is for students to engage in the larger issues that science fiction addresses. Rather than having students trace the way from *Do Androids Dream of Electric Sheep?* to *Blade Runner* in a mere search for the similarities and differences between novel and film, this lesson sequence uses both media to ask students to try to characterize the future scenarios, to observe both points of overlap and of divergence between the world they know and the one(s) presented in the book and the film, and to speculate on (the causes of) the developments that could lead to such future scenarios. A pivotal question in a fictionalized world in which androids possibly dream of electric sheep is: what it is that distinguishes or will distinguish humans from androids?

Given the large variety of Dick's works and the abundance of options this opens up, the following lesson sequence, illustrating how his science-fiction writing and the films derived from it can be approached practically in the classroom, needs to be understood as merely one of numerous possibilities. The following lesson sequence is designed for a tenth, eleventh, or twelfth grade English class, which corresponds to an advanced level of English as a foreign language and thus to the CEFR level B1.

As students' previous knowledge about the genre will differ, the sequence begins with one to two sessions of pre-reading/-watching activities, during which the students acquire vocabulary they will need to speak about the bleak future worlds projected by Philip K. Dick, and by extension, Ridley Scott. As students will be familiar with more mainstream science-fiction stories like *Star Wars* or *Star Trek*, creating a mind map of 'all things science fiction' can prove a rewarding exercise for students. Clustering the individual items they find into larger thematic units may result in such useful word fields as technologization and digitization, automation and cloning, spatial exploration and colonization, or encounters with life forms from outer space. Given recent endeavors, in Japan and elsewhere, to employ robots no longer only in industrial production but also in more social professions like nursing or caring for the elderly, there is an abundance of topical newspaper articles, documentaries, and critical cartoons available online, from which material can be drawn to familiarize students some more with the current state of affairs and prospects of robotics. Thanks to the dynamic vocabulary work surrounding the mind mapping and the reading exercise students have a solid lexical basis for discussing passages from *Do Androids Dream of Electric Sheep?* and *Blade Runner*.

As the next phase in this practice-orientated classroom approach, students will engage in the first while-watching activity. They will see a short sequence early on in the film, immediately following the opening sequence (00:03:03–00:04:09 mins.). The sequence begins with the written information on the setting, "Los Angeles, November 2019," and runs through the zoom-in onto somebody's eyeball. As they watch (there is only music at this point and no dialogue yet), they are expected to take notes on a worksheet which asks them to note down when the action is set, to observe the setting and find adjectives to characterize the setting, as well as to formulate hypotheses about what the situation is. Due to the fact that the fictional time of November 2019 lies in the immediate or near past, students can conclude that in November 2019 Los Angeles did not look the way it is depicted in the film and they can be easily encouraged to speculate on the reason(s) why it could be depicted this way in the film. After discussing the students' notes in class, a second while-watching phase will go further back in the film: only now do students watch the opening sequence, which provides them with the information as to the initial situation in the film and as to what replicants, the Nexus-6 unit, Tyrell corporation, and Blade Runners are, information which they are supposed to add to (the second page of) their worksheet (00:02:12–00:03:02 mins.). As homework for the next lesson, students are expected to read a passage from *Do Androids Dream of Electric Sheep?*[16] and look up unknown words at home.

This very passage will be central to the subsequent lesson, during which students will discuss what they have read at home. The excerpt given to them encompasses chapter four and parts of chapter five, in which Rick Deckard visits the Rosen Association and tries to determine with the help of the Voigt-Kampff profile scale whether Rachael is an android or not. The conclusion he draws, however, will not be part of what students read at home. Having read the passage in question, students will try to find answers to the following questions in a Think, Pair, Share approach: first on their own, then with a partner, and finally in small groups, they will 1) describe what the central idea behind the Voigt-Kampff profile scale is, 2) identify the traits that seem to be decisive for the distinction between humans and androids, according to this scale, and 3) argue why they believe Rachael is human or android. As homework for the next lesson, students are expected to read the rest of chapter five.[17] The next lesson will come back to chapter five and students will discuss Deckard's classification of Rachael. At this point, their attention will be drawn towards the direct juxtaposition of novel and film as students will be shown the sequence from the film in which Deckard arrives at the Tyrell Corporation and tests Rachael (00:16:17–00:21:16 mins.). Before watching, they will be briefed as to the importance of such elements as camera angles, costumes, make-up, set designs, and musical score.[18] A set of study questions provided on a worksheet will guide their watching as it asks them to pay attention to the mood created by the film, in comparison to the literary version they encountered before, to the actors' impersonation of the literary characters, as well as to the overarching question as to whether Rachael is human or not. The study questions can include the following:

- *What are Deckard and Rachael doing in the scene?*
- *Describe the atmosphere in the scene.*
- *Try to characterize Deckard and Rachael.*

- *What is the outcome of the scene?*
- *In your opinion, what features could be examined to tell apart humans from robots in a future in which you can't tell the difference by only looking at them?*
- *What could be considered 'typically human' or 'typically android'?*
- *In such a future, will it still matter if there is a difference? Why or why not?*

Results will be gathered in an ensuing group work phase. As homework for the next lesson, students are assigned a creative writing task, either a narrative or a screenplay that envisions the next encounter between Rick Deckard and Rachael Rosen, leaving students at complete liberty as to under which circumstances, at what point, and with what outcome this second encounter will take place.

In one or two final lessons, students will engage in post-reading/-watching activities that revolve around the themes discussed in the preceding sessions and that let them connect these themes to their own lifeworlds. Starting from the question of what could lie between the world they live in and the world(s) presented in the book and the film, students are asked to work together in groups and create posters that explain and depict a possible course of events from the real present to the fictional future. In a gallery walk approach, the entire class can subsequently scrutinize and evaluate each group's ideas and, optionally, designate a winning poster. Additionally or alternatively, to reflect more on the difference between androids and humans, and, by consequence on the idiosyncrasies of the human condition, students can be asked to play a role play/detective game, in which some participants, without the others' knowledge, assume the identity of androids. It is up to them to shape their role according to what they think makes androids androids. Others will be given the task to identify androids, much like in the book and the film, and to come up with methods and questions that will allow them to single out their non-human fellow role players. Another set of students will be asked to play 'themselves', i.e. impersonate humans and act as distractors from the androids in a (possible future) scenario in which androids and humans may live side by side.

Topic	The Future State of the World as Projected in *Do Androids Dream of Electric Sheep?* (1968) and *Blade Runner* (1982).
Objectives	To develop and practice: • vocabulary connected to science fiction, technologization, (dystopian) visions of the future • literary and film analysis: skills to read literary and filmic texts (on their own and/or comparatively) • critical thinking: reflect on and discuss causes of potential catastrophes in the form of global warfare and ecological collapse as well as means to prevent them
Age	Secondary students (15-17)
Level	CEFR level B1 and above
Time	5 lessons
Materials/media	Worksheets with introductory materials, excerpts from a novel with worksheet, film sequences with worksheet, role cards for role plays
1st lesson Before reading/watching Acquiring the necessary background	Ask students to think about the science-fiction works that they know and to come up with book or film titles, themes, or plots. With the help of a black/white or smartboard, collect students' ideas and thoughts in a mind map, which students are supposed to copy into their books. Ask students to read a topical article, annotated by the teacher, on automation/robotics and discuss central topics and questions. Homework: study new vocabulary from mind map and article.
2nd lesson While watching Getting into the film	Ask students to watch the sequence immediately following the opening sequence of *Blade Runner* (until the

	zoom on the eye). Ask students to take notes on what they observe and to formulate hypotheses on why Los Angeles looks the way it does in the fictional November 2019 on a worksheet. Ask students to watch the opening sequence and ask them to explain in their own words the initial situation in the film (e.g. what are replicants, Nexus-6, Blade Runners). Homework: read excerpt (chapter 4 and part of chapter 5, from "Maybe I'm worried…" through "…removed the adhesive patch from her cheek.") from the novel at home and look up unknown words.
3rd lesson While reading Getting into the novel	Ask students to think about and discuss (Think, Pair, Share) three study questions dealing with the excerpt from the novel they read as homework. Depending on the students' level, go deeper into literary analysis (e.g. plot development and creation of suspense, means of characterization) Homework: read the rest of chapter 5 from the novel at home and look up unknown words.
4th lesson While reading/watching	Ask students to summarize and comment on the rest of chapter 5. Familiarize students with the tools of film analysis. Ask students to watch the scene from the film that parallels the excerpt from the novel they read before and answer questions pertaining to (the comparison of) mood, characters, and Rachael in particular in the book and the film. Homework: creative writing task (write either a narrative or a

	screenplay envisioning the next encounter between Deckard and Rachael, detailing under which circumstances, at what point and with what outcome this second encounter will take place).
5th lesson After reading/watching Reflecting on one's own life world	Ask students to get together in groups of about 4 students. Ask each group to reflect on what could lie between the world they live in and the world(s) presented in the book and the film and to create a poster explaining and depicting a possible course of events from the real present into the fictional future. The sequence comes to an end with a gallery walk, during which the entire class looks at and evaluates each group's poster and possibly chooses the best one.

Table 1: A Lesson Sequence for Teaching *Do Androids Dream of Electric Sheep?*

4. Conclusion

This chapter proposes using Philip K. Dick's science-fiction narratives and their TV and cinema adaptations in the EFL classroom. The central aim is to provide students with a (guided) encounter with authentic literary and filmic science-fiction material which not only helps them explore the characteristics of this encompassing genre and discover the medial differences between book and film but also encourages them to ask more far-reaching questions about the future and the role that technology, (global) politics, the environment, and they themselves are going to play in this future. The depth of Dick's writings, the questions about human responsibility, agency, and empathy that they raise, and the dystopian character of his scenarios can serve as valuable tools to make young adults ponder the course of history, from past decades and ages, into our present moment, into a future that will be theirs.

Notes

1. Gunn, James E. (1992). *Inside Science Fiction: Essays on Fantastic Literature*. San Bernardino: Borgo Press, 42.
2. Dick, Philip K. (2007[1968]). *Do Androids Dream of Electric Sheep?* London: Orion Books, 36.
3. *Ibid.,* 12.
4. Parrinder, Patrick (1980). *Science Fiction: Its Criticism and Teaching*. London: Methuen, 119.
5. *Ibid.,* xiv.
6. Banks, Michael A. (1982). *Understanding Science Fiction*. Morristown, NJ: Silver Burdett, 72.
7. Vint, Sherryl (2014). *Science Fiction: A Guide for the Perplexed*. London: Bloomsbury, 6.
8. *Ibid.*, 4.
9. Jacobsen, Craig B. (2010). "Introduction: Teaching with Science Fiction." *Practicing Science Fiction: Critical Essays on Writing, Reading and Teaching the Genre*. Eds. Karen Hellekson et al. London: McFarland, 12.
10. Gunn (1992), 79-80.
11. Parrinder (1980), 121.
12. Though *Blade Runner 2049* is not an adaptation of a work by Dick, the end credits establish the connection to Dick's work by declaring that the film is "based on characters from the novel *Do Androids Dream of Electric Sheep?* by Philip K. Dick." *Blade Runner 2049.* Dir. *Denis Villeneuve*. 2017. Warner Bros.
13. Vint (2014), 61.
14. Bruck, Peter (2012). *Future Worlds*. Stuttgart: Ernst Klett, 7.
15. *Ibid.*, 7.
16. Dick. (2007[1968]), 30-43.
17. *Ibid.*, 44-52.
18. The materials provided in Bruck's *Future Worlds* on pages 100-104 are helpful at this stage. Cf. Bruck (2012), 100-104.

Bibliography

Primary Texts

Blade Runner. Dir. Ridley Scott. 1982. DVD. Warner Bros., 1997.

Blade Runner 2049. Dir. *Denis Villeneuve*. 2017. Warner Bros.

Dick, Philip K. (2002[1956]). *The Minority Report*. New York: Pantheon Books.

--- (2014[1962]). *The Man in the High Castle*. London: Penguin Books.

--- (2000[1966]). "We Can Remember It for You Wholesale." *We Can Remember It for You Wholesale: The Collected Short Stories of Philip K. Dick, Vol. 5*. London: Millennium, 157-174.

--- (2007[1968]). *Do Androids Dream of Electric Sheep?* London: Orion Books.

The Man in the High Castle. Created by Frank Spotnitz. 2015. Amazon Prime Video.

Secondary Literature

Banks, Michael A. (1982). *Understanding Science Fiction*. Morristown, NJ: Silver Burdett.

Bruck, Peter (2012). *Future Worlds*. Stuttgart: Ernst Klett.

Gunn, James E. (1992). *Inside Science Fiction: Essays on Fantastic Literature*. San Bernardino: Borgo Press.

Jacobsen, Craig B. (2010). "Introduction: Teaching with Science Fiction." *Practicing Science Fiction: Critical Essays on Writing, Reading and Teaching the Genre*. Eds. Karen Hellekson et al. London: McFarland, 7-12.

Parrinder, Patrick (1980). *Science Fiction: Its Criticism and Teaching*. London: Methuen.

Vint, Sherryl (2014). *Science Fiction: A Guide for the Perplexed*. London: Bloomsbury.

Sarah Nele Geiger (Königsbach-Stein)

Teaching the *Planet of the Apes* Franchise in the EFL Classroom

1. Introduction

Science fiction is of great value in the English as a foreign language (EFL) classroom as it raises thought-provoking issues and simultaneously provides entertainment. Due to its often estranged settings, it makes it possible to talk about real-world issues with a freedom of thought that is not as easily obtained through more realistic scenarios. The value of science-fiction texts, however, lies not only in their creative representation of the future, though this can be a motivating aspect, but in the way the genre deals with a variety of current issues that students can relate to. Moreover, since science-fiction topics often differ strongly from conventional topics in the EFL classroom, it is possible to reach and motivate students who would otherwise not be interested in English as a subject.

Since the early days of cinema, science-fiction texts have been brought to the big screen. One example of this trend is Pierre Boulle's novel *La planète des singes* (1963), which was published in English under its original title *Monkey Planet* in 1964 but shortly after reissued as *Planet of the Apes*. Since its original publication, the novel has inspired a franchise consisting of, for example, films, TV series, and comics. This contribution discusses the potential of the *Planet of the Apes* franchise for the EFL classroom, particularly illustrating how excerpts from the novel and the films can be used to encourage students to reflect on current issues, including, among others, racism,[1] discrimination, religion, and gender.

The first part of this article takes a closer look at the genre of the novel, which, despite Boulle's strong rejection, is commonly classified as science fiction. The following part then focuses on selected major themes from the novel as well as the reboot film series. It concludes by providing a detailed lesson plan centering on *Rise of the Planet of the Apes* (2011)[2] and showcasing how some of the films' major themes can be approached in the foreign language classroom.

2. The *Planet of the Apes* Franchise

La planète des singes tells the story of the two space travelers Jinn and Phyllis, who find a manuscript about the odyssey of the journalist Ulysse Mérou. Ulysse was invited to join Professor Antelle and his assistant Arthur Levain on their trip to the constellation of Beutelgeuse. As they land on an alien planet, which they name Soror, they find a society in which apes are the dominant species, while humans live like savage animals, bereaved of their ability to speak. Shortly after his arrival on Soror, Ulysse, together with other humans from the native tribe, is captured by the apes and transported to a biological research facility, where he is quickly identified as an 'intelligent animal'. During his imprisonment, Ulysse not only learns the simian language but also convinces the researcher Zira and her fiancé Cornelius to help him make a public speech in front of the ape community, disclosing his ability to speak and think. He is granted freedom and becomes a full member of the Ape society which, as we learn later in the novel, was created after the apes had rebelled against humanity and reversed the slave/master roles. When their lives come under threat, Ulysse, together with his human wife Nova and his son Sirius, attempt to leave the planet in a spaceship. Upon their landing on Earth, they are greeted by a gorilla, making Ulysse realise that his home planet has also been taken over by apes. At the end of the novel, Jinn and Phyllis are revealed to be space-travelling chimpanzees, who refuse to believe the story of an intelligent human.

Since the publication of the novel, the idea of apes replacing humans as the intelligent species has inspired a whole media franchise, which, in addition to video games, toys, and comics, includes a number of film adaptions, remakes, and reboots. The first film version of the novel, directed by Franklin J. Schaffner, was released in 1968 and, after the success of the first film, was followed by four sequels. Moreover, a television series was released in 1974. After more than thirty years, a *Planet of the Apes* remake by Tim Burton came to the cinema in 2001.[3] In 2011, ten years after the release of the remake, a reboot series consisting of three films started in 2011, reinventing the story of the chimpanzee Caesar, who already featured as a central character in two of the original films.

The original film series comprises five films, namely *Planet of the Apes* (1968), *Beneath the Planet of the Apes* (1970), *Escape from the Planet of the Apes* (1971), *Conquest of the Planet of the Apes* (1972), and *Battle for the Planet of the Apes* (1973). The series is loosely based on Boulle's novel, describing the fall of human society and the rise of ape dominance. In 2001, a *Planet of the Apes* remake was released. In 1974, the TV series *Planet of the Apes* came out. It is based on the films, featuring the adventures of human astronauts and their encounters with apes and humans in the ruins of the former United States. The *Planet of the Apes* reboot film series represents the latest addition to the franchise. The series includes three films, namely *Rise of the Planet of the Apes* (2011), *Dawn of the Planet of the Apes* (2014), and *War for the Planet of the Apes* (2017).

As we see, the continuous popularity of *Planet of the Apes* has led to a complex and elaborate opus in which the story undergoes several changes, although the basic storyline of Earth being taken over by apes remains the same.

3. *Planet of the Apes* – Science Fiction or Social Fantasy?

Science fiction remains a contested label, which, as Stableford points out in his introduction to *Science Fact and Science Fiction: An Encyclopedia*, has been "promiscuously applied".[4] In a similar vein, Milner argues that science fiction

> is a selective tradition, continuously reinvented in the present, through which the boundaries of the genre are continuously policed, challenged and disrupted, and the cultural identity of the SF community continuously established, preserved and transformed. It is thus essentially and necessarily a site of contestation.[5]

When Boulle's novel first came out, it was immediately classified as science fiction. This tradition was continued when later on the first film adaption was referred to as science fiction. Boulle, however, clearly rejected the label science fiction as the following quote illustrates:

> It is a story, and science fiction is only the pretext. I wouldn't even know how to define SF… I think it's the genre where you can deal with and imagine unhuman characters, but in my book my apes are men, there is no doubt. I believe it was triggered by a visit to the zoo where I watched the gorillas. I was impressed by their human-like expressions. It led me to dwell upon and imagine relationships between humans and apes.[6]

Boulle, author of the epic war story *Le Pont de la Rivière Kwaï* (1952), was not a science-fiction writer and space travel was only a 'necessary evil' to tell his story of a dystopian (future) world in which apes have evolved from humankind. In other words, Boulle not only rejected the label science fiction because he felt that it did not reflect the social impetus of his novel but also because he simply was not concerned with science fiction literature. Instead, he chose the term social fantasy,[7] a niche genre which aims to criticize the current political and economic order.

The label social fantasy, a still today largely unknown and theoretical genre, however, needs to be understood in the context of Boulle's time. Boulle was not particularly interested in technology and the potential effects it could have on human society but in the social fabric of society.[8] Moreover, as a former prisoner of war, Boulle, in *Planet of the Apes*, not surprisingly draws a protagonist who spends the better part of the narrative in a cage, exploring the psychological effects of long-term imprisonment and subjugation. As Chambers convincingly argues:

> *Planet of the Apes* is part of Boulle's literary canon that is bound up with the themes of subjugation, incarceration, and the dangers of complacency. These preoccupations perhaps draw upon his Second World War experiences – Boulle served as a resistance fighter in Burma during the war and was later subjected to forced labour after being captured as a prisoner of war.[9]

Moreover, Boulle was interested in exploring humanity and the relationship between humans and animals in a society that resulted from evolutionary reversal.

As Chambers points out, "[e]ach film was produced in a specific historical moment by different production teams, each with its own set of cultural concerns and interpretive potential".[10] However, some themes, such as race and religiosity[11] can be found not only in Boulle's novel but in all films. In the following, the treatment of animals and the image of the religious messiah will be discussed as examples.

4. Themes in *Planet of the Apes*

4.1. The Treatment of Animals

The end of the 1950s saw a public dispute about the death of the Russian space dog Laika. Politically exploited as anti-communist propaganda, the controversy nevertheless focused on mankind's ethical and moral responsibility towards animals. The debate triggered by Laika's death was the initiator for a growing animal rights movement that gained momentum at the end of the 1960s. With the radical description and sharp critique of big game hunts and animal experiments, Boulle's novel, published in 1963, delivered a literary treatise of animal rights that was ahead of its time. The big game hunt in the beginning is one of the more shocking scenes of the novel. Its intensity and cruelty are amplified by the fact that the typical roles of hunters and prey are reversed. The reader experiences the hunt through the eyes of the human first person narrator Ulysse and shares his feelings of terror.[12] Helplessly hidden away, Ulysse has to watch the death struggle of a man:

> [A]lready the man was racing like a mountain goat across open ground. The shoot rang out while he was still halfway across the field of fire. He gave a leap in the air, collapsed in a heap on the ground, and after a few convulsions lay motionless.[13]

Through the hunting and war imagery, Boulle also broaches the issue of the perverse ecstasy some humans derive from dominating and killing other lifeforms, which Boulle expresses through the "feverish pleasure"[14] on the face of the gorilla hunter. The scenes of carnage and senseless killing culminate in the depiction of the decadence of the simian society. With the admiration and applause of their wives,[15] the gorilla hunters display their game and prepare to be photographed:

> [T]he gorillas having themselves photographed first individually, in good poses, some of them placing one foot on one of their victims with a

> triumphant air; then as compact group, each of them putting an arm around his neighbor's shoulder. The she gorillas in turn were then photographed and assumed graceful postures in front of the slaughter, with their decorated hats well to the fore.[16]

The imagery of this scene not only reminds the reader of the trophy photographs taken after big game hunts in the beginning of the twentieth century but, more importantly, of war photography.[17] These associations are further evoked by Boulle's choice of words: the game has metamorphosed into "victims" and a sense of soldierly comradeship comes to mind by the triumphant gorillas "putting an arm around the neighbor's shoulder". The repeated use of military imagery implies a scathing critique on the lifestyle and behavior of the simian – and therefore also human upper class. The realistic mode of the narrative enforces the cruelty of the scene to such an extent that the imagery reminds the reader no longer of a hunt but of the pictures of atrocities committed during wars such as World War II, the Korean, and the Vietnam War.

The humans that are captured by the gorillas are later used in medical and zoological experiments. The medical experiments are criticized for their cruelty by the first-person narrator. After Ulysse's critique, the simian scientists' justification of their experiments sounds shallow and implausible:

> I admit these experimentations are rather bloodcurdling when you're not used to them. But you must bear in mind that thanks to them our medicine and surgery have made enormous progress in the last quarter of a century.[18]

The same argument is still used by human scientists worldwide. Like the simian scientists, they also make a point that the subjects experience no pain during surgery, but neglect to consider the consequences of the experiments. The consequences depicted for the human test subjects in *Planet of the Apes* are profound: "I saw men partially or totally paralyzed, others artificially deprived of sight."[19] It also provokes an association with the Nazis' experiments in the concentration camps. This resemblance sharpens the final critique on human as well as animal experimentation.

While the medical experiments are depicted in detailed cruelty, the description of the zoological experiments is odd and surprising. The life in cages causes an initial irritation in the human captives, but as they are treated well, they soon get used to their new surroundings. Even Ulysse adapts, at first finding the situation degrading, yet later describing it as pleasant:

> I must admit that I adapted myself with remarkable ease to the conditions of life in my cage. From the material point of view, I was living in perfect felicity: during the day the apes attended to my every need; at night I shared my litter with one of the loveliest girls in the cosmos.[20]

The description of the situation is questionable since Ulysse seems to find 'perfect felicity' in an environment that provides his basic needs, food and sex, but that deprives him of his freedom, intellectual challenges, and social interactions other than sexual intercourse.

Animal hunting and testing also represent prevalent themes in the reboot series of which the *Rise of the Planet of the Apes* may serve as an example. The film starts with mostly aerial shots of a group of chimpanzees trekking through the jungle, while some close-ups of their eyes serve to establish a connection between apes and audience as well as to humanize the primates. When the human hunters start their chase with wild, animalistic screams, there are hardly any close-ups and the hunters seem to lose their humanity. This point is emphasized in the final shot of the scene when the captured chimpanzee looks sadly through the small metal gap, her nostrils rising and falling rapidly in fear.

Yet, the hunt for test animals is justified and all the emotion, drama, and feelings of guilt this scene awakens in the audience are negated by the next scene when we see the captured chimpanzee happily solving the Tower of Hanoi in only twenty moves, thus proving that the drug development was successful.

Furthermore, at no point in the film is the process or ethical tenability of testing drugs on animals called into question as it is in the novel. The drug testing, and later the outbreak of the pandemic, seems more like a device to provide the appropriate setting for the plot, rather than a critique of the procedure: the main protagonist Will Rodman shows no moral qualms about animal testing. He is solely focused on developing a cure for Alzheimer's in order to save his father. The audience might feel bad when the director of the pharmaceutical company Jacobs orders the killing of all the apes involved in the testing "in the most cost-effective way"[21] but apart from the scene with Koba later in the film, no invasive testing or negative consequences for the animals are shown.

While the depiction of the experiments loses most of the terror they hold in the novel, Caesar's time in the primate shelter is shown as degrading and as physically as well as mentally challenging. Even though the primate shelter has a lovely front and play room, the back with its cells closely resembles a prison, as one of the animal handler's friend mentions during their tour of the facility in his derogative statement "More like a prison for hairy dudes".[22] Like a cruel prison guard, the animal handler Dodge finds pleasure in punishing and torturing the animals, whose lack of self-determination and reduction to property is emphasized by the fact that they are sold off to laboratories like Gen-Sys. Unlike in the novel, Caesar's time in the cage is not marked by perfect felicity but as a trial which he has to master before becoming the ape he is meant to be and taking up the responsibility of leadership.

4.2. The Role of the Religious Messiah

Religion features prominently in *Planet of the Apes*. A theocratic ape society governed by priest-like orangutans which stunt the evolution of simian culture by rejecting science and restricting knowledge.[23] The fact that in the first film series, Dr Zaius functions as both the Defender of the Faith and Minister of Science illustrates how simian society may serve as another example of how societal development is slowed down by religious fanatism.[24] The role of the religious Messiah represents another example.

In the third part of the novel, when he is in the luxury position of not having to fight for his life and rights as a rational being, Ulysse starts to presume a divine reason for his presence on the planet Soror.

> Nothing happens by chance in the cosmos. My voyage to the world of Betelgeuse was decreed by a superior consciousness. It is up to me to show myself worthy of this choice and be the new savior of this human race in decline.[25]

After learning that Nova is pregnant, Ulysse considers his son to be the 'means' by which he can fulfil his divine mission: "I now see exactly how the mission with which I have been entrusted can be accomplished".[26]

While his mission at first is only divine and could have resulted from any religious belief, it later takes on Christian characteristics due to the terms he uses to describe his son and the circumstances of his birth. The child "was lying on the straw like a new Christ"[27] and as the real Christ, who with his sacrifice took away people's sins, Ulysse expects his son to be the savior who causes the rebirth of the human race.[28] Furthermore, only with the birth of Ulysse's son do we see the appearance of the first spark of rationality in the indigenous human population: "I noted a marked change among the men. It was as though some mysterious instinct had notified them of the miraculous birth".[29]

Yet, when his life and the lives of his family are threatened, Ulysse fails in his divine mission. He and his little family flee from Soror and leave the humans there to their fate. Since there is no sacrifice, there also cannot be a divine rescue. With the unwillingness to give his life, Ulysse cements the final fate of a sapient humanity.

After Ulysse decides to escape from Soror, he feels the threatening doom for humanity. He tries to calm his feelings of guilt towards his fellow humans by justifying his actions and promising to return:

> Toward them [his fellow humans] I feel I am something of a deserter. Yet above all I must save my son and Nova. But I shall come back. Yes, later, I swear it on the heads of the captives in the cages, I shall come back with trump cards in my hand.[30]

Since his return would be at least 700 years into the future, his promise sounds as shallow as his previous declarations of being the divinely selected savior of the Sororian humanity.

Whereas Ulysse is a resounding failure as religious messiah, Caesar comes true as a savior for his fellow apes in the 2017 film *War for the Planet of the Apes*. When his tribe is imprisoned in the labor camps of the cruel colonel, he fights for their needs in disregard of his own survival. Again, the imagery of his trials is unquestionably Christian as he is crucified and nearly starved to death. The colonel, the antagonist to Caesar's messiah figure, either swayed by Caesar's bravery or his reasoning, provides the other apes with food and water. Thus Caesar's willingness for self-sacrifice is rewarded. However, the Christian imagery does not end there. At the end of the film, the mortally wounded Caesar leads his fellow apes to a promised land and like Moses has to cross a desert to find it.

5. Teaching *Planet of the Apes*

Watching films has become a popular leisure time activity for students and for most far outweighs the time spent on reading novels. According to Maley, the preeminence of audio-visual representation

> has created the need for us to make sense of this visual rhetoric. Moving pictures have a grammar and discourse all their own which we need to decode if we are to understand the meanings that they contain.[31]

Therefore, students have to learn about film language in order to understand how feelings and opinions can be manipulated through aspects such as camera angles or soundtrack. A contrastive look at the various film adaptations can help make film language more tangible for students as the same content presented with different means can result in a different interpretation. Additionally, students should gain confidence that they are capable of watching, understanding, and interpreting films in the English language. As Sherman points out, "there is a special thrill in being able to understand and enjoy the real thing".[32] Only if the viewing and discussion of the film is a positive experience will students start watching films in English in a private setting as well, thus extending the time they are exposed to authentic English language.

When confronted with the problem of choosing the right film for the language classroom, Bergala[33] argues that educators should always teach films which they like. His argument follows the line of thought that if educators do not like the film they are presenting, they will appear condescending. Yet, if they like a film, their enthusiasm will also motivate the students. For the author of this essay, this means teaching a science-fiction film. Since many pupils may believe that science fiction is only about spaceships, aliens, and sophisticated weapon systems, it is advisable to first introduce the genre of science fiction and provide students with examples of the most recent science-fiction films.[34] An example of this can be found in the first lesson of the lesson sequence.

One advantage of science fiction is that it not only offers a wide range of topics but is also extremely well suited for cross-curricular learning. Issues which are too challenging for students to discuss in English can be addressed in the students' shared language in other subjects such as art or history, while more relatable issues can be discussed in the English classroom. This approach does not only allow students to immerse in depth in the topics that are offered but also provides them with the positive experience of demonstrating that they understood the content of the film even if their ability to express themselves in English is still limited.

One interdisciplinary example of teaching *Rise of the Planet of the Apes*, which yielded great results in the past and is generally liked by the students, is a cooperation between art and English. After the viewing of the film, the students design an ad campaign. In the EFL classroom students will be introduced to the AIDA model[35] and following the steps of the model they create catchy slogans using stylistic devices. The art class provides the visual representation. Great topics that relate back to the film are an ad campaign on animal rights or for the San Francisco Zoo, and the promotion of a new drug against the Alzheimer's disease.

Topic	Science Fiction and *Planet of the Apes*
Objectives	To develop and practice: • listening and reading comprehension • expressing an opinion and acting in role plays • writing structured texts to a given topic • working with mind maps
Age	Secondary pupils (around 14-16 years old); German school system grade 9 (*Realschule*)
Level	CEF level A2/B1 and above
Time	7 lessons (585 mins.)
Materials/media	Projector and Blu-ray/DVD-Player, tablets, projector presentation, board and colorful chalk, posters and markers, worksheets, tags, trailer, internet connection, program to adapt films, feature films (*Rise of the Planet of the Apes* (2011), *Planet of the Apes* (2001), *Planet of the Apes* (1967), novel *Planet of the Apes* (1963), stills, speaking prompts, student access to internet for research.
Introduction	In this sequence, students will • gain a quick insight in what science fiction is • practice listening comprehension by identifying the general information as well as some details • learn about film analysis and features of film language

	• interpret roles and express an opinion that does not necessarily correspond with their own with the help of speech prompts • express their opinion in writing to a given topic in a structured way • collect and organize information in mind maps
1st lesson (90 mins.) Introduction to sf • Introduction to science fiction • Working with mind maps • Overview unit and criteria of film compendium	Materials: Projector presentation about science fiction, poster and pictures for mind map, instructions for film compendium Activities and classroom interaction: Teacher introduces topic with a projector presentation, which includes recent science-fiction film posters and trailers. From this starting point, the students create a mind map with the think-pair-share method. The teacher moderates the creation of the mind map and can guide the students to overlooked aspects through prompts and pictures. The mind map will remain in the classroom for the remainder of the unit. The lesson ends with the teacher giving a rough overview of the unit as well as explaining the criteria for a film compendium, which will document the unit. The students should take a photo of the mind map so that they can copy it into their compendium (which can be marked at the end of the unit). Homework: Students will start on their film compendium by creating a title page and copying the mind map
2nd lesson (135 mins.) Watching *Rise of the Planet of the Apes* • Watching a film • Personal impression (with double circle) • Comprehension check	Materials: Film *Rise of the Planet of the Apes*, worksheets Activities and classroom interaction: The students watch the film without any additional tasks so that they can become emotionally engaged and get a feeling for the atmosphere of the film. Only after the film do the students take notes on a worksheet. The focus is their personal impression, what they liked and disliked, and their favorite character. After completing their worksheets individually, the students gather in a double circle and tell each other about their opinions. Homework: In order to guarantee that all students understood the plot the students answer some multiple choice questions and put a scrambled summary of the plot in the correct order.

3rd lesson (90 mins.) Working with a trailer • Criteria of a film trailer • Voice-over for a trailer	Materials: Film trailer, film trailer without audio track (already uploaded on tablets), tablets, program to overlay trailer with new audio track, information sheet about criteria of a trailer Activities and classroom interaction: The lesson starts with the students watching a trailer for the 2011 film. From this trailer, students deduce typical features in think-pair-share (e.g. not a summary, no spoilers, but need to catch interest and have to give an idea what the film is about and what can be expected). Students get an information sheet about the criteria of a trailer so that they can reference it in the following task. Then the students work in pairs and write a new voiceover for the trailer. Each pair has their own tablet so that they can re-watch the trailer as well as do the voiceover (if the teacher marks the compendium, they should also mark the new trailers). For the recording, the students should have access to a quiet place, so several rooms will be necessary. Homework: The students write an essay about what home means for them. The essay should be at least 60 words. This homework is in preparation for the next lesson.
4th lesson (45 mins.) Discussing a topic • Mind map on home • Meaning of 'home' for Caesar	Materials: DVD/Blu-ray of 2011 film Activities and classroom interaction: The students fill in a mind map about 'home' on the board with ideas from their essays (and copy it for their compendium). Then the class re-watches the scene at end with Caesar saying 'Caesar is home'. In the think-pair-share method the class will discuss the following questions: *What does home mean for Caesar? What does he give up to be home? What does he gain?*

<table>
<tr><td>5th lesson (45 mins.)
Learning about film language

• Basic aspects of film language
• Gallery walk with stills of the film
• Transfer to Rise of the Planet of the Apes</td><td>Materials: Stills of the 2011 film, worksheet on film language, labels with names of shots and camera angles
Activities and classroom interaction: The teacher shows an example of an extreme long shot of the 2011 film. The students discuss what emotions are triggered by the shot and what the director's intention could have been. Then the students do a gallery walk: several stills of the 2011 film are pinned up in the classroom with a paper next to them for notes. Students do a walk around and write their impressions and the director's intentions on the paper next to the still. Next, the students fill out a worksheet on film language. Typical shots are shown with pictures and the students have to assign short text describing when/why the shots are typically used to each picture. After this, the content of the worksheet is transferred to the stills of the 2011 film and the students label the pictures on the walls with the correct terms and check whether their impressions correspond with what typically is intended by these shots/camera angles.</td></tr>
<tr><td>6th lesson (90 mins.)
Comparing a scene

Comparing the scenes of three different adaptations (1968, 2001, and 2011) with each other and the novel</td><td>Materials: Two different clips on YouTube (e.g. comedy and action), clips of hunting scenes (DVD/Blu-ray), tablets (with 1968 clip already opened on YouTube), scene from novel (copied), at least three different rooms/locations
Activities and classroom interaction: The teacher plays two very different scenes from films (e.g. a scene of romantic comedy and one of action film). With these scenes the class gathers/develops the criteria of comparing films (film language, music/soundtrack, setting, character, plot, personal impression/emotion, most important differences). The teacher provides the class with a table, in which the students take notes on the criteria above with the information collected in the following tasks. The hunting scene of the 2011 and the 2001 version of Planet of the Apes are shown three times, first normally, then without sound (to concentrate on film language), and then only sound but no picture/screen (to concentrate on music/soundtrack). After this, the students work in</td></tr>
</table>

	pairs to do the same with the hunting scene of the 1968 adaption, which can be found on *YouTube*. Due to the noise level several rooms are required for this task. Homework: The students read the hunting scene and fill in the column for the novel in the table. While the novel of course does not have a soundtrack, it provides the description of noises. The line for film language is left empty.
7th lesson (90 mins.) Discussing animal rights in Kenya • Preparing for roles • Role play: discussion (fish bowl) • Written discussion • Feedback on unit	Materials: Worksheets with information about the role, role cards with speaking prompts, tablets, tags with name/role, worksheet for feedback Activities and classroom interaction: The aim of this lesson is to have a lively discussion about animal rights in Kenya. The students will work in groups of three and prepare their arguments for their respective roles (representative of the farmers, environmental activist, animal rights activist, representatives for the tourism industry, moderators/hosts). Each group will get some information about their position as well as role cards with speaking prompts. Each group has a tablet, so that they can look up additional information or search for pictures to strengthen their arguments. The discussion will take place in form of a fish bowl, but each student has to sit down for the discussion at least once. Homework: The students put together a written discussion about drug tests on animals. They should write at least 120 words. The students should be encouraged to research the topic on the internet beforehand and then structure their ideas giving pro and contra arguments. Additionally, the students will give their feedback on the unit on a worksheet.

Table 1: *Teaching Planet of the Apes*

6. Conclusion

The *Planet of the Apes* franchise offers numerous possibilities for discussing critical themes and topics in the English as foreign language classroom. The experience the author has had over seven years using science-fiction films in general and the *Planet of the Apes* franchise in particular for teaching EFL to fourteen- to sixteen-year-olds has been overwhelmingly positive. Students' reactions and comments such as "this was the most fun I ever had in English" or "I never thought I will understand a movie in English", illustrate this. One student re-watched the 2011 film at home in order to do a character constellation, even though this student had not done any other homework before during the school year. This, together with many other positive experiences, supports the claim that science fiction offers a valuable addition to the traditional literary.

Notes

1 Cf. Greene, Eric (1998). *Planet of the Apes as American Myth. Race, Politics, and Popular Culture.* Hanover: Wesleyan University Press.

2 For a more detailed discussion of the film see Linder, Oliver (2015). "The Remade Prequel – *Rise of the Planet of the Apes* (2011)." *Remakes and Remaking: Concepts – Media – Practices*. Eds. Rüdiger Heinze and Lucia Krämer. Bielefeld: transcript, 23-40.

3 For a more detailed discussion of the 2001 remake cf. Lindner, Oliver. (2012). "'An Entirely Different and New Story': A Case Study of Tim Burton's *Planet of the Apes* (2001)." *Adaptation and Cultural Appropriation: Literature, Film, and the Arts*. Eds. Pascal Nicklas and Oliver Lindner. Berlin: De Gruyter, 117-131.

4 Stableford, Brian (2006). *Science Fact and Science Fiction: An Encyclopedia*. Abingdon: Routledge, xxi.

5 Milner, Andrew (2012). *Locating Science Fiction*. Liverpool: Liverpool University Press, 39-40.

6 As cited here: "Pierre Boulle." *Planet of the Apes – The Sacred Scroll*s. Fandom, n.d. Web. 6 December 2019 <https://planetoftheapes.fandom.com /wiki/Pierre_Boulle>.

7 Russo, Joe, Larry Landsman and Edward Gross (2001). *Planet of the Apes Revisited: The Behind-the-Scenes Story of the Classic Science Fiction Saga*. New York: St. Martin's Griffin, 4.

8 A simple Google search reveals that the novel is listed under a number of genres, including social fantasy, social satire, ironic social satire, or racial satire.

9 For a more detailed discussion of religiosity in *Planet of the Apes* see Chambers, Amy C. (2016). "The Evolution of *Planet of the Apes:* Science, Religion, and 1960s Cinema." *Journal of Religion and Popular Culture* 28.2-3, 107-122, 112.

10 *Ibid.*

11 *Ibid.*

12 It may be noted in passing that the chimpanzee which was on the spaceship is immediately strangled to death by the human Nova.

13 Boulle (1963), 61.

14 *Ibid.*

15 While the male gorillas are going out for the hunt, the female gorillas wait for 'their lords and masters' and praise their fortune in hunting "with little cries of admiration". *Ibid.,* 61.

16 *Ibid.,* 71.

17 Reminiscent perhaps of a recent event in which a Navy SEAL officer took a photograph of himself holding a teenager's head by the hair after stabbing the young ISIS prisoner to death and then sending the photograph to his friends.

18 *Ibid.,* 237.

19 *Ibid.,* 234.

20 *Ibid.,* 119.

21 *Rise of the Planet of the Apes*. Dir. Rupert Wyatt. 2011. DVD. Twentieth Century Fox Home Entertainment, 2011. 00:07:55.

22 *Ibid.,* 00:50:36.

23 Cf. Chambers (2016).

24 Cf. *Ibid.*

25 Boulle (1963), 219-220.

26 *Ibid.,* 225.

27 *Ibid.,* 250.

28 *Ibid.,* 251.

29 *Ibid.,* 256.

30 *Ibid.,* 259.

31 Maley, Alan (2001). "Foreword." *Film*. By Susan Stempleski and Barry Tomalin. Oxford: Oxford University Press, 9.

32 Sherman, Jane (2003). *Using Authentic Video in the Language Classroom*. Cambridge: Cambridge University Press, 2.

33 Bergala, Alain (2006). *Kino als Kunst. Filmvermittlung an der Schule und anderswo*. Bonn: Bundeszentrale für politische Bildung, 59.

[34] Due to didactic reduction, I only classify the overall genre science fiction as I found that talking about sub-genres is very challenging for students and they are not interested in labels but in context.

[35] The AIDA model is widely used in advertising. The acronym stands for attention, interest, desire, and action. The model illustrates the steps a consumer goes through from first coming into contact with the product (possible via an ad) until they decide to buy the product.

Bibliography

Primary Texts

Battle for the Planet of the Apes. Dir. J. Lee Thompson. 1973. Twentieth Century Fox.

Beneath the Planet of the Apes. Dir. Ted Post. 1970. Twentieth Century Fox.

Conquest of the Planet of the Apes. Dir. J. Lee Thompson. 1972. Twentieth Century Fox.

Boulle, Pierre (2001[1963]). *Planet of the Apes*. Trans. Xan Fielding. New York: DelRay-Ballatine.

Dawn of the Planet of the Apes. Dir. Matt Reeves. 2014. Blu-ray Disc. Twentieth Century Fox Home Entertainment, 2014.

Escape from the Planet of the Apes. Dir. Don Taylor. 1971. Twentieth Century Fox.

Planet of the Apes. Dir. Franklin J. Schaffner. 1968. DVD. Twentieth Century Fox Home Entertainment, 2004.

Planet of the Apes. Producer Herbert Hirschman. 1974. TV Series. *Twentieth Century Fox.*

Planet of the Apes. Dir. Tim Burton. 2001. DVD. Twentieth Century Fox Home Entertainment, 2001.

Rise of the Planet of the Apes. Dir. Rupert Wyatt. 2011. DVD. Twentieth Century Fox Home Entertainment, 2011.

War for the Planet of the Apes. Dir. Matt Reeves. 2017. Blu-ray Disc. Twentieth Century Fox Home Entertainment, 2017.

Secondary Literature

Bergala, Alain (2006). *Kino als Kunst. Filmvermittlung an der Schule und anderswo*. Bonn: Bundeszentrale für politische Bildung, 59.

Chambers, Amy C. (2016). "The Evolution of *Planet of the Apes:* Science, Religion, and 1960s Cinema." *Journal of Religion and Popular Culture* 28.2-3, 107-122, 112.

Greene, Eric (1998). *Planet of the Apes as American Myth. Race, Politics, and Popular Culture.* Hanover: Wesleyan University Press.

Lindner, Oliver (2012). "'An Entirely Different and New Story': A Case Study of Tim Burton's *Planet of the Apes* (2001)." *Adaptation and Cultural Appropriation: Literature, Film, and the Arts*. Eds. Pascal Nicklas and Oliver Lindner. Berlin: De Gruyter, 117-131.

--- (2015). "The Remade Prequel – *Rise of the Planet of the Apes* (2011)." *Remakes and Remaking: Concepts – Media – Practices*. Eds. Rüdiger Heinze and Lucia Krämer. Bielefeld: transcript, 23-40.

Maley, Alan (2001). "Foreword." *Film*. By Susan Stempleski and Barry Tomalin. Oxford: Oxford University Press, 9.

Milner, Andrew (2012). *Locating Science Fiction*. Liverpool: Liverpool University Press.

"Pierre Boulle." *Planet of the Apes – The Sacred Scroll*s. Fandom, n.d. Web. 6 December 2019 <https://planetoftheapes.fandom.com/wiki/Pierre_Boulle>.

Russo, Joe, Larry Landsman and Edward Gross (2001). *Planet of the Apes Revisited: The Behind-the-Scenes Story of the Classic Science Fiction Saga*. New York: St. Martin's Griffin.

Sherman, Jane (2003). *Using Authentic Video in the Language Classroom*. Cambridge: Cambridge University Press.

Stableford, Brian (2006). *Science Fact and Science Fiction: An Encyclopedia*. Abingdon: Routledge.

Christian Ludwig (Berlin) and Nadja Heß (Karlsruhe)

"The idea of gender – it is offensive to my people." – Developing Students' Gender Competence with *Star Trek: The Next Generation*

1. Introduction

Science fiction, for a long time, has been a (white) male domain. Both female and feminist science writers such as Ursula K. Le Guin, Alice Sheldon[1], and Joanna Russ, however, have criticised male-dominant cultural patterns, for example, through creating single-gender worlds where gender differences no longer exist. With the broadening of science-fiction readership and the social changes in the late 1960s, alternative genders and sexualities beyond the heteronormative norm slowly became more commonplace during the New Wave era. Since then, speculative fiction in general and science fiction in particular have increasingly extended the idea of gender, today including all forms of sex, gender, and sexuality from homo- or transexual humans to gender-fluid or even genderless alien humanoids and other forms of existence.

Taking this as a starting point and drawing on the exploration of gender in the large body of science-fiction literature, the present paper sets out to explore selected reconstructions of sex, sexuality, and gender in the *Star Trek* franchise in an exemplarily fashion, analysing one selected episode from the *Star Trek: The Next Generation* (*TNG*) series (1987-1994) in more detail. By doing so, it intends to shed light on how science-fiction narratives "speak to the present concerns of their specific moment in history"[2] while, at the same time, showing how selected examples from science-fiction TV series such as *Star Trek* can enrich a gender-sensitive contemporary English in the foreign language classroom (EFL), ultimately also training the students' audio-visual competence. In view of the cornucopia of taboo-breaking moments in *Star Trek*, it is surprising that the franchise, if at all, only plays a marginal role in EFL classrooms, especially considering the firm place films and TV shows have generally established in foreign language learning classrooms.

The first section of this paper briefly elaborates on the history of gender in science-fiction literature and moving images, arguing that science fiction represents the ideal genre for depicting alternative versions of sex, sexuality, and gender for a number of reasons. The second section then looks more closely at the potential role of TV shows in contemporary EFL classrooms and claims that they should gain their rightful place in foreign language classrooms not least with regard to their potential for developing students' audio-visual as well as gender competence. As far as gender is concerned, it will be argued that despite the growing number of publications in the field, addressing gender-related issues in the EFL classroom remains a desideratum. The fourth section then focuses on the cult series *Star Trek*, pointing out some milestones in the TV and cinema history of the franchise before moving on to discussing *Star Trek: The Next Generation*, the sequel of the original series in greater detail. The remaining part of this paper is of a more practical nature as it provides a more detailed analysis of one selected episode from *TNG*, i.e. "The Outcast", putting it not only in the context of its time of production and broadcasting but also offering more contemporary readings of the episode at hand. Despite its progressive theme, the episode caused a big public outcry at the time as it addressed the issue of homosexuality in a more subtle and indirect way instead of making a strong case for the LGBT[3] community.

Last but not least, the lesson plan provides suggestions for a close viewing of Soren's final speech before her planet's tribunal in which she makes a plea for the individual rights of the oppressed minority on her planet before experiencing severe brainwashing, ultimately conforming to the cultural norms of her society. Here, the main objective is to engage students in a contemporary (re-) interpretation by providing a transgender perspective on "The Outcast".

The ensuing section looks more closely at the intricate relationship between the genre of science fiction and gender.

2. Gender in Science Fiction

The fact that science fiction has been considered a male genre for a long time should not evoke the false impression that women have been entirely absent from science fiction as, quite the contrary, they have been present in the genre since science-fiction stories have been published in pulp magazines. The female writers of the 1950s who wrote under male pseudonyms, the feminist stories written by female authors from the 1970s onwards about societies entirely ruled by women may only serve as examples here.

Due to the complexity of the issue of gender in science-fiction narratives, the aim of this section is rather to provide a brief but enticing insight into the potential of the science-fiction genre for readers and viewers to engage with gender issues. Science fiction narrates stories which, as Ursula K. Le Guin once pointed out, have not happened.[4] More often than not these stories provide a social commentary on contemporary issues or as Merrick argues,

> [t]he narratives of 'Science' carry an implicit set of cultural assumptions about a whole series of relationships concerning subjectivity, knowledge, 'Nature' and gender, such that sf's central question 'what if?' ultimately cannot escape the analogous question 'what, then, becomes of us?' In what ways can we (re)imagine 'humanity'? Science fiction authors have employed a number of strategies to answer this question, in the process sometimes revealing, destabilizing or subverting normative understandings of gender.[5]

In a similar vein, Attebery argues that science fiction represents the ideal environment for exploring issues related to gender as both science fiction and gender represent systems which possess the ability to create.[6] For a long time, science fiction was based on the assumption that sex as well as gender can be classified into two distinct and opposite forms: masculine and feminine. Therefore, as Merrick emphasises, an "examination of work which challenges traditional notions of gender needs to be contextualized within the broader field of 'androcentric' sf." [7] Challenging this androcentric viewpoint lets us imagine alternative gender systems which

> attempt to disrupt gendered binaries have taken the form of a number of 'androgynous' solutions: merging the binary into a singular 'gender' (the

> hermaphrodite); collapsing the binary by refusing gender categorization altogether; or positing a multiplicity of genders which subverts dualistic oppositions.[8]

Gender experiments in science-fiction texts often illustrate the social constructedness of gender and expose "both how constructed and thoroughly naturalized ideas about sex, gender, and sexuality are in any given time and place".[9] Accounts of new gender norms on future Earth or alien planets, however, not necessarily have a positive effect as gender in science fiction can be "rendered in ways that either reinforce or subvert normative expectations".[10] No matter whether the former or the latter is the case, the science fiction 'Other' has the potential to challenge and question existing norms of gender and sexuality as well as confront the anxieties of certain groups in society.

To sum up, science-fiction texts play a vital role in questioning existing sexual norms, mainly through what Merrick refers to as 'defamiliarizing the familiar', i.e. processes of parodising or explicitly critiquing issues of gender. Ideally, these alternative viewpoints help make (formerly or still) marginalised groups visible in society and ultimately build a more egalitarian society. With regard to the foreign language classroom, the fact that science-fiction narratives "are not producing arbitrary fantasy but rather reworking key metaphors and narratives already circulating in the culture"[11] makes science-fiction texts a valuable resource that should not be left out of consideration.

Before coming back to the issue of gender in science-fiction series in greater detail in section four, the ensuing section concentrates on how to foster students' gender competence in the foreign language classroom settings by using TV series.

3. Developing Students' Gender Competence by Using TV Series in the EFL Classroom

As Sunderland already pointed out in her 1992 article "Gender in the EFL classroom",[12] there are three major ways in which gender "manifests itself in the EFL classroom, namely in form of the target language itself, the materials used in the classroom, and the classroom processes such as the interaction between teacher and students".[13] Moreover, the context, i.e. the background of the teacher and the students as well as the cultural context in which the classroom can be found also needs to be taken into consideration.

Gender-related issues in EFL learning contexts have become more important throughout the past two decades or so. Despite the still existing pay gap and the continuing oppression of (gender) minorities in many countries, the global population appears to have moved forward to a more progressive agenda when it comes to gender identities, accepting the fact that we tend to "define ourselves in less structured, more mutable ways".[14] To mention but two examples, there is not only a growing awareness that biological gender and cultural ideas about gender identity or even gender itself do not always overlap perfectly but also an increasing visibility of gender diversity in the public sphere. As far as the foreign language classroom (at least in many Western societies) is concerned, it can be noted that gender issues are more and more moving into the centre of interest.

Before we move on to the role of audio-visual media in talking about gender in EFL classroom settings, a few words on the term gender itself are necessary. The widespread use of the term gender erroneously leads us to believe to that gender is easy to define. According to Udry, gender describes "the relationship between biological sex and behaviour: a theory of gender explains that relationship. A gendered behaviour is one that differs by sex."[15] The "understanding and meaning of gender [however] can differ depending on the discipline in which it is studied or simply on the social group or individual that uses it".[16] As Aikhenvald clearly states:

> To different people, the word 'gender' means different things. [...] For a sociolinguist, a psychologist, and an anthropologist, 'gender' is a set of norms, attitudes, and behaviours that a given culture or society associates with the person's biological sex (male or female). A philosopher defines gender as 'social construction of male/female identity' distinct from 'sex, the biologically-based distinction between men and women'. [...] Gender is also defined as a set of ideas about relations and behaviours, and principles of social organization, to be understood within a social context [...].[17]

Gender-sensitive foreign language teaching and learning has been conceptualised under umbrella terms such as gender awareness, which subsumes a diverse set of competences.[18] Another term which has entered academic debates revolving around gender is gender competence, which, according to Volkmann, can be defined as "the ability to question the 'givenness' of gender identity and gender formations".[19] Here, the EFL classroom plays a vital role as it can function as an anxiety-free space where students can express their thoughts in the foreign language and even push the boundaries of their own but also society's gender norms.[20]

More recent publications[21] emphasise the key role of audio-visual media in critically reflecting on the "the socio-cultural constructedness of gender (as opposed to the biological sex) as well as the diversity of (sexual) identities which go beyond simple binary structures".[22] According to König, Lewin, and Surkamp, audio-visual materials

> allow the students insights into the lives of their characters – which always includes their position in terms of gender and sexuality. Through these perspectives, students can discover the condition of being male, female or queer in a given culture or historic context.[23]

TV series are easier to integrate into in EFL classrooms than films as they are shorter and often provide individual, self-contained episodes. In addition to this, their sometimes loose dependence on the overarching story line allows viewers to track a character's development over a longer period and even envision possible scenarios for their plotline where desirable.[24]

Audio-visual competence can be understood as the ability to receive, process, and produce material that function on a visual as well as audio level. However, the simultaneous or consecutive reception of foreign language input poses certain challenges to students.

As far as gender is concerned, the authors of this paper have argued elsewhere that "[d]ue to their 'real-life connection'"[25] and their closeness to students' lives, TV series have the potential to "trigger moments of self-realisation, also make them suitable to explore issues of culture and gender".[26]

The ensuing section now moves on to looking more closely at the *Star Trek* universe, mainly arguing that its potential for the classroom not only lies in the fact that it represents a media culture material out of which we not only "forge our very identities, our sense of selfhood, our notions of what it means to be male or female"[27] but also "our sense of class, of ethnicity and race of nationality and of 'us' and 'them'"[28] as the example of the (cold war) conflict between the United Federation of Planets and its long-time nemesis the Klingon Empire as an allegory of the Cold War era impressively elucidates.

4. The *Star Trek* Franchise

The catchphrase "Beam me up, Scotty" has made it into popular culture among Trekkies and non-Trekkies alike. Although the phrase was never used in this exact wording in what is retronymously referred to as *Star Trek: The Original Series*, which aired on NBC from 1966 until 1969, it has become part of popular culture to describe the desire to be somewhere else.[29] Since the cancellation of Gene Roddenberry's series about the deep space voyages of the crew of the starship Enterprise, whose mission was to explore new worlds, cultures, and civilisations, the series has spawned a mega-franchise consisting of, for example, additional TV series, films, books, comics, and games.

Almost twenty years after the original *Star Trek*, *Star Trek: The Next Generation* (*TNG*) once again featured the adventures of a star ship crew, now under the command of Captain Jean-Luc Picard. In contrast to the Constitution-class Enterprise-A, the Enterprise-D was a Galaxy-class ship whose mission was to explore not only the Milky Way but the entire Alpha Quadrant. Further series, such as *Star Trek: Deep Space Nine* (1993-1999), *Star Trek: Voyager* (1995-2001), also including the two prequels to the original series *Star Trek: Enterprise* (2001-2005) and the still ongoing series *Star Trek: Discovery* (2017-) followed.[30]

According to Thomas Richards, "there really is nothing like *Star Trek*".[31] In a similar vein, M. Keith Booker states that *Star Trek* is "arguably the best-known single work in the history of science fiction media [...] and has become the gold standard for science fiction television (SFTV) series".[32] *Star Trek*, as any other text, is a product of its time. In spite of that, or exactly because of that, it has always been known for addressing controversial issues such as race, ethnicity, class, or environmental destruction in a progressive way through the allegory of science fiction.

Gender and sexual diversity, however, largely remained a taboo topic for *Star Trek* until the early 1990s. The most prominent example of how the franchise broke significant ground in this area before the turn of the millennium is the well-known depiction of the first on-screen interracial kiss between Captain Kirk and Lieutenant Uhura in the 1968 episode *Plato's Stepchildren*.[33]

Although largely populated by human binary gender, the *Star Trek* universe is also inhabited by other variants of gender, including androgynous, transgender, and hermaphrodite species as well as species with more than two genders. In addition to humanoid bi-gender reproduction, there are also examples of tri-gendered or even multi-gendered ways of reproducing. A more systematic overview of existing forms of gender in Roddenberry's universe, however, are difficult as a large part of the information is non-canonical and thus often differs from fan-wiki to fan-wiki. Moreover, the different parts of the *Star Trek* franchise sometimes provide conflicting information on the species not only in the Alpha but also the other quadrants visited by Federation vessels or individuals.

To mention a few examples of the gender diversity in the Star Trek universe, the Vissians, a species first encountered in the 2150s, have three genders: male, female, and cogenitor, with the cogenitors being discriminated against in society. According to the Memory Alpha wiki, the third gender makes up only 3% of the population and is treated as inferior, existing only for facilitating reproduction between males and females.[34] Species 8472 has even five sexes.

Star Trek: *The Original Series* was largely concerned with issues of gender and race equality, such as "Angel One" (1x13), "The Offspring" (3x16), or "The Host", meeting the zeitgeist of American politics and society at the time. This changed with *TNG*, equally hitting the zeitgeist of the late 1980s and early 1990s. While it is also still concerned with more traditional topics such as women in the workplace – Dr Beverly Crusher as a widowed working mother may serve as an example here – the more progressive and liberal gender ideology of the late 1990s is strongly visible in the sequel. Moreover, it also explores other prevalent topics of its time such as the 1980s' anxieties over sexually transmitted diseases such as AIDS. One example of this is *The Naked Now* (1x3), in which the Enterprise crew is confronted with a contagious illness which causes manic behaviour.[35]

The ensuing section provides a detailed analysis of "The Outcast", which received critical public response not least due to its flaws in creating a genderless alien society.

5. Close Viewing of "The Outcast"

In this message episode, the Enterprise comes to the aid of an androgynous species, referred to as the J'Naii, who have lost one of their shuttles in a so-called null space, an area of space which until then only existed in theory. In J'Naii culture, all gender, sex, and sexuality issues are rendered illegal, and everyone stepping outside the norm is arrested and brainwashed to conform to the cultural idea of what is normal. Despite the hounding of individuals with a deviating gender identity, there is a group of individuals who live out their identities in secret, constantly being in danger of being discovered and prosecuted. Although the episode is not as daring as its obvious antecedent *The Left Hand of Darkness* by Ursula K. Le Guin,[36] in which a human male develops a friendship with an androgyne who becomes female during a mating cycle, in some ways it goes further, since Riker reciprocates both the emotional and sexual attraction that the alien Soren feels for him.

Similar to other episodes, the main plot of the episode is introduced by a voice over by Captain Picard: "Captain's log, star date 45614.6. We have been contacted by an androgynous race called the J'Naii to investigate the mysterious disappearance of one of their shuttlecraft." The log entry is directly followed by a close-up of the bridge crew of the Enterprise closely cooperating with J'Naii scientists. Here, their androgyny is mainly reconstructed through the 'Other'. In contrast to Starfleet staff, the J'naii are wearing loose-fitting one-piece suits and all have short hair, emphasising the conformity of their society as the following screenshot elucidates:

Fig. 1: Screenshot from "The Outcast" (00:00:18)

In the process of their investigation of the null space, Commander Riker learns more about both the J'Naii Soren (Melinda Culea) and the society she lives in. In the course of the episode, the viewer follows closely the development of a short but intimate relationship between Number One and Soren, who eventually opens up about her secret life as a gender-deviant. Similar to Riker, Soren enjoys their time together and seizes the opportunity to spend time among bi-gender people, exploring their views on gender norms and the roles of women and men in society from a diachronic as well as contemporary perspective.

The aspect of gender is already introduced during their first conversation when Riker expresses his confusion about the use of pronouns in a genderless society. Soren, however, does not offer an alternative to the traditional pronouns he/she but simply states that the pronoun the J'Naii use is non-translatable. Nevertheless, Riker appears to understand and apologises in advance for accidentally mis-labeling somebody:

Over a romantic lunch in Ten Forward, Riker and Soren further explore the differences between their societies. During their conversation, it becomes more and more evident that their relationship goes beyond a mere working one. In the course of their conversation, they aim for a more mutual understanding of their cultural differences. By doing so, they touch upon a diverse range of practical issues one can hardly imagine when living in a society that is based on a division between men and women. One example of this is the question of who leads in a dance:

> RIKER: Most people think so. But that's the kind of question that would take a lifetime to answer. Let me ask you, what's it like on a planet where the people have no gender?
> SOREN: I'm afraid I don't understand.
> RIKER: Well, who leads when you dance? If you dance.
> SOREN: We do, and whoever's taller leads.[37]

As already mentioned, for both Riker and Soren, it is difficult to grasp the characteristics of the other culture, alluding to the clear roles of males and females in a bi-gendered society. In line with his series character, Riker reveals himself as the omnipresent womaniser, his almost aggressive heterosexuality pushing Soren even closer to the feminine.[38]

During their mission in the shuttle craft, Soren very directly takes up the issue of the differences between the human binary system and her own genderless society as the following quote shows:

> SOREN: Commander, tell me about your sexual organs.
> RIKER: Er.
> SOREN: Is that an uncomfortable subject for humans?
> RIKER: No, but it doesn't tend to be a topic of casual conversation.
> SOREN: I'm interested in your mating practices. What is involved with two sexes?
> RIKER: Correcting course. Zero two one mark zero.
> SOREN: Mating?
> […]
> SOREN: The idea of gender. It is offensive to my people. You see, long ago we had two sexes, as you do. But we evolved into a higher form. I don't mean to sound insulting, but on my planet, we have been taught that gender is primitive.
> RIKER: Primitive?

SOREN: Less evolved.
RIKER: Maybe so, but sometimes there's a lot to be said for an experience that's primitive.
SOREN: Delta five grid map is fully plotted.

For Riker, talking about sexual organs is obviously unpleasant as his short and rather fact-based biological answers show. The situation thrives on the mix of their engineering endeavour and Soren's advances.

When Soren is injured during an accident and taken to sick bay, she continues her exploration of human gender culture when asking Dr Crusher what it is like to be a female, learning that despite their differences men and women are now considered equal in the human society of the 24th century. During the conversation, it becomes increasingly obvious that the J'Naii Soren is not simply interested in human gender history but even more so looking for a female role model who can help her to find ways of accentuating her own femininity.

When Soren and Riker's relationship gets more intimate, Soren ultimately opens up about her true gender identity and tells him about the underground networks of people with a distinct gender identity on planet as well as the consequences they face upon their discovery. Both Commander Riker's questions ("How long have you known that you were like this?") as well as Soren's answers ("I've known I was different all my life. But I didn't understand how or why until I was older.") resemble the characteristics of a homosexual coming-out description, particularly illustrating many homosexuals' experiences maintaining undercover identities in the fear of being ridiculed, despised, or even mistreated. Especially Soren's school memories of a young J'naii who preferred a male gender and was severely bullied for being different before being taken away and 'cured' by the authorities appears to be an obvious reference to the high number of teens being teased or bullied in our society for having a different sexual orientation or gender identity. Towards the end of their mission, Soren confesses that she identifies as female and that she is physically attracted to Riker. However, she also makes clear that she will not be able to live her gender identity due to the radical treatment she would undergo if she were discovered.

When Riker realises that he is willing to build a serious relationship with Soren, he learns that she has been arrested and taken before a tribunal. He immediately beams down to the planet to find out that the proceedings are already in progress. He pleads to the head of the panel of judges, Noor, for Soren's release. Soren, however, is tired of living her life in secret and makes a final plea for acceptance of herself and all the people with distinct gender identities on her planet:

> SOREN: I am tired of lies. I am female. I was born that way. I have had those feelings, those longings, all of my life. It is not unnatural. I am not sick because I feel this way. I do not need to be helped. I do not need to be cured. What I need, and what all of those who are like me need, is your understanding and your compassion. We have not injured you in any way. And yet, we are scorned and attacked. And all because we are different. What we do is no different from what you do. We talk and laugh. We complain about work and we wonder about growing old. We talk about our families, and we worry about the future. And we cry with each other when things seem hopeless. All of the loving things that you do with each other, that is what we do. And for that we are called misfits and deviants and criminals. What right do you have to punish us? What right do you have to change us? What makes you think you can dictate how people love each other?

Despite Riker's offer to take Soren to the Enterprise and grant her Federation asylum, Soren is taken away for immediate treatment the following day. When he meets Soren upon arriving on the planet once again, she has already been successfully brainwashed.

Even almost 30 years after its first broadcast, Soren's speech feels very contemporary and could easily be viewed in a different context. It supports the notion that transgender, homosexual or even gender-fluid individuals were born in a certain way and did not simply make a choice, as it is often suggested by conservative opinions. However, because Soren's words seem to have no impact and she is still 'cured' and later repents her behavior and feelings, the ending has the potential to leave viewers confused. While the show made a strong case against the discrimination of homo-or transsexual individuals and paints Soren as heroine*, the ending suggests that society might not be inclined to accept such individuals, and everything returns to the way it was before. For this and its conceptional flaws, the episode in question received severe criticism, especially from the *Star Trek* fanbase.

While the episode attempts to emphasise the androgynous nature of the J'Naii through appearance, dress, and behaviour, the J'Naii are entirely cast with women, evoking the image of a completely female (or even lesbian) society. Moreover, while the J'Naii are depicted as a species of androgynes that has moved beyond the concept of gender, their physiological state, apart from a brief and unclear reference to their reproduction, remains largely unexplained. While it is made clear that individuals are forbidden to act or feel like one single gender, also expressed through the lack of performative gender identities, it is not mentioned whether they are still structurally and functionally male and female, hermaphroditic or even asexual.

As already briefly mentioned, "The Outcast" has frequently been interpreted as an allegory about the discrimination homosexuals had to face especially around the time of the gay rights movement and in fewer cases continue to face until today. From a more contemporary perspective, the gay interpretation is even more questioned as the following fan quote taken from a blog shows:

> To me, the entire episode is much more about trans gender identity than anything else. The episode spoke about gender identity, possible gender fluidity, although they seemed to mean "sex" when using gender. I feel like it had some conflicting messages, but I found it a very interesting episode […].[39]

TNG executive producer Rick Berman even reacted to the episode's flaws and its lack to support the homosexual cause by stating that

> We thought we had made a very positive statement about sexual prejudice in a distinctively *Star Trek* way, but we still got letters from those who thought it was just our way of "washing our hands" of the homosexual situation.[40]

Yet, in addition to the general lack of any gay character in the series, homosexuality is not explicitly mentioned in the episode. When Riker and Crusher teach Soren about the achievements of gender equality and the nature of bi-gender relationships, they both exclusively adhere to a heteronormative understanding of gender and thus paint a very simplistic portrait of a society. Furthermore, there was discussion to cast a man as Soren, an idea which was even pushed by Jonathan Frakes, but the idea was dismissed.

Last but not least, the last section discusses the episode at hand from a practical classroom perspective, arguing that despite its flaws it represents a valuable resource for the EFL classroom.

6. Watching *Star Trek: The Next Generation* in the EFL Classroom

As far as explorations of gender identities are concerned, the portrayal of alien societies, often encompassing thought experiments of what alternative perceptions of gender might look like, provides students with the opportunity to explore their own ideas of their sense of self without being the focal point themselves.

Nonetheless, or actually because of its flaws and conflicting depictions of gender identities, the episode at hand is a useful example of the inevitably reciprocal relationship between TV series and society. The following ideas for watching and discussing the episode in the classroom represent a small selection of potential activities, aiming at both raising the students' gender awareness as well as audio-visual competence. While the first set of tasks concentrates on the episode itself and the context in which it was created, the second set of tasks 'beams' the episode to the 21st-century, encouraging students to analyse it from a more contemporary perspective as well as relating it to their own contexts and experiences. In order to provide a more structured approach to the episode, the first set is structured in a series of pre-, while-, and post-activities, while the second set follows a more task-based approach.

As already discussed in section two of this paper, understanding videos is a matter of decoding the language of moving images, including light, sound effects, cuts, dialogues, voice overs, and many more aspects. While students may be used to often passively consuming videos in their life outside the classroom, this does not necessarily mean that they possess the ability to unpack the full meaning of video content in a more analytical way. For this and other reasons, viewing activities should be done in small steps, particularly emphasising the purpose(s) of the viewings as well as the activities.

Before watching the beginning of the episode at hand, students should be told that they are going to watch and analyse one episode from the series *Star Trek: The Next Generation.* The authors' experiences from discussing the series in secondary as well as tertiary classrooms has shown that *Star Trek* is not always well known among the generation Z. Therefore, students should be asked if and what they know about *Star Trek*. One way of doing this would be to create as short classroom survey, for example including the following questions:

- *Have you ever heard of or even watched 'Star Trek'?*
- *(If answer to one is 'yes') What comes to your mind when you think of 'Star Trek'?*
- *Do you know the following characters from Star Trek: Captain Jean-Luc Picard, First Officer Riker, Lieutenant Commander Data?*

The advantages of survey tools like SurveyMonkey[41] are that they raise the students' interest in a topic and give them the opportunity to discuss a topic in a more interactive way as they create input for face-to-face classes. Furthermore, the students' media skills are trained while they simultaneously focus on both language and content. Once the students' answers have been discussed, the students are informed that they are going to listen to the beginning of one episode from *Star Trek: The Next Generation* with the title "The Outcast". Here, possible interim steps would be to collect students' ideas about why the series is called *The Next Generation or* what an episode entitled "The Outcast" could be about. Following this, the students are asked to close their eyes and listen to the first 41 seconds of the episode. The extract introduces not only the theme of the episode but also all of its major characters, already mentioning the aliens' distinct way of living. Tell students to listen to any sounds in the extract and to identify what the episode could be about. After the second listening, students open their eyes and write down everything they noticed. The results are then collected and discussed with the whole class. The advantage of listening to the beginning of the episode instead of watching it is mainly that the students' attention is entirely drawn to the sound level. Possible aspects which could be discussed here include: the captain's log-book entry, the androgynous nature of the J'Naii as well as the purpose of the mission. More detailed questions which could be asked here include:

- *What is the purpose of the Federation's cooperation with the J'Naii?*
- *Can you tell which of the voices belongs to the androgynous character? How?*
- *Which sound can you identify? How do they hint at the fact that the scene takes place on a spaceship?*

Following this, the students should be asked to draw or describe the androgynous race Captain Picard mentions in his log entry. Afterwards, the students are shown the scene they already listened to. Here, discussion questions regarding the J'Naii's gender identity such as the below could be based on the screenshot depicted in Figure 1:

- *How is the J'Naii's androgyny expressed here?*
- *How is the race's clothing used to establish conformity?*
- *What are possible purposes of the different colours they wear?*
- *Compare the Starfleet uniforms with the J'Naii's clothes. Where do you see similarities/differences?*
- *Are the J'Naii portrayed by male or female actors?*
- *What are the effects of the direct comparison between Worf, Data, Picard & Riker as well as the J'Naii?*

Moreover, the spatial proximity between Riker and Soren in combination with her distance to the J'Naii on the bridge already leads us to the following assumptions: She is higher in rank than the other J'Naii on board as she is not only allowed to speak but also sit next to the first officer on board the Enterprise. Furthermore, her physical closeness to Riker foreshadows the coming relationship between the two and her resulting disassociation from her planet's gender norms.

Following this introduction, the remaining part of the episode can be presented to the students either in either one or several sittings. Especially the conversations discussed in more detail in section three offer many opportunities for a more detailed scene analysis, especially in terms of a more discourse-oriented discussion of how gender is reconstructed in daily interaction. Here, while-viewing activities should give students the possibility to explore audio-visual communication techniques, gain a deeper understanding of the roles of the key elements of moving images as text, including but in no way limited to the characters, the narrative (for example, setting, structuring of time, point of view) as well as production elements (e.g. camera angles, lighting, sound, mise-en-scène), and assess the technical and aesthetic quality of audio-visual productions

In the following, the lunch scene between Commander Riker and Soren (08:24-12:45) will be used as an example of which questions to ask when analysing a scene in more detail. After having worked in the shuttle, Riker invites Soren for lunch in Ten Forward, the lounge facility of the Enterprise D. During the conversation, Riker and Soren continue their conversation about J'Naii culture and the growing attraction between the two is increasingly tangible. Their date comes to an abrupt end when they are joined by Soren's former flight trainer Krite, which causes Soren to quickly leave the table in order not to make Krite suspicious of the nature of her relationship with Commander Riker. In contrast to Commander Riker and Soren, who are spatially distant to each other, in the foreground of the frame, two people engaged in a conversation of an obviously more romantic nature can be observed. The sudden appearance of Krite not only serves as an additional contrast factor but also triggers an interesting change of behaviour in Soren.

In order to analyse the scene more closely, the class is divided into three focus groups, with each group concentrating on a different aspect of the scene. Each group is given a set of a while-viewing questions. In order to facilitate a better understanding, the scene should be viewed at least twice, each time giving the students ample time to write down their thoughts. After the second (or third viewing), the groups are given time to discuss their results and add missing information. The transcript of the scene can be handed out to more challenged students or groups. The following overview provides possible questions for each of the aspects suggested to be included in the analysis:[42]

Characters: *analyse the characters in the scene in more detail. Pay special attention to their physical attributes, voices, actions, and role(s). What are the characters' motivations? Where are the characters based in the frame? What are their key phrases?*

Narrative: *analyse the scene with regard to its setting (location, background), structuring of time, point of view, cause and effect, themes and issues, opening and closure. Possible questions include: What is the exact location of the scene and what is its relevance with regard to the plot? From whose point of view is the narrative presented? Which themes and issues are introduced in the scene?*

Production elements: analyse the scene with regard to its production elements (camera work, lighting, mise-en-scène, editing, sound, acting/performance). Possible questions include: *Which camera angles are used? What are the shot distances? What meaning is created for an audience by using different shot sizes, movement, and camera angles? Which lighting is used and which atmosphere does it create? How is atmosphere created via the sound design?*

The class having analysed this and/or other scenes in detail, post-viewing activities serve to encourage students to engage with the themes of the episode in even more detail, use the language that came from the video, or trigger different views of their own world. As far as the scene at hand is concerned, the following tasks could be set:

- *Find a soundtrack to accompany the scene. Justify your choice.*
- *Rewrite/continue the scene. What could have happened if they had not been interrupted by Krite?*
- *Write down the conversation of the couple in the background. How do they comment on Riker and Soren?*
- *Rewrite the conversation between Soren and Riker from today's perspective, considering that society has become more inclusive and that there is a variety of genders and sexual orientations visible in today's society.*

In addition, the old English nursery rhyme "What Are Little Boys Made Of?" which Riker quotes when asked by Soren to tell her more about the differences between males and females can serve as a basis for discussing past and present gender stereotypes.

The rhyme also offers a starting point for students to reflect on their own gender stereotypes. The video "Boys and Girls on Stereotypes",[43] which interviews children around the age of ten about their opinions on what it means to be a girl or a boy, can be employed to summarise still existing gender stereotypes about different genders and encourage students to collect their own stereotypes and critically reflect on them.

Other tasks going beyond a step-by-step analysis of individual scenes and taking a broader look at the episode with a primarily contemporary gender lens could include:

- *How can you tell that it is episodic television? How does the episodic character of the series influence the development of Riker and Soren's relationship?*
- *Why do you think the J'Naii were entirely cast with women? What are the effects of casting an androgynous race only with women?*
- *The corrective treatment Soren undergoes after her coming-out is said to be a reference to the conversion therapy approaches homosexuals had and still have to undergo when coming out as gay.*[44] *Do some research on the topic. Which different types of corrective treatment are there? Which techniques have been used by psychologists to change sexual orientation and gender identity? Find examples of where and in which contexts conversion therapy is still practiced.*

- *Research the actor Melinda Culea who played Soren. Why did she leave the famous TV series the 'A-Team' in the middle of season 2? What does it tell you about the role of women in the TV landscape of the 1980s?*
- *Captain Picard denies any help for Soren by referring to the Prime Directive. Discuss Starfleet's Prime Directive with regard to Soren's rights as an individual. How would you have reacted?*

Last but not least, the ensuing lesson plan suggests using the episode as a prompt to discuss the situation of transgender people in today's society, which is, in some way, comparable to the discrimination and fight for recognition homosexuals had to experience around the time of the gay rights movement.

Topic	*Star Trek: Next Generation* ("The Outcast")
Objectives	To develop and practise students' audio-visual competence vocabulary connected with gender concepts awareness of gender as a social construct knowledge of the situation of transgender individuals in today's society
Age	Secondary students (16-18)
Level	CEF level B2 and above
Time	90 mins.
Materials/media	Laptop, projector, board/white board, question sheet, empty note cards
Introduction	In this lesson, students will analyse selected scenes from *Star Trek: The Next Generation:* "The Outcast" and engage in discussions of the episode's references to transgender individuals. To do so, they are acquainted with the terms gender/transgender and presented with several scenes from the episode, asked to analyse them with regards to the reconstructions of gender and evaluate the connection to transgender individuals today.
1. Introduction to the topic (10 mins.)	Students watch "Like You" and briefly summarise the content.
2. Focus on vocabulary (previewing task 1) (10 mins.)	Students define the terms 'gender' and 'transgender' as well as biological sex, sexuality, and sexual orientation. Students make a list of

	problems transgender people encounter in today's society.
3. Introduction to the series (previewing task 2) (10 mins.)	Tell students that they are going watch one episode from the TV show *Star Trek: The Next Generation* which focuses on gender. Students complete a survey (see section 5 for possible survey questions). The answers are discussed in class.
4. Focus on the story: comprehension (15 mins.)	Students watch the first 41 seconds of the episode in form of a blind viewing. Students are given a viewing sheet with guiding questions (see section 5).
5. Extension 1: in-depth viewing (15 mins.)	Students are divided into 3-6 groups and analyse the lunch scene in their groups (see section 4 for transcript), particularly focusing on the reconstructions of gender in the show.
5.1 Differentiation	Transcript and/or vocabulary lists are provided.
6. Evaluation and discussion (10mins.)	Each group presents their results. Alternatively, each group analyses a different scene.
7. Extension 2: final-viewing (10 mins.)	Students watch Soren's speech (see section 4 for transcript) and the accompanying blog post (see section 5). Students discuss how the episode could be interpreted as having a transgender focus.
8. Setting homework (3 mins.)	Students select a scene from their favorite TV show, focusing on gender and bring it to class (video or transcript).
9. Optional follow-up task	Students watch the end of the episode when Soren undergoes conversion therapy. Students research whether conversion therapy is still used today and how it affects people who have undergone it.

Table 1: Lesson Sequence on Teaching *Star Trek*

The lesson starts off by asking the students if they know which group of people the term transgender refers to. Despite the fact that trans identities "were one of the most written about subjects of the late twentieth century",[45] it is unlikely that all students know what the term means and, even more so, what it entails to be transgender. Therefore, the following definition can be used to foster an understanding. According to the American Psychological Association the term transgender is

> [an] adjective that is an umbrella term used to describe the full range of people whose gender identity and/or gender role do not conform to what is typically associated with their sex assigned at birth.[46]

In addition, there is a plethora of online video sources available to familiarise students further with the issue. These include:
Beyond Gender - A short film by Daniel Brereton.[47] This short video depicts various gender-nonconforming people expressing their view on gender. It provides an insight into the complexity of gender and shows how different people interpret it within the context of their own gender expressions. The different viewpoints explored in this video illustrate how gender can be expressed in many ways and that it is possible to not conform to what society has deemed to be appropriate.

Like You – Trans Short Film[48]: this short film starts out as any other typical boy-meets girl story as a boy from England comes to work on a remote farm on an island and meets the daughter of the farmer. However, they soon realise that they have much more in common than they originally thought. The firm was produced by an all trans team and cast and briefly explores the struggles of growing up transgender and the importance of support and kinship.

Kids Meet a Gender Non-Conforming Person | Kids Meet | HiHo – Kids[49]: as alluded to in the title, the video depicts children and young teens meeting a gender non-conforming person. They are then allowed to ask questions and discuss topics like gender as a spectrum, gender expressions and personal pronouns. Because most kids in the video are aged between approximately six and twelve and, therefore, phrase their questions accordingly, this video might be more suited for a younger audience.

The students are then shown posts from a blog on "The Outcast" in which users criticise the 'gay interpretation' of the episode, mainly arguing that Soren is not attracted to the same sex but identifies as female and is attracted to men.[50] The blog posts can be read and discussed in class.

Last but not least, students look at Soren's final speech which she holds before the tribunal. Here, they can, for example, be asked to analyse the speech in more detail or change it to an apologia for other marginalised groups such as homosexuals or transgender people and discuss the effects it has on the audience. Here, changing the beginning "I am tired of lies. I am female." to "I am tired of lies. I am transgender." already changes the whole tone of Soren's public coming-out.

7. Conclusion

Science fiction has a long tradition of experimenting with alternative genders or even the absence of gender. This article focused on one selected episode from the realm of *Star Trek*. Despite the first rollouts for out gay characters in more recent *Star Trek* series, with "The Outcast" the authors of this paper deliberately chose an episode which seems rather quaint but remains as relevant as it did in 1992. The J'Naii depict a society which has evolved beyond gender, resulting in severe discriminatory practices of any gender deviant individuals comparable to the prosecution of homosexuals during the better half of the past century. The episode was discussed in its own right while, at the same time, shedding light on its potential for discussing gender-related issues in today's EFL classrooms, particularly focusing on its transgender interpretations.

Notes

1 Her stories were published under the male pseudonym James Tiptree, Jr.

2 Luckhurst, Roger (2005). *Science Fiction (Cultural History of Literature)*. Cambridge: Polity Press, 3.

3 Here, the acronym LGBT is used because this particular version was established in the 1990s with the rise of "bisexual, transgender, and queer movements". Iovannone, Jeffrey J. (2018). "A Brief History of the LGBTQ Initialism: How Did the LGBTQ Community Come to be Known as Such?" *Queer History for the People – Medium* 09 June 2018: n. pag. Web. 03 May 2019 <https://medium.com/queer-history-for-the-people/a-brief-history-of-the-lgbtq-initialism-e89db1cf06e3>.

4 Le Guin, Ursula K. (1993). "Introduction." *The Norton Book of Science Fiction.* Eds. Ursula Le Guin and Brian Attebery. Norton: New York, 15-44, 27.

5 Merrick, Helen (2003). "Gender in Science Fiction." *The Cambridge Companion to Science Fiction.* Eds. Edward James and Farah Mendlesohn. Cambridge: Cambridge University Press, 241-252, 242.

6 Attebery, Brian (2002). *Decoding Gender in Science Fiction*. Abingdon-on-Thames: Routledge.

7 Merrick (2003), 242.

8 *Ibid.*

9 Pearson, Wendy (2003). "Science Fiction and Queer Theory." *The Cambridge Companion to Science Fiction.* Eds. Edward James and Farah Mendlesohn. Cambridge: Cambridge University Press, 149-162, 149.

10 *Ibid.*

11 Seed, David (2011). *Science Fiction: A Very Short Introduction*. Oxford: Oxford University Press, 2.

12 Sunderland, Jane (1992). "Gender in the EFL Classroom." *ELT Journal* 46.1, 81-91.

13 *Ibid.*

14 Hughes, Sarah (2016). "Sexuality Today: How We Embarked on a New Age of Freedom and Tolerance." *The Guardian* 04 June 2016: n. pag. Web. 07 May 2019 <https://www.theguardian.com/society/2016/jun/04/same-sex-relationships-gender-fluid-queer-kristen-stewart>.

15 Udry, Richard J. (1994). "The Nature of Gender." *Demography* 31.4: 561-573, 561. Web. 10 November 2017 <https://www.unc.edu/courses/2006fall/econ/586/001/Readings/Udry_Nature_Gender.pdf>.

16 Eisenmann, Maria, and Christian Ludwig (2018). "Introduction." *Queer Beats. Teaching Gender and Literature in the EFL Classroom*. Eds. Maria Eisenmann and Christian Ludwig. Frankfurt am Main: Peter Lang, 17-38, 21.

17 Aikhenvald, Alexandra Y. (2016). *How Gender Shapes the World*. Oxford: Oxford University Press, 1.

18 As defined, for example, in publications such as Decke-Cornill, Helene, and Laurenz Volkmann (eds.) (2007). *Gender Studies and Foreign Language Teaching*. Tübingen: Narr and Elsner, Daniela, and Viviane Lohe (eds.) (2016). *Gender and Language Learning: Research and Practice*. Tübingen: Narr.

[19] Volkmann, Laurenz (2016). "Gender and Literature: Creating Gender Awareness." *Gender and Language Learning: Research and Practice*. Eds. Daniela Elsner and Viviane Lohe. Tübingen: Narr, 113-132, 119.

[20] Volkmann, Laurenz (2007). "Gender Studies and Literature Didactics: Research and Teaching – Worlds Apart?" *Gender Studies and Foreign Language Teaching*. Eds. Helene Decke-Cornill and Laurenz Volkmann. Tübingen: Narr, 161-184, 166.

[21] See, e.g. various articles in Eisenmann and Ludwig (eds.) (2018).

[22] Lohe, Viviane, and Britta Viebrock (2018). "Deconstructing Gender Stereotypes in EFL Classrooms Through Contemporary Movies." *Queer Beats. Teaching Gender and Literature in the EFL Classroom*. Eds. Maria Eisenmann and Christian Ludwig. Frankfurt am Main: Peter Lang, 413-438, 413.

[23] König, Lotta, Sonja Lewin and Carola Surkamp (2016). "What Does it Mean to Teach about Gender?" *Gender and Language Learning: Research and Practice.* Eds. Daniela Elsner and Viviane Lohe. Tübingen: Narr, 19-36, 26.

[24] Urisman, Svetlana (2014). "How to use TV Series, Trailers and Films in Language Class." *British Council.* Web. 10 November 2018 <https://www.britishcouncil.org/voices-magazine/how-to-use-tv-series trailers-films-language-class>.

[25] Heß, Nadja, and Christian Ludwig (2018). "'Look at that baby with those cream-puffs.' – Exploring LGBTQ Life Through American TV Series in the EFL Classroom." *Queer Beats. Teaching Gender and Literature in the EFL Classroom.* Eds. Maria Eisenmann and Christian Ludwig. Frankfurt am Main: Peter Lang, 359-384, 367.

[26] *Ibid.*

[27] Keller, Douglas (2011). "Cultural Studies, Multiculturalism and Media Culture." *Gender, Race and Class in Media: A Critical Reader.* Eds. Gail Dines and Jean MacMahon Humes. Thousand Oaks: Sage, 7-18.

[28] *Ibid.*

[29] "Beam me up." *Green's Dictionary of Slang*. 2019. Web. 07 May 2019 <https://greensdictofslang.com/search/basic?q=Beam+me+up>.

[30] In early 2020, CBS released the new *Star Trek* series *Picard* in which Captain Jean Luc Picard will once again be played by Patrick Stewart.

[31] Richards, Thomas (1997). *The Meaning of Star Trek: An Excursion into the Myth and Marvel of the Star Trek Universe.* New York: Random House, 4.

32 Booker, Keith M. (2008). "The Politics of Star Trek." *The Essential Science Fiction Television Reader*. Ed. Jay P. Telotte. Lexington: The University Press of Kentucky, 195-208, 195.

33 It has been controversially discussed whether this was actually a kiss or not. It is worth noting in passing that the original series also tackled gender-related issues such as stereotypes in "Turnabout Intruder" (1969).

34 Memory Alpha. "Vissian." *Memory Alpha.* FANDOM. Web. 06 May 2019< http://memory-alpha.wikia.com/wiki/Vissian>.

35 *Star Trek: Discovery* shows an even greater gender diversity in Starfleet. To mention but one example, the series features the gay relationship between Paul Stamets and Hugh Culber. Largely ignoring any common stereotypes about homosexuals, it is the normality of their relationship which is emphasised in the series. It is also worth noting that both actors are openly gay.

36 Shipley, Elizabeth (2018). "'She was probably male': Exploring Gender with Science Fiction in the EFL Classroom." *Queer Beats. Teaching Gender and Literature in the EFL Classroom.* Eds. Maria Eisenmann and Christian Ludwig. Frankfurt am Main: Peter Lang, 175-194.

37 All transcripts are taken from this website: Chrissie's Transcripts Site. "The Outcast." Web. 07 May 2019 <http://www.chakoteya.net/NextGen/217.htm>.

38 In this episode, other characters weigh in on the gender debate as well. Worf's masculine side is accentuated as, for example, in the poker game scene. Through scenes like this one, varying notions of masculinity and femininity are displayed and debated.

39 Blog post taken from this website: Reddit. "r/startrek." Web. 07 May 2019 <https://www.reddit.com/r/startrek/comments/5mcra6/for_me_tngs_the_out cast_is_more_about_trans/>.

40 Berman in Nemecek, Larry (1992). *The* Star Trek The Next Generation *Companion.* New York: Pocket Books, 217.

41 Survey Monkey. Web. 06 May 2019 <https://de.surveymonkey.com>.

42 Australian Centre for the Moving Image: Education Resource. "Guide to Film Analysis." ACMI Masaryk University. Web. 07 May 2019 <https://is.muni.cz /el/1421/jaro2017/AJ18085/film_analysis.pdf?lang=en>.

43 "Boys and Girls on Stereotypes." (2019). *YouTube*. Web. 07 May 2019 <https://www.youtube.com/watch?v=aTvGSstKd5Y>.

44 Ramaswany, Chitra (2018). "'I still have flashbacks': The 'Global epidemic' of LGBT Conversion Therapy." *The Guardian* 08 August 2018: n. pag. Web. 2 March 2020 <https://www.theguardian.com/world/2018/aug/08/i-still-have-flashbacks-the-global-epidemic-of-lgbt-conversion-therapy>.

45 Whittle, Stephen (2006). "Foreword." *The Transgender Studies Reader.* Eds. Susan Stryker and Stephen Whittle. New York: Routledge, 11-16, 11.

46 American Psychological Association (2015). "Guidelines for Psychological Practice with Transgender and Gender Nonconforming People." *American Psychologist* 70.9, 832-864, 863.

47 "Beyond Gender – A Short Film by Daniel Brereton." (2019). *YouTube*. Web. 07 May 2019 <https://www.youtube.com/watch?v=TCwUL0iak5U>.

48 "Like You – Trans Short Film." (2019). *YouTube*. Web. 07 May 2019. < https://www.youtube.com/watch?v=Y3LddZubx88>.

49 "Kids Meet a Gender Non-Conforming Person | Kids Meet | HiHo Kids." (2019). *YouTube*. Web. 07 May 2019 <https://www.youtube.com /watch?v=DZsBei4nCkU>.

50 Reddit. "r/startrek." Web. 07 May 2019 <https://www.reddit.com/r/startrek /comments/5mcra6/for_me_tngs_the_outcast_is_more_about_trans/>.

Bibliography

Primary Texts

"Angel One." *Star Trek: The Next Generation.* Dir. Michael Rhodes. 1988. First-run syndication.

"Beyond Gender – A Short Film by Daniel Brereton." (2019). *YouTube*. Web. 07 May 2019 <https://www.youtube.com/watch?v=TCwUL0iak5U>.

"Boys and Girls on Stereotypes." (2019). *YouTube*. Web. 07 May 2019 <https://www.youtube.com/watch?v=aTvGSstKd5Y>.

"The Host." *Star Trek: The Next Generation.* Dir. Marvin V. Rush. 1991. Syndication.

"Kids Meet a Gender Non-Conforming Person | Kids Meet | HiHo Kids." (2019). *YouTube*. Web. 07 May 2019 <https://www.youtube.com /watch?v=DZsBei4nCkU>.

Le Guin, Ursula K. (1969). *The Left Hand of Darkness*. New York: Ace Books.

"Like You - Trans Short Film." (2019). *YouTube*. Web. 07 May 2019. < https://www.youtube.com/watch?v=Y3LddZubx88>.

"The Naked Now." *Star Trek: The Next Generation.* Dir. Paul Lynch. 1987. First-run syndication.

"The Offspring." *Star Trek: The Next Generation.* Dir. Jonathan Frakes. 1990. First-run syndication.

"The Outcast." *Star Trek: The Next Generation.* Dir. Robert Scheerer. 1992. First-run syndication.

"Plato's Stepchildren." *Star Trek: The Original Series.* Dir. David Alexander. 1968. NBC.

Star Trek: Deep Space Nine. Creator Rick Berman. 1993-1999. Syndication.

Star Trek: Discovery. Creator Alex Kurtzman. 2017-. CBS.

Star Trek: Enterprise. Creator Rick Berman. 2001-2005. UPN.

Star Trek: The Next Generation. Creator Rick Berman. 1987-1994. First-run syndication.

Star Trek: The Original Series. Creator Gene Roddenberry. 1966-1967. NBC.

Star Trek: Picard. Creator Alex Kurtzman. 2020-.CBS.

"Turnabout Intruder." *Star Trek: The Original Series.* Dir. Herb Wallerstein. NBC

Star Trek: Voyager. Creator Rick Berman. 1995-2001. UPN.

Secondary Literature

Aikhenvald, Alexandra Y. (2016). *How Gender Shapes the World.* Oxford University Press: Oxford.

American Psychological Association (2015). "Guidelines for Psychological Practice with Transgender and Gender Nonconforming People." *American Psychologist* 70.9, 832-864.

Attebery, Brian (2002). *Decoding Gender in Science Fiction.* Abigndon-on-Thames: Routledge.

Australian Centre for the Moving Image: Education Resource. "Guide to Film Analysis." ACMI Masaryk University. Web. 07 May 2019 <https://is.muni.cz/el/1421/jaro2017/AJ18085/film_analysis.pdf?lang=en>.

"Beam me up." *Green's Dictionary of Slang.* 2019. Web. 07 May 2019 <https://greensdictofslang.com/search/basic?q=Beam+me+up>.

Booker, Keith M. (2008). "The Politics of Star Trek." *The Essential Science Fiction Television Reader.* Ed. Jay P. Telotte. Lexington: The University Press of Kentucky, 195-208.

Chrissie's Transcripts Site. "The Outcast." Web. 07 May 2019 <http://www.chakoteya.net/NextGen/217.htm>.

Decke-Cornill, Helene, and Laurenz Volkmann (eds.) (2007). *Gender Studies and Foreign Language Teaching*. Tübingen: Narr.

Eisenmann, Maria, and Christian Ludwig (2018). "Introduction." *Queer Beats. Teaching Gender and Literature in the EFL Classroom.* Eds. Maria Eisenmann, and Christian Ludwig. Frankfurt am Main: Peter Lang, 17-38.

Eisenmann, Maria, and Christian Ludwig (eds.) (2018). *Queer Beats. Teaching Gender and Literature in the EFL Classroom.* Frankfurt am Main: Peter Lang.

Elsner, Daniela, and Viviane Lohe (eds.) (2016). *Gender and Language Learning: Research and Practice*. Tübingen: Narr.

Heß, Nadja, and Christian Ludwig (2018). "'Look at that baby with those creampuffs.' – Exploring LGBTQ Life Through American TV Series in the EFL Classroom." *Queer Beats. Teaching Gender and Literature in the EFL Classroom.* Eds. Maria Eisenmann and Christian Ludwig. Frankfurt am Main: Peter Lang, 359-384.

Hughes, Sarah (2016). "Sexuality Today: How We Embarked on a New Age of Freedom and Tolerance." *The Guardian* 04 June 2016: n. pag. Web. 07 May 2019 <https://www.theguardian.com/society/2016/jun/04/same-sex-relationships-gender-fluid-queer-kristen-stewart>.

Iovannone, Jeffrey J. (2018). "A Brief History of the LGBTQ Initialism: How Did the LGBTQ Community Come to be Known as Such?." *Queer History for the People – Medium* 09 June 2018: n. pag. Web. 03 May 2019 <https://medium.com/queer-history-for-the-people/a-brief-history-of-the-lgbtq-initialism-e89db1cf06e3>.

Keller, Douglas (2011). "Cultural Studies, Multiculturalism and Media Culture." *Gender, Race and Class in Media: A Critical Reader.* Eds. Gail Dines and Jean MacMahon Humes. Thousand Oaks: Sage, 7-18.

König, Lotta, Sonja Lewin and Carola Surkamp (2016). "What Does it Mean to Teach about Gender?" *Gender and Language Learning: Research and Practice.* Eds. Daniela Elsner and Viviane Lohe. Tübingen: Narr, 19-36.

Le Guin, Ursula K. (1993). "Introduction." *The Norton Book of Science Fiction.* Eds. Ursula Le Guin and Brian Attebery. Norton: New York, 15-44.

Lohe, Viviane, and Britta Viebrock (2018). "Deconstructing Gender Stereotypes in EFL Classrooms Through Contemporary Movies." *Queer Beats.* EFL Classrooms Through Contemporary Movies." *Queer Beats. Teaching Gender and Literature in the EFL Classroom*. Eds. Maria Eisenmann and Christian Ludwig. Frankfurt am Main: Peter Lang, 413-438.

Luckhurst, Roger (2005). *Science Fiction (Cultural History of Literature).* Cambridge: Polity Press.

Memory Alpha. "Vissian." *Memory Alpha.* FANDOM. Web. 07 May 2019 <http://memory-alpha.wikia.com/wiki/Vissian>.

Merrick, Helen (2003). "Gender in Science Fiction." *The Cambridge Companion to Science Fiction.* Eds. Edward James and Farah Mendlesohn. Cambridge: Cambridge University Press, 241-252.

Nemecek, Larry (1992). *The* Star Trek The Next Generation *Companion.* New York: Pocket Books.

Pearson, Wendy (2003). "Science Fiction and Queer Theory." *The Cambridge Companion to Science Fiction.* Eds. Edward James and Farah Mendlesohn. Cambridge: Cambridge University Press, 149-162.

Ramaswany, Chitra (2018). "'I still have flashbacks': The 'Global epidemic' of LGBT Conversion Therapy." The Guardian 08 August 2018: n. pag. Web. 2 March 2020 <https://www.theguardian.com/world/2018/aug/08/i-still-have-flashbacks-the-global-epidemic-of-lgbt-conversion-therapy>.

Reddit. "r/startrek." Web. 07 May 2019 <https://www.reddit.com/r/startrek /comments/5mcra6/for_me_tngs_the_outcast_is_more_about_trans/>.

Richards, Thomas (1997). *The Meaning of Star Trek: An Excursion into the Myth and Marvel of the Star Trek Universe.* New York: Random House.

Seed, David (2011). *Science Fiction: A Very Short Introduction*. Oxford: Oxford University Press.

Shipley, Elizabeth (2018). "'She was probably male': Exploring Gender with Science Fiction in the EFL Classroom." *Queer Beats. Teaching Gender and Literature in the EFL Classroom.* Eds. Maria Eisenmann and Christian Ludwig. Frankfurt am Main: Peter Lang, 175-194.

Sunderland, Jane (1992). "Gender in the EFL Classroom." *ELT Journal* 46.1, 81-91.

Survey Monkey. Web. 06 May 2019 <https://de.surveymonkey.com>.

Udry, Richard J. (1994). "The Nature of Gender." *Demography* 31.4: 561– 573. Web. 10 November 2017 <https://www.unc.edu/courses/2006fall /econ/586/001/Readings/Udry_Nature_Gender.pdf>.

Urisman, Svetlana (2014). "How to use TV Series, Trailers and Films in Language Class." *British Council.* Web. 10 November 2018 <https://www.britishcouncil.org/voices-magazine/how-to- use-tv-series-trailers-films-language-class>.

Volkmann, Laurenz (2007). "Gender Studies and Literature Didactics: Research and Teaching – Worlds Apart?" *Gender Studies and Foreign Language Teaching*. Eds. Helene Decke-Cornill and Laurenz Volkmann. Tübingen: Narr, 161-184.

--- (2016). "Gender and Literature: Creating Gender Awareness." *Gender and Language Learning: Research and Practice*. Eds. Daniela Elsner and Viviane Lohe. Tübingen: Narr, 113-132.

Whittle, Stephen (2006). "Foreword." *The Transgender Studies Reader.* Eds. Susan Stryker and Stephen Whittle. New York: Routledge, 11-16.

Dennis Weißenfels (Duisburg-Essen)

Yet Another "Giant Leap for Mankind": Teaching *The Martian* and a Human Mission to Mars to Students in Upper Secondary Education

1. Introduction

This paper will take a closer look at the 2015 science-fiction film *The Martian*, highlighting ways in which it could be implemented in the English as a foreign language (EFL) classroom in upper secondary education. Directed by Ridley Scott, the film stars Matt Damon as Mark Watney, the hero of the story, who ends up stranded alone on Mars and has to work his way to be rescued. In the way it is set up, it offers a vivid and exciting depiction of a humanity that has successfully landed on Mars. Its audience is one that lives in a time that is only one small step away from witnessing a real-life human mission to the red planet. Due to its multifaceted nature, the film opens up great opportunities to connect with a variety of different subjects in school curricula, such as physics, biology, politics, history or economics. This paper will highlight its potential to elucidate psychological contexts in the EFL classroom in particular, which can be further related to the subjects of pedagogy, sociology, ethics and religion.

The Mars mission is a topic of great cultural importance. If one glances over the science fiction sections on online media-services providers such as Netflix or Amazon, one does not need to search long until one will stumble across films or series featuring human missions to colonise Mars. Be it the 2016 semi-documentary series *Mars*, the 2015 film *The Martian* or the 2015 science-fiction series *The Expanse*, the prospect of human travel to Mars for the purpose of establishing a permanent settlement seems to capture the imagination of a wide audience. Similarly, a *YouTube* search of 'Mars Mission' will conjure up a great variety of videos including documentaries, explanations by professionals and visions by enthusiasts and adventurous LEGO and Playmobil episodes for children.

In fact, there have already been a number of mission proposals in which people could send applications to become members of potential Mars missions. Mars One was one example of this. According to its website, its goal was to "establish a permanent human settlement on Mars", inviting the public to "Come along!"[1] Due to financial issues, the project was cancelled early in 2019. However, out of more than 200,000 people interested in the project, a total of 4,227 people had officially registered for the program, indicating a serious public desire for the mission.[2] The most prominent and probably also the most promising proposal of that sort has been made by SpaceX, a private American aerospace manufacturer founded by entrepreneur Elon Musk. Under the slogan "Making Life Multiplanetary", the company made it their aim to send humans to Mars as early as 2024 to eventually establish "a self-sustaining civilization on Mars", captivating visitors of their website with their latest generation of real space transportation technologies such as their Starship.[3]

Students growing up in this day and age find themselves in a world that exhibits a renewed fascination with space travel that had been limited to the world of fiction in previous decades. And while it is still unclear when the first actual mission will be launched, both the will and the technology to accomplish it are now a reality. It is no surprise that SpaceX's test launches of their Falcon Heavy rocket have drawn the interest of the public and become global media events. Reaching a total of more than 2.3 million views, their launch in 2018 became the second biggest *YouTube* livestream in history, second only to the Red Bull Stratos jump in 2012, "which racked in a ridiculous 8 million concurrent views".[4] That both events are related to space travel is a fact which should most certainly arouse suspicion that something big is going on in that field. And while SpaceX's Falcon launches are certainly more interesting from a technological perspective, the fact that the Stratos jump involved Felix Baumgartner as a human pushing the boundaries while putting himself at severe risk is definitely a factor that led to the large number of viewers. Human endangerment always evokes greater emotional responses from an audience than technological display.

A human mission to Mars is on the crossroads between real contemporary technology and the world of science fiction. While for the most part, science fiction in the tradition of *Star Trek* largely produced visions of a distant future on the basis of theoretical science, the type of science fiction that deals with Mars missions connects to a foreseeable future that will probably become a reality in most of our very lifetimes. This gives teachers a unique opportunity to capture students' imagination through a phenomenon in their own *Lebenswelten* that still has one foot in the excitement of the adventurous unknown.

In order to provide teaching suggestions for the film *The Martian* as a manifestation of those cultural trends in the EFL classroom of upper secondary education, this paper will first put the Mars mission into a brief historical context. In the chapter following this, I will analyse *The Martian* as a specific type of science fiction. And in the final chapter, I will present a possible lesson plan with key tasks for teaching the film, concentrating on competences related to English but also suggesting connections to competences related to other subjects that have a psychological dimension.

2. The Mars Mission in Context

Mars has been an object of continuous fascination for humans at least since the late nineteenth century. For a long time, ever since its discovery by Galileo in 1610, humans have speculated what the red planet might have in store for human visitors. Speculations of that sort went as far as to assume that Mars did not only provide a habitable environment but that it actually was inhabited by human-like intelligent civilisations. Most of that speculation came to a definite halt with the Mariner 4 flyby of Mars in 1964, which revealed the red planet to be a heavily cratered and desolate world with a thin atmosphere that has not much more to offer than rocks and deserts. However, it would continue to be considered a world that could potentially be reached and even colonised by humans.

The first realistic proposal for a human mission to Mars was made by Wernher von Braun, the chief rocket scientist of Nazi Germany, who worked for NASA and became a US citizen after the end of the Second World War. Von Braun was the chief architect for NASA's Saturn V program, that put the US ahead of the Soviet Union in the Space Race that resulted in the USA sending human astronauts to the moon for the first time in 1969. Yet even with those successes, von Braun's foremost ambition was to send humans to Mars in the long run. However, the enthusiasm for manned space travel declined after the failed moon landing mission of Apollo 13 almost resulted in the death of its astronauts. And apart from that, with the thrill of the first lunar landing having worn off, public interest in space travel lost its momentum. Besides, the fact that the race for the moon was predominantly motivated by political reasons was another strong factor that led to the decline in willpower. So the time of serious human space travel came to an end in 1972, only three years after the first successful moon landing, leaving Apollo 17 astronaut Eugene Cernan the last person to walk on the surface of the moon.

As the public will to send people out on dangerous missions became weaker and weaker, President Richard Nixon issued the formal end to any ventures of that sort for the following decades. Two programs were proposed to Nixon by NASA. One program was less costly and far less daring, the other was highly expensive and extremely difficult. The first was the Space Shuttle, the second a mission to Mars. Feeling the lack of public support to invest in continuing the space program, Nixon decided to go with the Space Shuttle.[5] Very soon after that decision, seeing his dreams of Mars shattered, Wernher von Braun retired from NASA.

However, in spite of the slow progress of space technology after the Apollo program, there have been some noteworthy steps forward. In 1986, the Soviet Union sent their space station Mir into the earth's orbit, which operated until 2001 when it was eventually deorbited. Overlapping this time frame, the International Space Station (ISS) was launched into orbit in 1998 and after being continuously upgraded, it is still in operation. The ISS marks a significant multinational effort, which is a necessary precondition for a successful Mars mission.

Further, exploration of Mars has continued with a number of unmanned missions. Apart from some early attempts in the 60s and 70s, Martian probes have gathered a lot of knowledge about the red planet since the late twentieth century.[6] Be it landing missions, such as the Curiosity rover, or orbital ventures, such as the Mars Orbiter Mission, Martian exploration is taking many steps to gather intelligence of Mars that are necessary if one ever plans to send humans to our neighbouring planet.

However, it is only with the extremely ambitious undertakings of SpaceX that a human mission to Mars has become conceivable in the near future. Above all, a sustainable human mission to Mars would depend on developing reusable rockets for a variety of reasons. SpaceX is the first manufacturer that ever managed to build a rocket that could successfully launch and land back safely to be reused for a later launch, with their first successful landing taking place in 2015. Previous rocket technology had the rocket destroyed after launch, which is not only wasting valuable materials but also would not allow a potential Martian crew to leave the red planet again after landing.

Apart from all that, the enthusiasm cannot overshadow the extreme difficulties and dangers connected with the endeavour. Apart from technological and intelligence-based challenges that come with a human mission to Mars, there is another factor that makes such a mission extremely difficult: humans. One rather obvious difficulty is physiological in nature. The prospect has been likened to polar expeditions, where humans had to cope with an extremely hazardous environment that is adverse to life. Apart from that, the psychological challenges are no less threatening. As a Mars mission would take several months of journey and possibly a prolonged stay on the red planet, its crew members would have to live together in a very confined space surrounded by the lethal environment of empty space or the uninhabitable atmosphere of Mars. Basically, the attempt would involve "stuffing crewmembers inside hermetically sealed cans for months at a time".[7] The psychological pressure of those circumstances is probably not what comes to mind first when thinking about the dangers of a Martian mission. However, it should not be underestimated, as it poses one of the biggest challenges of the mission.

In fact, there are projects to simulate the unique challenges a Martian mission would pose to its crew. HI-SEAS (Hawai'i Space Exploration Analog and Simulation) locks up a crew in a habitat similar to those that would be used on Mars, primarily in order to see what a Martian crew would have to cope with psychologically.[8] All of that only accounts for a successful mission. If something went wrong in those circumstances, there is no telling as to what the effects would be on the crew. *The Martian* takes an extreme approach to those horror scenarios. Instead of dealing with the challenges that confining a group of humans to a small space brings, it shows the challenges that being left completely alone poses. Leaving Mark Watney stranded alone on Mars is probably the worst-case scenario that a human being conceivably could face. And it is especially this context that will be the foundation for the teaching suggestion in this paper.

In the following, I will give a brief overview of *The Martian* and contextualise it in the science fiction genre, highlighting specific contexts and aspects of its narrative setup that could be used to teach psychological and social issues in the EFL classroom.

3. *The Martian* in Context

Before putting *The Martian* into the context of the science fiction genre, it should be stressed that my discussion of the material is limited to the 2016 film and does not consider the novel on which it is based. This limitation is set for pragmatic reasons, as it is much easier to implement a feature length film, even one as long as *The Martian* (142 minutes) in the limited scope of the EFL classroom. In addition to that, the technological accessibility of the film is another good argument to use it instead of the novel. Most students probably have private access to Netflix, on which this film is available. So even if the curriculum makes it hard to engage in a watching of the film together in class, it is certainly possible that students would watch the complete film at home. Even if not every individual student has access to the platform, it is easy to share one's access with others or even get together to watch the film in small groups. With a little cooperation, potential barriers could easily be overcome. Indeed, a decentralised approach is probably advantageous in many respects, as students can easily switch subtitles on and off, stop, rewind or rewatch the film to suit their individual needs and maybe even watch it in their native language first and then watch selected scenes in English. Based on that, it is much easier to take a "clip approach" to watching the film in class, in which only "one scene or a sequence of several scenes" of varying length is shown in class.[9]

One question one has to ask first is how the film fits into the greater context of the genre. While science fiction as a genre is notoriously difficult to define, *The Martian* corresponds rather nicely even to a relatively restrictive definition of the genre as "a narrative of an imaginary invention or discovery in the natural sciences and consequent adventures and experiences".[10] As the Mars mission is only a small step away, it takes only very little imagination to believe in its slightly advanced technology to make the story work. Yet even in this almost matter-of-factual way, the wonders of this recent technology never cease to amaze the audience. It is not so much the invention of new technology but rather its implementation for a human mission to Mars that creates excitement for the story.

Among the numerous sub-genres of science fiction, such as "hard sf, space opera [or] science fantasy",[11] *The Martian* is a rather 'down-to-earth' manifestation of hard sf (pun intended). *Interstellar*, another science fiction film that aired just a year before *The Martian*, starts with a dystopian setting in which Earth is a desolate planet on the brink of becoming completely inhospitable to humans. In this particular context, space travel is not undertaken in an exploratory spirit, but it is a sheer necessity for a population of eco-refugees. In addition to that, *Interstellar* takes its audience into the most exotic and speculative marvels of the universe such as black holes and wormholes, including much more imaginative technological advances.[12] *The Martian* neither sets out with any dystopian premises nor showcases any exotic marvels of the universe. While it makes occasional references to a future necessity for a multiplanetary humanity, it presents space travel in a very optimistic fashion. Here, humans set out on their space journey completely in the spirit of exploration and discovery. Yet the film does not embark on any utopian musings either. Unlike *Star Trek*, which largely presents a utopian human society in which all problems of human civilisation on earth have been solved, *The Martian* highlights political and organisational conflicts on earth that make universal human endeavours difficult. Indeed, the film manages to present a highly optimistic outlook and mixes it with impressions of the brutal and destructive elements of extra-terrestrial nature, while simultaneously not downplaying difficulties connected to humanity as such. Yet just like *Star Trek*, *The Martian* highlights the sense of adventure that comes with space travel.

In addition to that, *The Martian* is also quite 'down-to-earth' with respect to its reliance on special effects. A lot of recent science fiction films could be shrugged off "primarily [as] a compendium of special effects whose story merely frames a display of cinema's magical possibilities".[13] *The Martian* uses minimalist yet believable computer-generated imagery to bring the story forward, making it one of those films that are "fascinating because of their illusory power",[14] without feeling the need to include myriads of effects just because it could. Its effects never distract from the story and are done well enough not to break the suspension of disbelief.

The film starts in the midst of a mission accomplished, not featuring any scenes of a journey to Mars but right on the surface of Mars as the astronauts attend to their specific tasks during the mission. It is not even supposed to be the first human mission to Mars in the film's timeline. The astronauts are members of the "Ares III" crew, which implies that at least two earlier manned missions have taken place. So it is hard to draw a parallel between that particular mission and the first moon landing. However, it is interesting that this depiction of the mission to Mars features a female commander. For the Ares III mission at least, Neil Armstrong's cliché quotation would have to be slightly modified. Indeed, the first human to touch the surface of Mars in this film would most certainly have called this "one small step for a woman". By featuring a female mission commander, the film participates in a tradition of increasingly gender-conscious science fiction that can be traced back to the 1960s and 70s.[15] This is only one of the elements that add notions of diversity to the prototypical American story. Several characters in the film that play vital roles in the story are of diverse backgrounds and ethnicities. The crew's pilot is of Latino origin, the chemist a German, NASA astrophysicist Rich Purnell is an African American, and the rescue mission is only made possible by the Chinese offering their help in providing a rocket to resupply the Martian crew.

Further, the transnational nature of the endeavour is often highlighted by references to legal implications of the mission. For example, towards the film's finale, Watney jokes about being the first official 'space pirate' in human history, as he has to claim a mission rocket on Mars for his escape (1:38:14).[16] As no nation can lay claim to any area that is not on Earth, he has to capture the spacecraft on his own accord on Mars, which is technically lying in international waters. This most certainly humbles any national sentiments with respect to interstellar colonisation. Indeed, it alludes to the somewhat American prototype of having a far-away colony gain independence. In the same spirit, the concept of colonisation is also put in a more innocent framework in the film. Mark Watney is told that it was only his successful growing of plants on Mars that constituted the act of colonisation rather than any conceivable military endeavours or drawing arbitrary borders (~1:00:13).

As far as its plot structure is concerned, *The Martian* follows the archetypal formula of the hero's journey. It throws its protagonist from the border of the realm of habitable order into the deepest depths of chaos. The successful Martian mission marks the edge between habitable order and chaos. Abandoned on a lethal world in the depth of space, Mark Watney is forced back into the small confines of the HAB (a module for astronauts to live in), the only bit of relatively safe space left on the planet. Trapped in that small space almost like Jonah in the belly of the great fish, Watney has to assess his situation and work on a solution. He has to keep pushing the boundaries further and further, thus creating a greater sphere of habitable order out of the chaos of hostile Mars. This is achieved by his gradual harvesting of available resources, such as Martian soil, leftover mission equipment, deserted Martian probes of the past, his crew members' personal items and even his own excrement, to mention a few. However, probably more importantly, he has to harvest the resources hidden in his own mind, adapting them to a new and challenging situation. It is predominantly his innovative spirit in combination with his extensive training, his thinking quickly on his feet and his extremely resilient character that give him the edge in his battle for survival on Mars. In a way, Watney's story is somewhat like Robinson Crusoe, just minus the cannibals, Friday, water or air.

Mark Watney is far from being a stereotypical hero figure. Of all the different personages on the mission, being a botanist, he is arguably the 'least important' crew member for the actual mission. Throughout the film, the other crew members and Watney himself joke about this circumstance. This may surely make him more relatable to a greater audience, who themselves are not experts in highly technical fields of study. However, as Watney is thrown into the circumstance of being stranded on Mars without sufficient supplies, his botanist skills make him the most likely to survive the stay. In this sense, the least shall be first. Arguably no other crew member could have successfully grown enough food to survive until the rescue mission could take place.

Thus, Mark Watney is not a hero by default, but he becomes the hero of the story by overcoming all the challenges that his dire circumstances pose to him. As Watney survives even in the face of some major setbacks, such as his complete potato plantation being destroyed in an accident, he manages to survive long enough to wait for his crew to come back to rescue him. In a scene that is nothing short of a mythological descent to the underworld journey, his female mission commander descends from the ship just about far enough to pick up the starving hero from the underworld of the Martian orbit and bring him back home to the surface of Earth and therefore back to life. The fact that it is a female character that descends to save the hero from the underworld is as much embedded in recent cultural trends of gender consciousness as it is set in an ancient tradition of the underworld journey, where it was predominantly the role of female characters to do bring the hero back.

However, in spite of those setbacks, challenges and even pains Mark Watney has to endure, one of the most intriguing aspects of the film is that he does so with an unconquerable lightness of spirit. For instance, when realising the sheer number of problems that he will have to deal with if he is to survive on Mars, instead of being frightened or frustrated, Mark Watney concludes that he will "have to science the shit out of this" (~36:00). Indeed, whenever he is struck by a devastating tragedy or facing next to impossible odds, Watney delivers a funny line that alleviates the tension. Those moments of comic relief that the protagonist creates for himself are one of three major factors which help him to maintain his psychological health. The second factor is that he keeps a diary in the form of log entries on the station's computer. On the one hand, this may give a detailed record of his solo mission to NASA in case he will not make it. On the other hand, this type of soliloquy helps him to think out aloud and solve the problems ahead of him via a communicative process. In addition to that, it allows the film to pass on vital information to the audience, who need to have access to Watney's mind for the story to make sense. The third factor is the establishment of communications with Earth. Even though his initial system of communication is relatively minimal, as he can only put up signs and have NASA point an old camera from the late 90s to a specific sign, the fact that he has contact with other humans is a major benefit to his maintenance of sanity. The further he proceeds, the more sophisticated his means of communication with NASA become.

A major part of Mark Watney becoming the hero of the story is the fact that he manages to stay calm and sane throughout his prolonged stay in isolation. His extraordinary character and personality inspire the audience in ways that other characters could not. This intriguing part of the story offers a great source of continuous interest to the audience, which can be used as a vehicle for teaching a variety of issues to learners engaging with the film. In the next chapter, I will propose a particular plan of teaching the material to students in the EFL classroom.

4. *The Martian* in the EFL Classroom

This chapter will lay out a lesson sequence and exemplary lesson procedure for teaching *The Martian* in the EFL classroom. The lesson procedure highlights the psychological challenges that a Martian mission poses to humans. In this, the topic can be used to connect with other subjects that have a psychological dimension, such as pedagogy, sociology or religion, for instance.

First of all, I will organise the thematic field in a coherent and conceivable lesson plan. In order to make a systematic assessment of competences possible, this sequence relies on a task-based approach to learning, in which learners learn "language as a living entity through using it and experiencing its use during task completion".[17] The content matter of this sequence serves as a narrative vehicle through which that experience is made possible. A thinkable sequence of lessons could look like this:

Lesson topic	Task
1. Introducing a human mission to Mars: Planning human resources	Make a list of the types of professions and personalities you would want to take on a mission to Mars.
2. Watching *The Martian*	Complete the observation-sheet while watching the film
3. Describing *The Martian*: Evaluating the observation-sheet	Create an overview of the main plot and the main characters of the film.
4. Character constellation: Characterising the Ares III crew members	Create character cards for each of the crew members and evaluate their importance for the mission.
5. What type of person is Mark Watney? Characterising the protagonist	Use selected scenes to score Mark Watney in the list of the "Big Five personality traits" and evaluate how fit he is to serve as the hero of the story.

6. What isolation can do to a person: Identifying the challenges of a Martian mission	Identify the psychological dangers that a mission to Mars poses to its crew and compare that to the extreme situation Mark Watney is in.
7. A comic figure in a tragic scenario: Explaining how Mark Watney copes with his dire situation	Explain how Mark Watney manages to remain mentally healthy and how that also benefits the audience of the film.

Table 1: Lesson Sequence on Teaching *The Martian*

This is only a minimal plan, which could be extended or contracted in several places depending on the thematic focus teachers may want to take. Further, it may require some modifications for practical application. As different learners and groups of learners have different needs, it might be necessary to add extra lessons into the plan to prepare learners sufficiently for the tasks to come. At the beginning of this sequence, it is recommended to thematically introduce the Mars mission in general, using some of the materials and contexts laid out at the beginning of this paper. After that general introduction, the topic has to be narrowed down to its psychological dimensions, using character constellations as a guiding thread. Further, as mentioned above, students should ideally watch the film at home, with session two of this plan indicating where in the process that watching would take place.

In the following, lesson seven of this plan will be exemplified in detail, as it brings together many of the competences trained in previous lessons.

Topic	A comic figure in a tragic scenario: Explaining how Mark Watney copes with his dire situation
Objectives	To develop and practice • Vocabulary connected with mental health, isolation, social contact and humour • Grammar: clauses of cause and reason
Age	Upper Secondary Education (15+ years of age)
Level	CEF level B1 and above
Time	45 mins.
Materials/media	Quotes/hypotheses, film clips, sheet with useful expressions
Introduction	In this lesson, students will write a commentary on one of the specific factors that contributes to Mark Watney's

	psychological endurance. Based on three different quotations[18] about the requirements of mental health in combination with specific film scenes, students explore non-pragmatic functions of things Mark Watney does on his mission, such as delivering funny lines, using the mission log as a diary and establishing communications with NASA.
1. Introduction to the topic (5 mins.)	Ask students to brainstorm factors that contribute to Mark Watney's psychological endurance
2. Focus on the story (10 mins.)	Ask students to use one of the following hypotheses to discuss Mark Watney's behaviour in the corresponding film clips • "Of a sane man there is only one safe definition. He is the man who can have tragedy in his heart and comedy in his head." (G.K. Chesterton) ➔ Watney's funny lines (e.g. clip: 35:28-36:05) • "I would consider my diary serves the same purpose as going for a walk or a run. They are all physical ways of clearing a mental landscape." (Chet Faker) ➔ Watney's log entries (e.g. clip: 20:55-21:35) • "We don't function well as human beings when we're in isolation." (Robert Zemeckis) ➔ Watney making contact with NASA (e.g. clip: 48:32-49:25)
3. Extension (10 mins.)	Ask students to write a short commentary on one of the three factors that contribute to Mark Watney's psychological endurance
4. Oral extension (10 mins.)	Ask students to present their commentaries to the rest of class
5. Oral extension II (10 mins.)	Ask students to discuss what effects those three factors have on the audience of the film

Table 2: Lesson Plan for Teaching *The Martian*

5. Conclusion

The materials used in this lesson invite a cooperative learning approach. This is not only feasible because cooperative learning fosters a "greater transfer of learning from one situation to another", which is important for the sequence this lesson is embedded in.[19] This specific scenario is a case in point for cooperative approaches since they are also thematically part of the topic at hand – a successful Mars mission depends on committed human cooperation. In this particular lesson, students would cooperatively work on the material, having each group deal with another quotation and film clip and present their results to the rest of the class. At some point in the sequence, the connection between cooperation in the classroom and cooperation in a human mission to Mars should be reflected upon. The tasks of this sequence are laid out in a way that "common elements of effective cooperative learning strategies [...] should occur naturally" in the language classroom.[20] Thus, individual lessons of this sequence will lend themselves easily to cooperative teaching methods that teachers might choose.

Ideally, students should often reflect upon communicative tasks and processes and transfer them to situations in their own *Lebenswelten*, which involves the pedagogical tasks of those lessons relating to target tasks in real-life communication.[21] This might help to increase their motivation and commitment to the tasks and make it easier for them to participate in discussions and think more thoroughly about the issues at hand.[22] The fact that the film might easily connect to their pastime pursuits might be greatly benefit that aim.

In an alternative or additional assessment to the oral extension II in the plan, students could reflect on the importance of the three factors in their own lives instead of taking a reader-response approach from the perspective of the film's audience. Depending on the group of learners, it might be more feasible to engage with their personal lives and experiences instead of trying to shed more light on how the film works as a narrative. Yet a reader-response approach is an interesting endeavour, as it forces students to think about the question whether or not "our various responses to literary works produce the same (or similar) readings".[23] Especially with regards to Mark Watney's soliloquies in the mission log, the audience becomes an "actively mediating presence",[24] as each individual watching the film will engage in another communicative relationship with the protagonist.

Throughout this sequence of lessons that uses *The Martian* as their basis, students engage with a variety of questions that are of profound interest to the puzzles of human nature. They learn to look at the great adventures of humanity with a sense of admiration on the one hand, and with a sense of terror on the other. This dual nature of all human enterprises has the capacity to bring to the surface that which is best about humanity and is something that could unite humanity in spite of their tensions and conflicts. As students cooperate to complete the tasks in front of them and draw meaningful conclusions about them for their own lives, *The Martian* and a human mission to Mars becomes a vehicle to motivate, engage and inspire them to facilitate what is best about themselves and how much more they themselves could grow to become.

Notes

1 Mars One. Official Website, 2019. Web. 20 June 2019 <https://www.mars-one.com/>.

2 See Kraft, Norbert (2015). "The Science of Screening Astronauts." 27 May 2015. Web. 20 June 2019. <https://community.mars-one.com/blog/the-science-of-screening-astronauts>.

3 Space Exploration Technologies Corp. "Mars." SpaceX, 2017. Web. 20 June 2019 <https://www.spacex.com/mars>.

4 Singleton, Micah (2018). "SpaceX's Falcon Heavy Launch Was YouTube's Second Biggest Live Stream Ever." *The Verge* 6 Feb. 2018: n. pag. Web. 20 June 2019 <https://www.theverge.com/2018/2/6/16981730/spacex-falcon-heavy-launch-youtube-live-stream-record>.

5 See Lambright, W. Henry (2014). *Why Mars: NASA and the Politics of Space Exploration*. Baltimore, Maryland: Johns Hopkins University Press, 52-53.

6 Cf. Stooke, Philip J. (2015). *The International Atlas of Mars Exploration: From Spirit to Curiosity* (Volume 2: 2004 to 2014). Cambridge: Cambridge University Press.

7 Seedhouse, Erik (2015). *Survival and Sacrifice in Mars Exploration: What We Know from Polar Expeditions*. Cham et al: Springer, xvii.

8 See University of Hawai'i. "HI-SEAS. Hawai'i Space Exploration Analog and Simulation." University of Hawai'i, 2013. Web. 20 June 2019 <https://hi-seas.org/>.

9 Thaler, Engelbert (2014). *Teaching English with Films*. Paderborn: Schöningh, 151.

10 Bailey, James Osler (1972). *Pilgrims through Space and Time*. Westport, CT: Greenwood, 10.

11 Wolfe, Gary K. (2011). "Theorizing Science Fiction: The Question of Terminology." *Teaching Science Fiction*. Eds. Andy Sawyer and Peter Wright. New York: Palgrave, 38-54, 46.

12 It is interesting that, just like *The Martian*, *Interstellar* features Matt Damon playing an astronaut stranded alone on another planet, waiting to be rescued. Yet unlike *The Martian*'s protagonist Mark Watney, Dr Mann (Damon's role in *Interstellar*) does not take his calamity with humour and optimism. Instead, the prospect of dying alone on a foreign planet, together with his prolonged isolation, turns him into a psychologically unstable and sinister character. A comparison of both characters might be turned into a useful task in class.

13 Bould, Mark (2003). "Film and Television." *The Cambridge Companion to Science Fiction*. Eds. Edward James and Farah Mendlesohn. Cambridge: Cambridge University Press, 79-95, 80.

14 Gunning, Tom (1990). "The Cinema of Attractions: Early Film, Its Spectator and the Avant-Garde." *Early Film: Space, Frame, Narrative*. Ed. Thomas Elsaesser. London: British Film Institute, 56-62, 57.

15 Attebery, Brian (2011). "Teaching Gender and Science Fiction." *Teaching Science Fiction*. Eds. Andy Sawyer and Peter Wright. New York: Palgrave, 146-161, 146.

16 All references to parts of the film will correspond to the time stamps in the Netflix version: *The Martian*. Dir. Ridley Scott. 2015. Online Video. Netflix.

17 Long, Mike (2015). *Second Language Acquisition and Task-Based Language Teaching*. Malden: Wiley, 249.

18 Chesterton, Gilbert Keith (2007). *Tremendous Trifles*. Mineola, NY: Dover Publications, 170; Chat Faker in Zuel, Bernard (2014). "Chet Faker: Out in the open." *The Sydney Morning Herald* 19 April 2014. Web. 23 June 2019 <https://www.smh.com.au/entertainment/music/chet-faker-out-in-the-open-20140416-36r56.html>; Robert Zemeckis in Kehr, Dave (2000). "FILM; 'Cast Away' Director Defies Categorizing." *The New York Time*s 17 December 2000. Web. 23 June 2019 <https://www.nytimes.com/2000/12/17/movies/film-cast-away-director-defies-categorizing.html>.

19 Jolliffe, Wendy (2007). *Cooperative Learning in the Classroom: Putting it into Practice*. London: Sage, 6.

20 Digby, Annette (2013). "Cooperative Learning in Secondary English: Research and Theory." *Secondary Schools and Cooperative Learning: Theories, Models, and Strategies*. Eds. Jon E. Pedersen and Annette D. Digby. New York: Routledge, 229-250, 231.

21 See Nunan, David (2004). *Task-Based Language Teaching*. Cambridge: Cambridge University Press, 1.

22 See Borsch, Frank (2015). *Kooperatives Lernen: Theorie – Anwendung – Wirksamkeit*. 2nd ed. Stuttgart: Kohlhammer, 10.

[23] Davis, Todd F., and Kenneth Womack (2002). *Formalist Criticism and* Reader-*Response Theory*. New York: Palgrave, 51.

[24] Fish, Stanley E. (1972). *Self-Consuming Artifacts: The Experience of Seventeenth-Century Literature*. Berkeley: University of California Press, 384.

Bibliography

Primary Texts

The Expanse. Producer Naren Shankar. 2015-. Legendary Television Distribution.

Kraft, Norbert (2015). "The Science of Screening Astronauts." 27 May 2015. Web. 20 June 2019 <https://community.mars-one.com/blog/the-science-of-screening-astronauts>.

Mars One (2019). Official Website. Web. 20 June 2019. <https://www.mars-one.com/>.

The Martian. Dir. Ridley Scott. 2015. Online Video. Netflix.

Mars One. Official Website, 2019. Web. 20 June 2019 <https://www.mars-one.com/>.

Space Exploration Technologies Corp. "Mars." SpaceX, 2017. Web. 20 June 2019 <https://www.spacex.com/mars>.

University of Hawai'i. "HI-SEAS. Hawai'i Space Exploration Analog and Simulation." University of Hawai'i, 2013. Web. 20 June 2019 <https://hi-seas.org/>.

Secondary Literature

Attebery, Brian (2011). "Teaching Gender and Science Fiction." *Teaching Science Fiction*. Eds. Andy Sawyer and Peter Wright. New York: Palgrave, 146-161.

Bailey, James Osler (1972). *Pilgrims through Space and Time*. Westport, CT: Greenwood.

Borsch, Frank (2015). *Kooperatives Lernen: Theorie – Anwendung – Wirksamkeit*. 2nd ed. Stuttgart: Kohlhammer.

Bould, Mark (2003). "Film and Television." *The Cambridge Companion to Science Fiction*. Eds. Edward James and Farah Mendlesohn. Cambridge: Cambridge University Press, 79–95.

Chesterton, Gilbert Keith (2007). *Tremendous Trifles*. Mineola, NY: Dover Publications.

Davis, Todd F., and Kenneth Womack (2002). *Formalist Criticism and Reader-Response Theory*. New York: Palgrave.

Digby, Annette (2013). "Cooperative Learning in Secondary English: Research and Theory." *Secondary Schools and Cooperative Learning: Theories, Models, and Strategies*. Eds. Jon E. Pedersen and Annette D. Digby. New York: Routledge, 229-250.

Fish, Stanley E. (1972). *Self-Consuming Artifacts: The Experience of Seventeenth-Century Literature*. Berkeley: University of California Press.

Gunning, Tom (1990). "The Cinema of Attractions: Early Film, Its Spectator and the Avant-Garde." *Early Film: Space, Frame, Narrative*. Ed. Thomas Elsaesser. London: British Film Institute, 56–62.

Jolliffe, Wendy (2007). *Cooperative Learning in the Classroom: Putting it into Practice*. London: Sage.

Kehr, Dave (2000). "FILM; 'Cast Away' Director Defies Categorizing." *The New York Time*s 17 December 2000. Web. 23 June 2019 <https://www.nytimes.com/2000/12/17/movies/film-cast-away-director-defies-categorizing.html>.

Lambright, W. Henry (2014). *Why Mars: NASA and the Politics of Space Exploration*. Baltimore, Maryland: Johns Hopkins University Press.

Long, Mike (2015). *Second Language Acquisition and Task-Based Language Teaching*. Malden: Wiley.

Nunan, David (2004). *Task-Based Language Teaching*. Cambridge: Cambridge University Press.

Seedhouse, Erik (2015). *Survival and Sacrifice in Mars Exploration: What We Know from Polar Expeditions*. Cham et al: Springer.

Singleton, Micah (2018). "SpaceX's Falcon Heavy Launch Was YouTube's Second Biggest Live Stream Ever." *The Verge* 6 Feb. 2018: n. pag. Web. 20 June 2019 <https://www.theverge.com/2018/2/6/16981730/spacex-falcon-heavy-launch-youtube-live-stream-record>.

Stooke, Philip J. (2015). *The International Atlas of Mars Exploration: From Spirit to Curiosity* (Volume 2: 2004 to 2014). Cambridge: Cambridge Cambridge University Press.

Thaler, Engelbert (2014). *Teaching English with Films*. Paderborn: Schöningh.

Wolfe, Gary K. (2011). "Theorizing Science Fiction: The Question of Terminology." *Teaching Science Fiction*. Eds. Andy Sawyer and Peter Wright. New York: Palgrave, 38-54.

Zuel, Bernard (2014). "Chet Faker: Out in the open." *The Sydney Morning Herald* 19 April 2014. Web. 23 June 2019 <https://www.smh.com.au/entertainment/music/chet-faker-out-in-the-open-20140416-36r56.html>.

Jonathan Shipley (Fort Worth)

Dinosaurian Legacy: The Role of Reptilian Sentients in Science Fiction and Fantasy

1. Introduction

From the Draconians of *Doctor Who* (1963) to the Gorns of *Star Trek* (1966) to the lizard-like Visitors of *V*, traditional science fiction often portrays human-like saurian races as archetypal antagonists of humanity. Can it be, as Sagan postulated in *Dragons of Eden* (1977), that the 'reptile brain' in humans, which controls our aggression, causes humans to fear the dragon inside of themselves and others? As a writer who explores saurian cultures in my own writing, I am curious if these saurian depictions are a universal response. As a teacher of creative writing, I had the perfect opportunity. Using my high school class, I asked students to imagine and write about a threatening monster of nightmare. If the reptilian antagonist is an archetype created by the 'reptilian brain', menacing saurians should claim a place in any random assortment of depictions of predatory, threatening creatures. One of the consistent themes within the genre of science fiction is the exploration of what it means to be human. One thread of this exploration is posthumanism, the comparison of what we are with what we could become, whether that be mutation, cybernetics, evolution, or even a post-death state. One of several posthuman concepts is based on "the idea that the human species is in the process of transforming itself through a phase of transhumanism into a final posthuman state of superior intelligence, in which the human species is both eliminated in its present form and at the same time attains a form of immortality through transformation".[1] But the exploration of being human also extends to close comparisons of what we are with what we are not. In the late eighteenth century, Georg Wilhelm Friedrich Hegel described the Other as a method of defining ourselves,[2] but this concept has been expanded in more recent postmodern literature into the monstrous Other, "a complex phenomenon with broad implications for the politics of subjectivity and the future of social and political justice" which "poses significant challenges for the ongoing tenability of normative notions of the human".[3] The genre of science fiction is ideally suited to depict the monster stereotype as the darkened mirror that tests humanity by showing what is beyond the limit of humanness. Conjectured worlds are perfect hosts for the unknown that humans encounter outside of their own sphere of carbon-based evolution, as part of a different system of physiology and physics than the one which shaped us. Randomness in itself could create monsters by simply combining unhuman traits into an alien species, but perhaps we are not dependent on randomness. Perhaps there are certain patterns that occur in our monsters over and over again because the human mind has a tendency to define 'monstrous' in predictable ways. As art and literature fulfill the function of holding up the mirror to human society, so do they also hold up the darkened mirror to show that which most repels us. Surveying a range of legends, children's tales, and modern graphic and cinemagraphic science-fiction portrayals, do we find the same players repeatedly cast in the role of the monstrous Other? It appears to be exactly that. In the repetition of certain stereotypes, it appears that reptilian aliens have captured that role for reasons that extend far back into our own human development.

2. Myth and Fantasy

2.1. The Serpent in Our Midst

Centuries before we entered the conceptual realm of alien species, we explored Otherness in the form of Man versus Beast.[4] This can be seen as an actual physical conflict in Neolithic cave paintings showing pride in survival. Perhaps it was man versus mastodon or man versus wolf, but as myths and tales evolved, we see a shaping of the conflict into man versus monster where the monster takes on certain aspects in early recorded writings. In Norse legend, this manifested as the Midgard Serpent, also known in Egyptian and Greek cultures as the Worm Ouroboros, the great serpent that encircles the world and swallows its own tail, thus having no beginning or ending, or the Biblical serpent in the Garden of Eden that seduces humankind and orchestrates the Fall from Grace, or the Plumed Serpent Quetzalcoatl that held court in Mesoamerican legend, or the reference in Genesis to the great serpent Leviathan that dwells at the bottom of the sea. All of these images share an ophidian commonality that could point to a deeply embedded sensitivity to snakes at the species level. Certainly ophidiophobia is a frequently encountered phobia in modern society. Of all of the possibilities that one would hate to find when throwing back the covers of the bed in preparation for sleep, a coiled snake would rank high on the list. As we move forward in time and widen the scope of phobias slightly, we arrive at herpetophobia, the fear of not just snakes, but reptiles in a more general sense, and the stage is set for the long medieval conflict with that greatest of all reptilian foes, the dragon.

2.2. Here Be Dragons

In dragons we see a conceptual evolution of serpent to reptile, traceable by geographical region. We can surmise that this creature of legend began life as a great serpent. In Asia and the Middle East, we see this most strongly with Mesopotamian serpents as adversaries to be struck down by the local gods and their Asian counterparts as legged but serpentine creatures associated with fortune and wisdom. In Europe during the Middle Ages, however, a winged, fire-breathing super-reptile emerged as the most fearsome of adversaries for heroes to battle. Although the word dragon can be deconstructed all the way back to the Sanskrit 'eye' because of the terrible power of a dragon's eye,[5] these European creatures were clearly something new on the monster horizon. It was as if several persistent terrors of the medieval mind – snakes, fire, flight – were conflated and distilled into their worst aspects. If it stopped there, the dragon would be simply a fearsome beast, a flying shark, so to speak; however, it does not stop there. Dragons are typically imbued with other, non-animal characteristics – cunning, ancient knowledge, greed for gold – that elevate them from the realm of beasts to that of sapient creatures. Moreover, they possess a combination of traits that makes them uniquely dangerous and even positions them to challenge humans as rulers of the Earth. We have arrived at the great antihuman, the primary monstrous Other of fantasy literature.

Some of the most powerful fantasy draconic images are those where dragon is closely related to humans. Speaking becomes an important trait; indeed, speech may be expanded to the power of dragonspell over an unwary listener or the power of knowledge granted to the hero gifted enough to talk to dragons unscathed. We see this in J.R.R. Tolkien's Smaug the Golden in *The Hobbit* (1937), and in Ursula K. Le Guin's Dragon of Pendor in *A Wizard of Earthsea* (1968), also in BBC One's 2008 television production of the *Merlin* series. Within George R.R. Martin's more recent *Game of Thrones* series (1996-2011), the Mother of Dragons is mistress of a creature of physical power more than intellectual danger, similar to J.K. Rowling's very physical dragons in the *Harry Potter* series. These particular dragons have stepped back from the monstrous Other to become simply monstrous beasts.

A step in the other direction would be the dragon Fafnir in the Germanic legends from which Richard Wagner drew inspiration for his operatic *Ring Cycle*, and the dragon the boy Eustace becomes in C.S. Lewis's *The Voyage of the Dawn Treader* (1952), the third volume of his Narnia series. Both of these dragons have the very monstrous quality of being humans, or near-humans, transformed into reptiles, a transformation which eerily echoes posthumanism, though in each case this transformation is clearly presented as a curse, not an evolved state. Both of these characters gain a hoard of gold and fearsome power, but in the process unwillingly forfeit their humanity and descend into a state of misery. The fact that the transformation is possible, albeit under unique circumstances, gives rise to the question, 'Are dragons our cousins?' This cross-species connection is utilized without explanation in the folktale collected by the Brothers Grimm as "The Dragon and his Grandmother", where three soldiers indentured to a dragon's service in exchange for whips that can snap gold out of thin air come across an 'old granny', presumably completely human in form, who turns out to be "the dragon's own grandmother". The granny agrees to help the soldiers solve the riddle that is their key to freedom from her "dragon-boy".[6] In this tale, the dragon is clearly a fire-breathing, winged beast of great cunning and persuasiveness, the soldiers are clearly human, and the grandmother is somehow connected to both species. Ursula Le Guin plays with this same human/dragon crossover in the later *Earthsea* books. I explored another twist to the concept in my own short story, "Fruits of Victory", where at the conclusion of the War of Order against Chaos, the Great Dragons choose a humanoid form for their offspring in order to take advantage of the changes in the evolving universe that will henceforth give mammalians an advantage.[7] Here dragons are transmuting into humans as a planned evolution. Throughout all of the varieties of permutations, the consistent image is that the two species are close enough for an unlikely transformation to take place between them. In the range of these crossovers, it becomes unclear whether dragons are filling the role of monstrous Other or are portraying humanity's monstrous self. Perhaps there is no difference. Either way, the connection could be deeply embedded in our primal brains.

2.3. Dinosaurs in Our Brains

Sagan in *The Dragons of Eden* speculates that "[t]he pervasiveness of dragon myths in the folk legends of many cultures is probably no accident".[8] He ties human responses to reptiles back to the earlier ages of evolution and a possible conflict in the Mesozoic hundreds of millions of years ago. Although the Age of Mammals began in the Cenozoic 65 million years ago as a successor era to the Age of Reptiles that lasted 300 million years prior to the Cenozoic, there was a period of overlap, perhaps even a hundred million years, when mammals were small and fearful and survived by running from the great reptiles that ruled the Earth. Perhaps this is the clue to our definition of monsters. The most primitive part of the human brain, the so-called reptilian brain, is a 400 million-year-old collection of neurons folded deep inside the human brain and has been linked to the evolution of mammals and certain behaviors. It is the paranoid, primitive nerve center that processes everything in term of fight or flight.[9] What if it is more than an instinctual throwback to an earlier version of humanity? What if the reptilian brain carries within it the vague memories of an earlier species? Sagan posits that somehow, somewhere, humanity, perhaps only in primal dreams, intersected dinosaurs and carry with them an imprint of responses to the great lizards. This intersection has manifested itself in art and literature for as long as there has been art and literature. On the most basic evolutionary level, the quintessential monsters of all mammals could be their non-mammalian predecessors from the Age of Reptiles. The relationship of these small first mammals with their massive dinosaurian elders was flight – not fight or flight, but strictly flight. Fear was the glue that bound one species to the other. Fast forward millions of years and we see that same fear codified in myth and literature in predictable forms.

> The implacable natural hostility between men and dragons, as exemplified in the myth of St. George, is strongest in the West. (In Chapter 3 of the Book of Genesis, God ordains an eternal enmity between reptiles and humans.) But it is not a Western anomaly. It is a worldwide phenomenon. Is it only an accident that the common sounds commanding silence or attracting attention seem strongly imitative of the hissing of reptiles? Is it possible that dragons posed a problem for our protohuman ancestors of a few million years ago, and that the terror they evoked and the deaths they caused helped bring about the evolution of human intelligence? [. . .] When we feared the dragons, were we fearing a part of ourselves? One way or the other, there were dragons in Eden.[10]

If we see ourselves very broadly not as human, but as mammals with mammalian behaviors that developed in the Mesozoic hundreds of millions of years ago, the inference can be made that the opposite of all that is mammalian is all that is reptilian and that this divide has defined monsters ever since.

2.4. Crocodile Smiles

The category of reptiles broadly includes snakes, lizards, turtles, crocodiles, and a multitude of extinct dinosaur types. Where once dinosaurs were the most fearful of monsters, the literary mantle of monster fell predominantly to serpents and dragons, but with one prominent excursion into the realm of crocodilians. Crocodilians are ancient, but literary crocodiles have a much shorter resume than dragons, the most famous example being James M. Barrie's 1911 novel *Peter Pan*. The Crocodile in *Peter Pan* ate the hand of the villainous Captain Hook and liked the taste so much that it devoted its existence to stalking the captain with the intention of devouring the rest of him. And it was no subtle stalking. The Crocodile was as persistent and inevitable as death itself and was the one thing that could arouse instant panic in the wicked pirate's heart. [11] The Crocodile's function throughout the story was basically to provide a symbol of fear until that morphs at the end into a symbol of death. Here we can view Captain Hook as the Other of Peter Pan, for they represent polar opposites, but the Crocodile wins the role of monstrous Other much more so than any of the wicked pirates. The 1911 century timing of this one important crocodile image is interesting as it fills a gap between fantasy's dragons and science fiction's reptilian aliens. Had Barrie lived forty years later, it is easy to see Neverland's location of "second star to the right and straight on 'til morning"[12] becoming the coordinates of a different planet, the theme of a boy who refused to grow up becoming the quest for high-tech immortality, and the human-hungry Crocodile morphing into an alien species.

3. Reptilians as the Bogeymen of Science Fiction

3.1. Early Pulp Fiction Images (1940-1960)

How has the baggage of mammalian evolution and medieval legends presented itself in the 20th and 21st centuries within the genre of science fiction where all things are possible? Can we expect aliens to be very alien life-forms that have no relation in either form or function to carbon-based life from Earth? The answer is no. When humans reach for the stars in the future, they seem to take their baggage with them. While there is a wide range of aliens, some very non-humanoid, there is also a persistent recurrence of reptilian aliens that in 1950 pulp fiction can be generically dubbed 'lizardmen' from the use of the term to describe multiple reptilian races in comics, gaming, and Dungeons and Dragons. These are typically scaled-down, humanized T-Rexes with green scales, claws, long snouts, and menacing teeth. Their function seems to be to threaten mankind with mindless brute strength. In my futuristic short story, "Brooklyn", the main character views a xenophobic propaganda billboard on Brooklyn Bridge where a monstrous alien lizard is presented as "coming to rape, pillage, and destroy".[13] This image is straight out of 1950s pulp science fiction where aliens were invariably hostile and tended to either be tentacled or reptilian. The bitter irony of the "Brooklyn" propaganda is that the neo-fascist militaristic government uses it as justification to oppress and enslave segments of the human population and ultimately to sell cheap slave labor to alien corporations. The actual 50s images, however, were less ironic and more patently xenophobic, and reptilian aliens tended to be scaled-down versions of Godzilla who first appeared in a Japanese horror movie in 1954 and was still headlining movies as of May, 2019. These scaled-down lizardmen populated the inner Earth worlds of

Skartaris, Subterranea, and the Savage Land of comic majors Marvel and DC in the 1960s and 1970s, while the 1954 movie *Creature from the Black Lagoon* (Fig. 1) perpetuated the image on the silver screen.

Fig. 1: Advertising Poster for *Creature from the Black Lagoon*

Fig. 2: Still from *Creature from the Black Lagoon* Showing 'The Pose'

In Fig. 2, one can see 'The Pose', as I label it for the purpose of this discussion. It presents the strong reptilian hovering threateningly over the weaker human lying helpless on the ground. While this still from *Creature From the Black Lagoon* seems to embody 1950s sexism in the way it depicts the helpless female, The Pose turns out to be less sexist than humanist. In Fig. 3 of Batman #35 from June 1946, The Pose is enacted with Robin as the helpless human about to go under the claws of a T-Rex, and in Fig. 4 from the Original Star Trek's 1967 "Arena" episode, Captain Kirk is the helpless human on the ground.

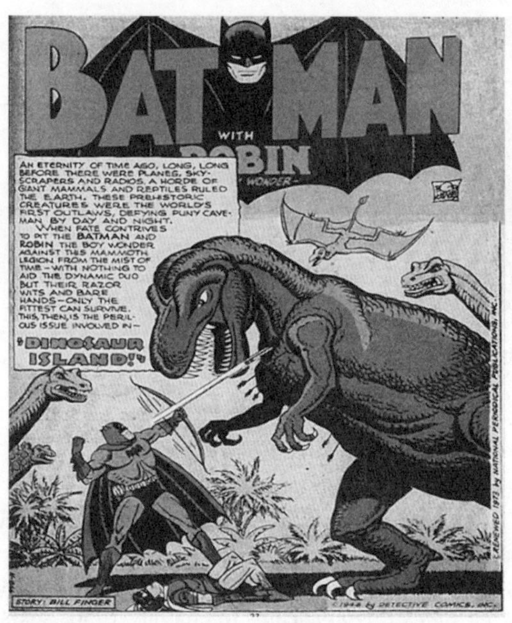

Fig. 3: Cover of *Batman* #35 Showing 'The Pose'

Fig. 4: Still from *Star Trek's* "Arena" Episode Showing 'The Pose'

3.2. *Star Trek* Representations (1967-2004)

The *Star Trek* "Arena" episode perhaps represents a shift in science-fiction lizardmen. There is no denying that lizardmen make convenient villains with little or no explanation needed, but "Arena" made an effort to play upon the prevailing stereotype while simultaneously arguing against it. The original *Star Trek* was famous in the 1960s for breaking social barriers with strong statements against racism and discrimination – and the first interracial kiss on prime time television. It makes a statement also in the "Arena" episode where Captain Kirk is pitted in an unarmed fight to the death with a newly encountered hostile race called Gorns. These Gorns are the stereotypical lizardmen of 1950s pulp fiction, bigger, stronger, and more predatory than humans. The twist comes when Kirk gains the upper hand but shows unexpected mercy toward his Gorn adversary by sparing his life. The highly evolved Metron who has orchestrated the spectacle of brute strength is surprised to find the evolved quality of mercy present in a primitive species and sees it was promising for the future of humans.[14] The interesting subtext of the ending is that as humans view lizardmen, so do Metrons view humans – primitive and savage – with essentially no difference between humans and Gorns developmentally. The episode does not go against the pulp fiction stereotype of lizardmen. If anything, the lumbering, scaled, captain of the alien ship is exactly the stereotype. What goes counter to stereotype, however, is that stereotypes do not dictate action. Where fight or flight is the standard human reaction to lizardmen, Kirk defies convention, shows mercy, and breaks the cycle.

The other *Star Trek* series continue to use lizardmen as part of their alien line-up. Within the story arcs of both *Voyager* and *Next Generation*, the role of monstrous Other is given for the most part to the Borg, who represent another science-fiction trope, the computer as unfeeling master, taken to a terrifying extreme; however, the militaristic, oppressive Cardassians of *Deep Space Nine* have scaled skin reminiscent of reptiles. The Cardassians eventually ally themselves with the Federation when an even more oppressive species of lizardmen, the Jem'Hadar, invade the quadrant. In terms of oppressive reptilian stereotypes, there is irony to that political shift. The later series *Enterprise* takes the stereotype a step further returning to lizardmen as the Great Enemy in 2003 and 2004. The five-raced Xindi culture that is intent on destroying Earth as a far-forward-thinking act of survival is comprised of Aquatics, Arboreals, Primates, Insectoids, and Reptilians, Avians having gone extinct with their homeworld's apocalypse. Within one culture, we see cross-species interaction and stereotyping. Of these five, the Insectoids and the Reptilians are most determined to continue the plan of destruction, even when the other races are swayed by human arguments. In the final attack, it is the Reptilians who are pushing forward, even to the point of betraying their fellow Xindi.[15] There is no redeeming quality to these lizardmen who are coming to "rape, pillage, and destroy"[16] the Earth. It is the old 1950s stereotype of lizardmen.

3.3. *V-The Visitors* (1984/2009)

Among other science fiction presentations of menacing reptilians is the television miniseries *V-The Visitors,* released originally in 1984, then followed by additional televisions series and films in the same universe. What is new in this portrayal is the aspect of reptilians masking themselves as humans in order to gain the trust of the Earth population, and the masking technique involves covering their green, scaled bodies with a layer of smooth, human-like skin that also reshapes any incongruities of form into human-appearing features. The disguise adds an additional layer of menace to the old trope of aliens taking over the world because the visual deceit is so effective and because it is accompanied by a massive propaganda effort (Fig. 5) to win the hearts of humans. This method arouses the paranoia of 'the enemy walks among us' and gives us hints what that enemy actually is through small slips in behavior or masking. One of the memorable moments of the original series is when the main antagonist Diana is caught in hostile fire that shreds one side of her human mask, providing a glimpse the green, scaled visage beneath (Fig. 6).[17] This moment was even memorialized by DC as a cover to their *V* miniseries comic. Like the dragons that shift between human and draconic form, these Visitors blur the line between human and reptilian because the masking is not only visual, but also behavioral. At least one of the gentler souls among the Visitors joins the human opposition, in essence allowing the human mask to become the dominant nature. Does this character become truly human, or perhaps even more human than some psychopathic souls? In terms of lizardmen, the Visitors add the twist of deceit to reptilians coming to "rape, pillage, and destroy",[18] and add a range of personality to the standard stereotype. Some are brutal and evil, as stereotype would dictate, but others are sympathetic and unsure about the morality of the mission of conquest their leadership has mandated. The subtext of the series, perhaps, is that evil is a function of nature, not appearance, and that surface appearances can only be believed at our own peril.

Fig. 5: Visitors' Propaganda Poster

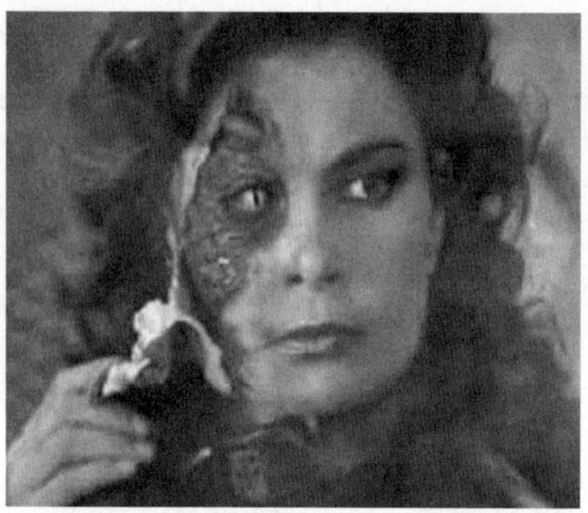

Fig. 6: The True Face of the Visitors

4. Saurians in the Shipleyverse

I explored the boundaries of species stereotyping in "Pale as the Noonday Sun" (2015), a short story from the point of view of a seven-foot, carnivorous 'voraciraptor'. The inherent drama in the piece comes from the viewpoint saurian Vergesh encountering a human refugee and having to deduce what this very different mammal wants, how it thinks, and whether it can be trusted. Some physical traits come very much into play. The saurians are possessed of an extremely sensitive sense of smell and use it more than sight to negotiate the world. They are also very tail conscious. Tails for them are not only natural weapons along with claws and teeth, but also indications of status and hierarchy. The attitude toward a 'poor, tailless mammal' is very much one of pity. Physically the human is no match for Vergesh, but the two find common ground as manipulative opportunists. In that, they are more alike than they are different.

A third character in the story also represents an old stereotype. This is the ophidian Skal, who is hunting the human refugee as bounty. The Skal are large snakes with small arms and as carnivorous as the saurians. Voraciraptors and Skal would seem to be natural allies, but they are not. Vergesh despises this new hunter as a newcomer with no pedigree or nobility and, more importantly, without the acute sense of smell possessed by all the reptilian Old Noble Races.[19] The fact that Vergesh allies himself with a 'pathetic mammal' against the Skal shows a complete departure from the lizardman stereotype and shows that a reptilian point of view can also be a rational point of view. This shift in narrative viewpoint is one of the bases of the classroom project "Make Your Own Monster" and "Pale as the Noonday Sun" can easily be incorporated into that project.

5. Classroom Project

5.1. Monster Concepts and Sensory Details

If reptilians are embedded as monsters deep within the human psyche, then there ought to be continuing manifestations independent of the body of film and literature. To explore this question, I created a short activity to allow the self-definition of monsters and assigned this activity to high school students in my creative writing class at Fort Worth Country Day School, a private college-preparatory school in Fort Worth, Texas, USA. The class is an English Department elective open to juniors and seniors, and its nature allows for a fluid curriculum in the realm of writing.

This exercise is couched in terms of either a monster in a haunted house or an invasion of terrifying aliens. I create opening prompts for each of these scenarios that stop when the door opens, then allow students to fill in the blank with anything that strikes them as alien and horrific. Besides being an exercise of the imagination in describing aliens, this activity solidifies a class discussion of sensory details as an important form of vivid fiction writing. Appealing to the five senses – sight, sound, smell, touch, taste – is a way of drawing the reader into a story by supplying them with pseudo stimulation within a verbal context. The important point to stress in discussion is that not all description is sensory. Visual descriptions abound in fiction, but only those descriptions that supply light and color, or conversely darkness as lack of color, trigger sight perceptions in the brain. For example, to write that "the obese clown lumbered down the aisle of the supermarket and fell heavily on his face in the dairy section," is vivid writing in that it is specific with details and employs a strong verb. It is not, however, sensory, merely specific action. To become sensory, the action must be overlaid with light and color: "The obese clown in a red-and-blue jacket lumbered down the dark aisle of the supermarket and fell heavily on his green-painted face in the dairy section." To make the same sentence even more vivid, the writer could make appeal to more than one sense: "The obese clown in a red-and-blue jacket lumbered through the buzzing crowd in the supermarket aisle and fell heavily on his green-painted face in the chilly dairy section." Here are appeals not only to sight, but also to sound (buzzing) and touch (chilly). In the context of a supermarket, it would also be easy to add in smells, though at some point the poor sentence would sink under the weight of too many tightly packed sensory details.

For the purpose of the monster activity, some senses work better than others. Sight is most important, but sound and smell can also be significant. For touch to function, there would have to be a less likely tactile interaction between the narrator and the alien, and the taste of the alien is very unlikely to come into play. For my students, I specified sight, sound, and smell as requirements. I also assigned other non-monster writing exercises where all five senses are required as a follow-up to the sensory discussion.

5.2. Making the Monsters

Because are no limits placed upon the aliens, students can imagine in a variety of directions, but if the premise of the ophidian/draconian /saurian presence being hardwired into the human brain is true, then a prevalent direction ought to be towards lizardmen in some shape or form. One would expect that to be truer for the alien invasion scenario than for the haunted house. In reality, while the range of monsters was different using the haunted house scenario as a Halloween activity, the lizard quotient remained consistent with both scenarios. The two writing concepts that the project emphasizes are sensory details and narrative viewpoint, and all the discussions come back to those core concepts.

5.3. Discussion and Analysis

In the exercise, nothing unexpected was uncovered, nor was I able to prove anything about stereotypes in this small classroom sampling. What I did discover, however, was the opportunity for productive expansion of the exercise into a series of three or more lessons that include classroom discussion and student analysis of each other's work. Stereotyping, of course, is a much broader topic than reptilian characters in science fiction, but the exercise represents an inroad into the broad topic, specifically the final discussion where students are asked whether writing from the monster's viewpoint changed their attitude toward the monster. There exists the opportunity for growth in thinking and perspective that affects more than reptilians.

5.4. Extension Readings

The classroom project is designed to function with the writing and discussion sections outlined in the lesson plan below, or to be expanded with readings that thematically tie into the discussions. Both of the possible readings from the Shipleyverse are free online for classroom use.

Prior to Lesson One, "Fruits of Victory" could be read. This short story has a strong subtext of sensory details, not only as they are used for description, but also as a plot device that shows the narrator becoming entranced by the sensuousness of experiencing certain sights, smells, and tastes for the first time. This reading could serve as an introduction to the sensory details discussion, especially how the viewpoint character's mind, and therefore the course of the story, is fundamentally changed by sensory details. "Fruits of Victory" is free for classroom use, available online.[20]

In conjunction with Lesson Three "Pale as the Noonday Sun could be read. This short story explores the flipped viewpoint and utilizes a reptilian sentient as the viewpoint character who interacts with a human. There are two possible uses of this extension reading. This could be used as preparation for the students flipping viewpoints in their own scenarios, or could be a reading assignment after the second written scenario. Either way, this can be a part of the discussion along with the students' scenarios. The particularly interesting questions from this story are 1) How sympathetic is the saurian viewpoint character, 2) How sympathetic is the human character through saurian eyes, and 3) Could the very unsympathetic Skal snake character become sympathetic as a viewpoint character? "Pale as the Noonday Sun" is available as a free ebook for classroom use.[21]

Topic	Creating and describing your personal monster in the most vivid way
Objectives	To develop and practise: • vivid writing: sensory details • vocabulary: unique words connected with each sense • figures of speech: similes and onomatopoeia • oral presentation skills: individual readings analysis: identification of words and senses from the examples
Age	High School aged 15-18
Level	English Native Speaker, CEFR C2
Time	3 lessons of 70 minutes each • Lesson 1: Present sensory detail concepts and examples; begin writing assignment • Lesson 2: Share writing assignments; analyze sensory details; begin second writing assignment Lesson 3: Share second writing assignments; discuss both sensory description and the effectiveness of flipping viewpoints
Materials/media	Projection of written materials for discussion, both before and after the writing time
Introduction	In these lessons, students will discuss the five senses (sight, sound, smell, taste, touch) and listen to examples that evoke the senses through description. Students then will write their own examples by completing one of the prepared opening paragraphs about monsters. Students are encouraged to include three senses. Upon completion, students will share their scenarios and let others identify which three senses are evoked and which words create that sense. The teacher may designate a Best of Sight, Best of Sound, etc. and explain why this example was especially effective. A second writing assignment continues to use sensory descriptions but focuses on flipping the viewpoint narrator from human to monster. The discussion afterward includes both sensory analysis and viewpoint responses.
Procedure – Lesson 1 Summary	Teacher will present sensory details; class will discuss examples; students will write a monster scenario
Present and Discuss	PRESENT TO STUDENTS: Using sensory details in description is a 'show don't tell' method of vivid

	writing. There are five senses – sight, sound, smell, taste, touch – but sight is used more often than all the others combined, not because it is better, but simply because it is easier. As writers, you want to appeal to all five senses. Adjectives are the main words used in description, but the figures of speech of simile and onomatopoeia are also very useful. What words and devices do you find in the following examples? SIGHT: Emphasizes colors and light, or lack of light EXAMPLE: An aged woman in a dark, flowing cloak burst through the door and commandeered a stool at the dirty counter. (all adjectives) SOUND: Onomatopoeia is always a sound sensory detail EXAMPLE: The steady drip-ping-drip echoing from the tiled bathroom drilled into his head like a slow jackhammer. (onomatopoeia and simile) SMELL: Often describes food or an unpleasant stench EXAMPLE: The gritty aroma of bacon wafted down the hall from the kitchen, followed by a gust of sweet blueberry from the pancake batter. (all adjectives) TASTE: Most often describes food, but can be a bitter, unpleasant sensation in the mouth as well EXAMPLE: In stony silence he devoured the stew, the earthy taste of mushrooms smothered under a layer of tart allspice and melted butter. There would be time to talk later. (all adjectives) TOUCH: Always refers to feeling a texture under the fingers, never feeling as an emotion EXAMPLE: She picked up the glowing amulet, marveling at the contrast in texture – glassy smoothness on one side and coarse, pebbly grit on the other. (all adjectives)
Discuss again	PRESENT TO STUDENTS: Which words and devices create which sensory details in these two introductory paragraphs? Intro 1: The three children pushed on the front door of the old, abandoned mansion at the edge of town. The carved oak door opened with a loud creak to reveal a

	long hallway covered in dust and cobwebs that shone white in their flashlights. The house had obviously not been opened in a long time for a strong musty smell like wet socks came from all of the rooms. The children moved down the hallway, running their hands over the polished wood of the staircase banister as they passed by. At the end of the hall was the door they had heard about at school, the door to the cellar of the house. Taking deep breaths to summon their courage, they each raised a hand to knock on the door in unison – once, twice, three times. Then they waited. At length they heard shuffling steps coming up the cellar steps and saw the door handle slowly turn. As the door swung open, they gasped as they saw what they had summoned. Intro 2: The Battle for Earth was over and humanity had lost. All people could do was wait anxiously for their new overlords to arrive. A crowd gathered at the airstrip north of town, and townspeople dressed in gray overcoats and mud boots milled listlessly around the open space. The sky was overcast with dark clouds, and the air was heavy with the scent of burning cars that the aliens had incinerated from above. Suddenly, a shrill humming filled the air, and a dark globe appeared in the sky far overhead. It descended rapidly, and the people below pressed back to give it ample room on the airstrip. The globe came to a halt and a drawbridge-like aperture opened downward. The gathered crowd gasped as the first of the aliens came down the drawbridge into view.
Write	ASSIGNMENT FOR STUDENTS: Choose one of the two opening paragraphs and write the rest of the scene. You want to focus on two things: creating a vivid monster and using three sensory details as part of that description. You may start the writing today in class so that it is ready to present next class period.
Procedure – Lesson 2 Summary	Students will read their monster vignettes Class will discuss sensory details of each Teacher will lead a summary discussion about types of monsters Students will write a second monster vignette
Presenting	Each student will read his/her prepared vignette

Discuss Sensory Details	After each reading, ask students to identify the three sensory details and whether adjectives, similes, or onomatopoeia are used.
Discuss Types of Monsters	After all the readings, poll the class on categories of monsters used. Were they strange aliens with tentacles, or vampires, or giant cockroaches? Was there a difference in type of monsters according to which intro paragraph was used? Did the haunted house lend itself to ghosts, ghouls, and vampires, and the spaceship to bizarre aliens, or was there no pattern? Which particular monster felt the scariest to you the listeners? Did one type of monster feel scarier than another type?
Discuss Viewpoint	PRESENT TO STUDENTS: What is narrative viewpoint? It is the character through whose eyes the scene is being told. While it is possible to have an omniscient viewpoint, vivid writing often focuses on the experiences of one character. In the first vignette, the story was told from the viewpoint of a human looking at monsters. In the second vignette, that will be flipped around.
Write a Second Vignette	ASSIGNMENT FOR STUDENTS: Rewrite the monster scene from the viewpoint of the monster being summoned or landing on the airstrip. What sights, smells, and sounds is it most aware of. How does it view the humans in front of it? How does it describe the humans? Have this scene ready to present next class period.
Procedure – Lesson 3 Summary	Students will read their second scenarios Class will analyze sensory details of each Teacher will poll the class which viewpoint is more effective
Presenting	Each student will read his/her prepared second scenario
Discuss Sensory Details	After each reading, ask students to identify the three sensory details and whether adjectives, similes, or onomatopoeia are used.
Discuss Viewpoint	Ask students which viewpoint was more interesting and why? *Which viewpoint was more vivid in description?*
Discuss Overall Conclusions	After all the readings, ask if there is a class trend in viewpoint. *Was the human or monster viewpoint more interesting? Did the monsters cease to be monsters by telling the scene through their eyes?*

	Who was more monstrous – monsters through human eyes or humans through monster eyes?

Table 1: Make Your Own Monster

5.5. Retrospective – Responses to the Lessons from my Students

Because I assigned Intro One and Intro Two as two different activities on different days, students never had as full a range of monsters to experiment with. With Intro One, the results were, predictably, skewed more toward Halloween monsters than aliens, and with Intro Two, the aliens tended toward, unpredictably, distortions of human images. Of the dozen Intro One responses, five were human-based monsters – vampires, reanimated corpses, faceless men in tuxes – in keeping with traditional Halloween characters. But two fell broadly into the stereotypical lizardmen category with a "green, rough" monster and a human body with a snake head. What was universal in this sensory detail exercise was the vivid use of smell in all the vignettes. All the monsters stank, which is not unexpected with dead corpses, but less expected of random creatures. No one described how the monsters tasted. Of the dozen Intro Two responses, four were very alien with tentacled, amorphous, or multi-limbed bodies. The strangest result was giant noodle creatures. Six responses were distorted human beings, but very recognizably human beings, and two responses fell into the lizardmen category with beings that were green with diamond-shaped eyes or, as one student described them, "ugly lizard-looking aliens". The fact that each scenario consistently produced two reptilian responses was different than my expectations, as was the result that a number of students saw humans as the greatest monsters. That in itself could be worth some exploration. I did not expand either exercise to a full multi-lesson project with discussions, readings, and multiple writings, but I would do so in the future in order to solidify the concepts of sensory details and narrative viewpoint. Flipping a character from unsympathetic to sympathetic by flipping the viewpoint is an especially valuable lesson in possibilities for young writers. Often in the creation of fiction, it is not just the sequence of events that determines the success of the story, but also through whose eyes the story is told.

6. Conclusion

The reptilian presence in the science fiction genre is enduring but not consistent in its usage over time. There seems to be a tacit acknowledgment that reptilian lizardmen are intrinsically non-human, perhaps threateningly non-mammalian in nature, but with the possibility of being merely different, not monstrous. Writers are aware of the stereotype and support it or counter it as fits the nature of the immediate story. Where the writing counters the stereotype, it is a step back from the monster stereotype, but does that mean a different alien race then becomes the monsters of the storyline?

The whole lesson project could serve as an introduction to a more philosophical discussion of human nature. As the blurring of lines between human and reptilian is explored in various ways by various writers without any consensus, so could those ideas be explored in the classroom: Are we cousins to dragons? Do humans have inner dragons waiting to emerge? Do dragons have inner humans? Who is more dangerous? Are we more the same than we care to admit? None of these questions have answers or resolution, but their value is in the exploration. For some students and some classes, the abstraction level of this discussion may be too high, but with other classes, there may be an opportunity, even though it could easily turn into a dark discussion that is less about posthuman transformation than an acknowledgment of what is already within our inner nature that may emerge through circumstances. While a positive spin might be that humans innately long to fly, and flight is our connective link to dragons, what we see repeated in literature and graphics is that the shared link between human soul and dragon soul seems to be the darker shades of behavior – greed, violence, deceit, and destruction. Within the context of creative writing, however, the connection can be anything we decide will tell our story well, and therein lies the power of the writer.

[1] Ludwig, Christian, and Elizabeth Shipley (2019). "Reading and Creating the Posthuman in the Primary and Secondary EFL Classroom – Report of a Posthuman Teaching Experiment with Graphic Novels, Children's Books and Visual Media." *Teaching the Posthuman*. Eds. Roman Bartosch and Julia Hoydis. Heidelberg: Winter, 45-74, 46-47.

[2] Hegel, G.W.F. (2014[1807]). *The Phenomenology of Mind.* Trans. J.B. Baillie. Web. 8 August 2019 <https://ebooks.adelaide.edu.au /h/ hegel/phenomenology_of_mind/ complete.html>.

[3] Adkins, Roger A. (2010). "The 'Monstrous Other' Speaks: Postsubjectivity and the Queering of the Normal." *University of Oregon Scholar's Bank*. Web. 8 August 2019 <http://hdl.handle.net/1794/10875>.

[4] Man versus Beast appears sexist, but Human versus Beast conveys less of the feeling of the original.

[5] "Dragon." *Webster's New International Dictionary of the English Language*, Second Edition, Unabridged. 1948.

[6] Grimm, Jacob Ludwig Karl, and Wilhelm Carl Grimm (1936[1857]). "The Dragon and His Grandmother." *Tales from Grimm.* Trans. Wanda Gag. New York: Coward-McCann.

[7] Shipley, Jonathan (2017). "Fruits of Victory." *Cosmic Roots and Eldritch Shores*. Web. 3 March 2020 <https://cosmicrootsandeldritchshores.com /fiction>.

[8] Sagan, Carl (1977). *The Dragons of Eden: Speculations on the Evolution of Human Intelligence.* New York: Ballantine Books, 149.

[9] Budson, Andrew (2017). "Don't Listen to Your Lizard Brain." *Psychology Today* 3 Dec. 2017. Web. 8 August 2019 <http://www.psychologytoday.com /us/blog/ managing your memory/201712>.

[10] Sagan (1977), 150.

[11] Barrie's original title *Peter and Wendy* became better known under the title *Peter Pan.*

[12] Barrie, J.M. (1911). *Peter and Wendy.* New York: Charles Scribner's Sons, 43.

[13] Shipley, Jonathan (2019). "Brooklyn." Unpublished manuscript.

[14] "Arena." *Star Trek: The Original Series.* Creator Gene Roddenberry. 1967. Desilu Productions.

[15] "The Xindi." *Star Trek: Enterprise*. Creator Rick Berman. 2003. Paramount Domestic Television.

[16] "Brooklyn." (unpublished).

17 *V: The Original Miniseries*. Creator Kenneth Johnson. 1983. Warner Bros. Television.

18 "Brooklyn." (unpublished).

19 Shipley, Jonathan (2016). "Pale as the Noonday Sun." *The Worlds of Science* Fiction, *Fantasy, and Horror, Vol. 1*. Ed. Robert Stephenson. Adelaide: Altair Australia Pty Ltd.,166-180.

20 "Fruits of Victory" is available at the Cosmic Roots and Eldritch Shores website at <https://cosmicrootsandeldritchshores.com/fiction-all/myths-legends-and-fairy-tales/fruits-of-victory/>.

21 "Pale as the Noonday Sun", part of *The Worlds of Science Fiction, Fantasy and Horror Vol 1* anthology, is available at <https://www.smashwords.com/books/view/607089>.

Bibliography

Primary Texts

The Adventures of Merlin. Creator Julian Jones et al. 2008. Shine Limited Television Series.

Barrie, J.M. (1911). *Peter and Wendy.* New York: Charles Scribner's Sons.

Creature from the Black Lagoon. Dir. Jack Arnold 1954. Universal Pictures.

Grimm, Jacob Ludwig Karl, and Wilhelm Carl Grimm (1936[1857]). "The Dragon and His Grandmother." *Tales from Grimm.* Trans. Wanda Gag. New York: Coward-McCann.

Lewis, C.S. (1952). *The Voyage of the Dawn Treader.* London: Geoffrey Bles.

Le Guin, Ursula (1968). *A Wizard of Earthsea.* Berkeley, California: Parnassus Press.

Martin, George R.R. (1996-). *A Song of Ice and Fires.* New York: Bantam Spectra.

Rowling, J.K. (2000). *Harry Potter and the Goblet of Fire.* New York: Scholastic.

Shipley, Jonathan (2016). "Pale as the Noonday Sun." *The Worlds of Science Fiction, Fantasy, and Horror, Vol. 1*. Ed. Robert Stephenson. Adelaide: Altair Australia Pty Ltd., 166-180.

--- (2017). "Fruits of Victory." *Cosmic Roots and Eldritch Shores*. Web. Web. 3 March 2020 <https://cosmicrootsandeldritchshores.com/fiction>.

--- (2019). "Brooklyn." Unpublished manuscript.

"The Xindi." *Star Trek: Enterprise.* Creator Rick Berman. 2003. Paramount Domestic Television.

"Arena.". *Star Trek: The Original Series.* Creator Gene Roddenberry. 1967. Desilu Productions.

Tolkien, J.R.R. (1937). *The Hobbit.* New York, Ballantine Books.

V: The Original Miniseries. Creator Kenneth Johnson. 1983. Warner Bros. Television.

Secondary Literature

Adkins, Roger A. (2010). "The 'Monstrous Other' Speaks: Postsubjectivity and the Queering of the Normal." *University of Oregon Scholar's Bank*. Web. 8 August 2019 <http://hdl.handle.net/1794/10875>.

Budson, Andrew (2017). "Don't Listen to Your Lizard Brain." *Psychology Today* 3 Dec. 2017. Web. 8 August 2019 <http://www.psychologytoday.com/us /blog/ managing your memory/201712>.

"Dragon." *Webster's New International Dictionary of the English Language, Second Edition, Unabridged.* 1948.

Hegel, G.W.F. (2014[1807]). *The Phenomenology of Mind.* Trans. J.B. Baillie. Web. 8 August 2019 <https://ebooks.adelaide.edu.au /h/hegel /phenomenology_of_mind/ complete.html>.

Ludwig, Christian, and Elizabeth Shipley (2019). "Reading and Creating the Posthuman in the Primary and Secondary EFL Classroom – Report of a Posthuman Teaching Experiment with Graphic Novels, Children's Books and Visual Media." *Teaching the Posthuman*. Eds. Roman Bartosch and Julia Hoydis. Heidelberg: Winter, 45-74.

Sagan, Carl (1977). *The Dragons of Eden: Speculations on the Evolution of Human Intelligence.* New York: Ballantine Books.

Jürgen Wehrmann (Oldenburg)

Teaching the Form of Science Fiction: Introducing and Using Critical Terminology in Analytical, Intertextual and Creative Tasks

1. Introduction

When science fiction is discussed in the English as a Foreign Language Classroom (EFL) classroom, the focus is usually on the content, whereas formal elements and narrative strategies specific to the genre tend to be neglected. This chapter argues that formalist studies on science fiction offer teachers and students insights into the genre that enable a deeper interaction with texts and films as well as, consequently, a more holistic access to their themes. First, some reasons will be given why genre definitions and critical terminology are significant and at least necessary evils, before a synthesis of some main formalist theories of science fiction is attempted. This synthesis will enable me to describe the ways teachers can use critical terms for analysing science fiction both in preparation of lessons and as technical terms during classroom discussions. Lastly, I will include a plan for a lesson sequence in which genre definitions and other critical terms are introduced.

During all of these steps, the argumentation will mainly refer to one example, the young-adult novel *The Hunger Games* (2008) by Suzanne Collins, chosen because of its immense popularity and its potential for the EFL classroom.[1] *The Hunger Games* is set in a future post-apocalyptic dystopian society and tells the story of sixteen-year-old Katniss Everdeen, who has to take part in a sadistic reality TV show: together with 23 other teenagers and a battery of weapons, she is thrown into a huge outdoor arena. Only the last person alive wins. In telling how Katniss struggles to survive and maintain her personal integrity in this extreme situation, the novel raises political and ecological questions and alludes to various cultural discourses, which can be explored in the EFL classroom.

2. Cutting Words: The Risks and Benefits of Definitions and Critical Terminology

Literature, or at least good literature, is assumed to be fluid, ambiguous and unpredictable. The act of putting something as strange, complex and multi-faceted as a well-written literary text into a little box like a genre, a period or a formal category will usually seem somewhat inadequate and of limited relevance to lovers of the art form. Therefore, one does not expect two experienced, highly respected writers, each known to be an admirer of the work of the other, to publicly argue about whether a novel should or should not be subsumed under a certain genre. Yet this is exactly what happened when Ursula Le Guin reviewed Margaret Atwood's *The Year of the Flood* (2009) and criticised Atwood's statement that she did not write science-fiction novels.[2] Atwood answered graciously, claiming that the divergent classifications were only a matter of words and obscured an agreement in principle. At the same time, however, she insisted on the very differentiation between playfully fantastic science fiction and a more serious and demanding speculative fiction that Le Guin had opposed.[3]

Le Guin, whose work, in contrast to Atwood's, has almost completely been published under the labels of science fiction and fantasy, had too much experience with the damaging effects of exclusive, prescriptive and derogatory genre definitions to believe that Atwood's distinction could be meant or understood as value free. Not only has 'science fiction' been used as a pejorative term for decades, associated with juvenile adventure stories spun around mad scientists, tech gadgets and extraterrestrial monsters, but also within the genre itself and its subcultural community of fans, authors and critics, waves of prescriptive distinctions have followed each other, all of them attempting to raise the status of one group of texts by devaluating another: science fiction demarcated against fantasy, hard science fiction against soft science fiction, and speculative fiction against space opera. This is why Le Guin argued for an inclusive, descriptive use of the term 'science fiction', based on typical formal elements and strategies as general as possible, which allows readers to appreciate the individual work against the background of similar and divergent forms.

Obviously, genre politics as complex and contradictory as the one practised by and against the science-fiction community is a fascinating object of cultural study. Science-fiction studies have accordingly shifted from a predominantly synchronic perspective on the genre to a diachronic one that considers science fiction as a historical process rather than a fixed, universal entity.[4] Such an approach makes a general definition of science fiction virtually impossible:

> In fact, the only genre definition [...] adequate to the historical paradigm would be a kind of tautology, an assertion that the genre is whatever the various discursive agents involved in its production, distribution and reception say it is.[5]

However, the historical paradigm appears to be much less fruitful in teaching literature in the EFL classroom than in cultural studies. To trace the discursive constructions and reconstructions of science fiction and its subgenres in history is not an efficient or motivating task for language learning. In contrast, the formalist attempts to describe structures and strategies specific to a large group of texts marketed and read as 'science fiction' offer inclusive, descriptive critical terms that can be very useful for discussing films, novels and short stories in the EFL classroom. These critical terms and definitions may not be perfect and equally applicable to each and every text of the field, but they enable students to understand the phenomenon 'science fiction' better and they allow teachers to develop effective analytical, creative and intertextual tasks for the EFL classroom.

For reliable critical terms are essential in order to achieve an integration of analytical, creative and intertextual reading strategies in the classroom. Critical terms allow us to focus on and talk about forms in a more precise manner. Discussing the content of a text without including its form will often result in a vague, superficial interpretation or might even lead to serious misunderstandings because obviously "form shapes meaning".[6] Without some knowledge of the form of a text, teachers will also find it hard to identify possible creative tasks that can be used to work with the text, and if critical terms are available in order to describe creative allusions to, modifications of and departures from the original texts, action- and production-oriented tasks can be more effectively included in lessons.[7] Furthermore, forms serve as intertextual markers, refer back to pretexts with similar forms and position texts in or between cultural discourses, so that they can be employed as starting-points for intertextual tasks.

While the formalist paradigm in science-fiction studies thus provides knowledge that, in a simplified version, is directly applicable in the classroom, the historical paradigm can sensitise educationalists and teachers to the problematic usage of genre terms in a lot of teaching material. It is remarkable that curricula and teaching material predominantly refer to 'utopian' and 'dystopian literature', supposedly genres clearly distinguishable from 'science fiction', which seems less worth being taught.[8] Yet many critics are of the opinion that it is virtually impossible to consistently separate utopias and dystopias from science fiction as independent genres, either in a historical or systematic perspective, since the 1950s, describing Ray Bradbury's *Fahrenheit 451* (1953) as the point when the science-fiction magazine tradition and the more established utopian and dystopian traditions merged.[9] 'Young-adult dystopia' is a term that enables publishers to market books without the subcultural, nerdy connotations of science fiction. It allows literary critics and educationalists to isolate a popular group of texts and films for study from a wider transmedial context and from the criticism discussing this larger field, although the group of texts does not substantially differ from many other science-fiction films and texts. Thus, the usage of the term continues a tradition in the classroom that, knowingly or unknowingly, excludes and devalues large portions of science fiction. However, in an educational context, it appears to be particularly appropriate to use neutral, inclusive and descriptive terms, and also students will find terms that can be applied to a wider field of cultural production more useful than terms of a limited range.

3. Mapping Alternative Worlds: A Synthesis of Theories of Science Fiction

Instead of relying on one of many theories of science fiction, teaching science fiction should build on a synthesis of different approaches. Literary critics tend to concentrate on one specific perspective on science fiction, for example, the relations of the text to the world, to other texts or to the reader. These various perspectives should be integrated when defining key critical terms that can help discussing science fiction in the classroom.

3.1. Relations between Text and World in Science Fiction

A particularly influential theorist of science fiction, Darko Suvin, considers the relation between text and world as most important to science fiction. Science-fiction texts do not only contain people, places or events non-existent in the empirical world, but fundamental conditions are changed, like knowledge, technology, social and political systems or types of intelligent agents. Suvin uses the term *novum* for such fundamental elements of the storyworld that are significantly different from the world known and understood at the time of writing the text. According to Suvin, a *novum* is an "estrangement" of the author and implicit reader's world that, in science fiction, has to be "cognitive", that is: reconcilable with the contemporary state of scientific and academic thinking.[10] Obviously, this is a very restrictive definition, so that Freedman has suggested considering the cognition in science fiction primarily as a device *internal* to the text, as a "cognition effect". In order to class a text or film as science fiction, it is sufficient to examine whether it *presents* its *nova* as if they were reconcilable with a scientific world view, notwithstanding the question whether they really are.[11]

The functions of *nova* can be complex and multilayered. In many science-fiction texts, they are more than spectacular props for exciting action. Undoubtedly, the cruel TV event called the Hunger Games enables Suzanne Collins to achieve in her novel what Hegel describes as reconstruction of individual independence ("die Rekonstruktion der individuellen Selbständigkeit").[12] In the arena, there are no laws and institutions within which the tributes have to act; they are, though in a perverse manner, set free to produce justice from within themselves. Thus, the *novum* of the Hunger Games creates a space for heroic violence and for an action-packed plot. However, the *novum* can also be understood as an experimental hypothesis: if young people had to play a game in which they had to fight each other to death and only one of them could win, how would they act? At the same time, the Hunger Games can be read as a satire of reality television or as a symbol for the struggle of young people to find a place in a highly competitive world dominated by an unreliable, irresponsible older generation.[13] Finally, the *novum* of the Hunger Games is an element of the *novum* of a highly unjust, oppressive future society situated in North America, Panem. This overarching *novum* implies a fictitious historical narrative that puts the present America into a new context: as the past out of which Panem has emerged. Like *The Hunger Games*, many science-fiction films and novels present *nova* that combine these main four functions; while propelling the action, they are symbols, experimental hypotheses and meditations on the future course of history at the same time.

Science fiction is a very diverse genre, encompassing quite different types of texts and films. As Malmgren has shown,[14] the genre can, to a large extent, be mapped out according to the parts of the fictional world formed as *nova*:

World component changed to a *novum*	Subgenres
Character	Intelligently acting beings appear in the plot that do not exist in reality, for example aliens (alien encounter sf), robots (robot sf) or artificially created human beings.
Social and political order	An alternative society is depicted (social sf). This society can be better than our society or even ideal (utopia), but it can also be much worse (dystopia).
Objects	A newly invented technology plays a central role in the plot (gadget sf), or a new natural phenomenon is discovered.
Place	The story is set in outer space or on another planet (space sf) or depicts a radical change of places on Earth (apocalyptic sf, disaster movies, post-apocalyptic sf).
Basic assumptions: historical facts, natural laws and other theories	Some films and texts show another timeline, an alternative past or present based on the assumption that key historical events had a different outcome, for example. Germany won World War II (alternate history). Others deny facts and theories that were common knowledge at the time of writing (science fantasy).

Table 1: Subgenres of Science Fiction Based on Types of *Nova* (Simplified Adaptation of Malmgren's Table)

Obviously, science fiction often contains combinations of several *nova* rather than having one *novum*, so that mixtures are widespread. *The Hunger Games* is set in a world radically transformed by climate change (post-apocalyptic sf) and depicts a society significantly worse than the one we live in (social sf, dystopia), a society in which the ruling class commands technology more advanced than ours (gadget sf). Interestingly enough, the ecological catastrophe is referred to only in a few passages, and nature seems to have largely recovered, while tech gadgets merely play minor roles and the socio-political structure of Panem is hardly more than roughly sketched, sometimes even surprisingly naively and inconsistently (what rulers in their right mind would mutilate a proven enemy of the state and then use her as a servant ["Avox"], opening their homes and other sensitive places to her, or what system could survive forcing parents to watch on TV how their children are murdered for 75 years?). It seems evident that the dominating *novum* of Collins' novel is the ritual/ show of the Hunger Games themselves, and that the book's tremendous power primarily stems from the intensive depiction of the Hunger Games through the eyes of a fascinating heroine – and from the symbolical value and the historical references of this *novum*. Correspondingly, many texts will not comfortably fit into the systematic subgenres as distinguished by Malmgren but will be clearly recognisable as science fiction according to the definition by Suvin and Freedman.

3.2. Relations Between the Text and Other Texts in Science Fiction

Science fiction does not need to be based on original extrapolations and speculations. Often, we recognise science-fiction films and texts as such simply by conventional motifs like robots, spaceships, time machines and artificial intelligence, the sum of which Broderick has described as the "mega-text" of science fiction, stabilising both the genre and the single text.[15] Indeed, most science fiction adopts, varies and develops *nova* already established in the genre. At the same time, science fiction has proven that it can assimilate all kinds of themes, motifs, plots and types of material beyond the mega-text, transforming the old into something new and futuristic.[16] The highly intertextual character of the genre has been considered as endangering its cognitive content but also as implying a subversive, critical potential, since it can be used to sell an age-old story once more in a futuristic costume without any truly significant changes or it may be employed to form thought-provoking montages of various discourses.[17] Hallet has shown that the complex intertextual references of some science-fiction texts can be starting-points for exploring political discourses of the target culture in the EFL classroom.[18]

The Hunger Games are not an original *novum*. Similar reality TV shows appear in several texts and films (for example, *Battle Royale* [novel 1999, film 2000] and *The Running Man* [novel 1982, film 1987]). Yet, since killing as reality TV is not a canonic, generally known element of the mega-text of science fiction, the intertextual references clearly marked in the text are more relevant to interpretations of the novel. According to Suzanne Collins, the idea for *The Hunger Games* emerged by an accidental montage of two different visual discourses when she "was lying in bed channel-surfing between reality TV and coverage of the Iraq War".[19] Interestingly enough, the novel itself, in contrast to the film, never represents reality TV as a text directly from the perspective of the audience or the gamemakers. Rather, it shows reality TV as a practice through the eyes of one of the victims/players.

Like in much science fiction, neologisms serve as intertextual markers in *The Hunger Games*. Newly invented words are more frequent in science fiction than in any other genre, and, at first sight, finding a name for a *novum* appears to be a moment of complete linguistic independence, allowing the author to freely connect sounds to an extralinguistic (even if imagined) object for the first time. In fact, however, neologisms in science fictions are usually not isolated creations but intersections between texts, well-calculated instruments that integrate *nova* in cultural discourses. For example, new scientific discoveries are mostly named with newly combined words, prefixes and suffixes adopted from Greek and Latin, in imitation of established scientific practice in order to enhance the cognition effect.[20] Neosemes, known words with a new meaning, are also a frequent device in science fiction, which emphasises cultural changes and marks historical connections.[21]

The most important neologism in *The Hunger Games* is 'Panem', the name of the future state depicted. On the one hand, 'Panem' can be understood as a form of 'Pan Am', short for 'Pan American', mainly familiar from bombastic names of companies like Pan American World Airways. Changes in the way the word is written and pronounced might suggest the passing of time and underline the historical and cultural transformations that have taken place since our present. On the other hand, 'Panem' is the accusative of the Latin word *panis*, meaning 'bread' and referring to a famous quotation from Roman satirist Juvenal, "panem and circenses". Juvenal criticised that the Roman emperors had destroyed the Roman Republic while distracting the citizens with gladiator fights and donations of bread.[22] Thus, the name of the fictitious state hints at parallels between the Hunger Games and the Roman circus and connects an expanded US or American hegemony to discourses of Roman tyranny, decline and decadence. Other neologisms derived from Latin like 'avox' and the usage of Roman first names for almost all characters from the Capitol reinforce the association of Panem with Ancient Rome. Furthermore, 'Capitol', as the name for the capital of Panem a neoseme, alludes to the idea of a *translatio imperii*, widespread from the eighteenth century onwards, which imagined America as the heir of the Roman Empire[23] and which also inspired Jefferson to name the American congress building after the temple *capitolinum*, the holy religious and political centre of the Roman Empire.[24] According to the founding fathers, the challenge that the young union had to face was how to emulate the virtues of the Roman Republic while avoiding their perversion in the Roman Empire. The *Hunger Games* trilogy was written under the impression of the Bush presidency, whose unilateralist foreign policy was described as imperialist by some and triggered new comparisons between the US and the Roman Empire. "Arc We Rome?" asked the title of a popular political book in the year before *The Hunger Games* was published.[25]

3.3. Relations Between Text and Reader

One of the most astonishing facts about *The Hunger Games* is the novel's tremendous success especially among teenagers but also many adult readers. While *The Hunger Games* was primarily written and marketed for young adults, nevertheless a particular affinity of the age group to science fiction in general has always been observed, prompting the famous statement: "[T]he real golden age of science fiction is twelve".[26] Obviously, the genre satisfies needs of a significant group of young people. Many texts lend themselves to a romantic reading that focuses on empathy with heroines and heroes crossing boundaries of space, time, knowledge, culture and biology.[27] Science fiction can frequently offer "an intense experience of being translated from the mundane to imaginary worlds and ideas that exceed the familiar and the habitual".[28] The 'sense of wonder' created by the genre has been described through the categories of the sublime and the grotesque: science fiction can evoke natural and technological phenomena of enormous size and power, and it teems with interstitial beings like the "muttations" in the *Hunger Games* trilogy, defying known rational distinctions between culture and nature, human and animal, or person and thing.

Due to its garish effects and sensational themes, science fiction is considered an easy read by many. Yet, in fact, reading a science-fiction text involves specific challenges, as the genre imagines worlds in which fundamental conditions are changed. In order to identify and understand the *nova*, information is needed, and science-fiction texts differ regarding the amount of that information and their helpfulness towards the reader. Some texts contain characters mediating between the world of the reader and the fictitious world transformed by the *nova*. These mediators either, like the narrator in H.G. Wells' *The War of the Worlds* (1898), experience how the *novum* irrupts into their world, which is initially quite similar to the reader's, or they, like the time traveler in *The Time Machine* (1895), travel to the strange, changed world. In both cases, the readers can follow the learning process of the mediating characters. More difficult texts are seemingly written from the point of view of the changed world, so that the existence of the *nova* is presented as taken for granted. Consequently, the readers are plunged into a strange world in which they have to look for clues in order to understand the nature and consequences of the *nova*. The knowledge needed to decipher a complex science-fiction text can be quite diverse: knowledge concerning word formation and its discursive and societal contexts to understand neologisms; historical, scientific and technological knowledge; and last but not least knowledge about ideas, motifs and techniques from the mega-text of science fiction.[29]

Thus, a truly competent reading of science fiction asks for an impressively wide range of reading styles: a romantic, empathetic reading is needed to enjoy the plot and sensational effects of science fiction. A speculative reading will focus on the *novum* as a thought experiment, anticipating and reflecting on the implications and consequences of significant changes in the storyworld from the world as known to the reader.[30] Allegorical and intertextual readings look for figurative representations of and allusions to the present and its discourses, while an analytical reading focused on the form enables the appreciation of specific techniques of the genre. Almost as basic to the enjoyment of science fiction as a romantic reading is a reading style that can be called ethnological: if a science-fiction text or film does not only present an exciting technology but depicts a whole society significantly changed by *nova*, the reader encounters a different, fictitious culture that she tries to understand, either by following the hermeneutic efforts of the mediating figures or by treating the whole text like a source from another time or culture.

Indeed, Suvin's analysis of what happens when a science fiction text is read resembles descriptions of intercultural understanding:

> [Science fiction's] specific modality is a feedback oscillation that moves from the author's and implied reader's norm of reality to the narratively actualized novum in order to understand the plot-events, and now back from those novelties to the author's reality, in order to see it afresh from the new perspective gained. This oscillation, called estrangement by Shklovsky and Brecht, is no doubt a consequence of every poetic, dramatic, scientific, in brief *semantic* novum. However, its second pole is in SF a narrative reality sufficiently autonomous and intransitive to be explored at length as to its own properties and the human relationships it implies.[31]

The readers must activate knowledge about their own cultural background and compare known cultural elements to the strange fictitious culture of the science-fiction text in order to grasp similarities and differences between them. Yet this oscillation does not only result in a better understanding of the fictitious culture of the text but enables a distancing from the norms of the readers' world. In Trans- and Intercultural Learning, the critical and creative potential emerging in such an oscillation is described with terms like "critical cultural awareness"[32] and "symbolic competence".[33]

Compared to many science-fiction texts, *The Hunger Games* is quite easy to read. Although the autodiegetic narrator Katniss has grown up in the changed world of the novel, she is, in her ideas and ways of thinking and feeling, very close to contemporary readers. The narration in the present tense, enhancing the suspense and immediacy of the story, also occludes the situation in which the story is told. Still, Katniss does not assume that any important facts about Panem are known to her audience but continuously weaves basic information into the plot. Therefore, the beginning is no typical *heinleining*, as the reader's immediate immersion in the science-fiction world without mediating figures is usually called.[34] However, an important change of perspectives is achieved when readers look at the affluent society of the Capitol, so similar to the West today in many respects, through the eyes of Katniss who is used to shortages of food and starvation in her district.[35]

4. Backstage and On-Stage Uses: Critical Terminology in Teaching Units on Science Fiction

Theories of science fiction and their critical terminology are already useful when texts for teaching units are selected. In addition to general criteria like length, authenticity, linguistic difficulty, potential for identification and thematic interest for the respective group of learners, science-fiction studies suggest aspects specific to the genre that should be taken into consideration. Teachers might tend to evaluate science fiction like any other prose text based on style, characterisation and the perceptive representation of events and interactions. Yet a text can be well written and still seem unsatisfactory as science fiction, which is the reason why not every "invasion from above"[36] – that is attempts at science fiction by authors renowned for texts of other genres – has been successful. The quality of science fiction mainly depends on the quality and the consistent development of its *nova*, whereby the potentially multilayered speculative, allegorical or extrapolative functions of *nova* should be taken into account. A science-fiction text might be readable as a well-conducted thought experiment that casts an interesting light on ethical or political questions. Another is an effective satire or allegory of aspects of our society, while still other science fiction sketches a compelling fictitious historical narrative. Moreover, the intertextual connections to extra-literary discourses or to the science-fiction mega-text might be useful to understand the target culture or the transmedial genre science fiction better.[37] When reflecting on the accessibility of the text for the respective group of learners, teachers should pay attention to the way the *nova* are introduced, the density of neologisms and the usage of *heinleining* or mediating characters.

An understanding of the form of science fiction can also orient teachers planning a teaching unit or task sequence. If a *novum* presents an interesting experimental arrangement, the teacher can let students conduct a thought experiment based on the *novum* as a pre-reading task. In some cases, it might be more interesting to formulate a thought experiment that changes some variables of the plot in the post-reading phase in order to open up other perspectives. Although all kinds of thought experiments can be conducted based on science-fiction texts, moral, political and existential ones are the most interesting because they usually include that the experimenters have to imagine themselves in a specific situation and reflect on their possible actions and reactions. Perspective change here uses extreme circumstances to explore one's own ideas and feelings directly, instead of adopting the perspective of a person with a different cultural background and coordinating this perspective with one's own like in Intercultural Learning.[38] Moral, political and existential thought experiments in philosophical texts differ from science fiction in that, firstly, their experimental arrangement is usually much more limited, they form, secondly, not a closed narrative but expect the experimenter to adopt the roles of protagonist and co-author, and, thirdly, they are framed by a specific question to be answered and an argumentation on the outcome. Using science-fiction texts for thought experiments thus involves the *selection* of suitable experimental hypotheses, a task arrangement that allows the *immersion* of the experimenter into the experimental situation and a *framing* of the experiment by research questions and an evaluation of the results. Either the teacher alone selects a *novum* und, if necessary, adapts it as an experimental arrangement, or the class as a whole looks for *nova* suitable for thought experiments. Immersion is usually achieved by creative tasks like writing, continuing or performing a story, diary entry or scene. Framing can take place through class discussions or writing essays on the implications of the experiment.[39] Yet as I taught *The Hunger Games*, I decided for an abstract discussion of the different options that a person has when entering the Hunger Games because I thought that the scenario was too gruesome to encourage students to immerse too deeply and personally in it. At the same time, I was of the opinion that the central *novum* of *The Hunger Games* was not a very productive experimental hypothesis. The class developed a decision tree, which we used to understand and discuss the moral choices that Peeta and Katniss have to face.

Of course, science fiction can be read in class without introducing any specific critical terminology, which might be particularly sensible in groups of younger learners. However, older, more advanced students aged sixteen or older will benefit from knowing terms like 'novum', 'cognition effect' and 'neologism' in order to focus on specific elements of science fiction and to be able to talk about their functions and effects. Having identified *nova* and neologisms by analytical tasks, students can then explore the contexts of the text. A close reading of *The Hunger Games*, for instance, should be combined with a wide reading: groups of students can choose inter- and extratextual references of the text and do research on subjects like reality TV, circus and its political functions in Ancient Rome, the Roman Republic and the Roman Empire as models for the United States as well as the reasons for hunger and poverty in the world today. The results should be presented on posters and used for deepening the interpretation and discussion of the novel.[40] Neologisms can also be the starting point for product-oriented tasks that entertainingly create awareness of word formation in the target language.

That science fiction offers opportunities for Global Education has been repeatedly pointed out.[41] Science-fiction texts often focus on global issues like hunger and the ecological crisis in the case of *The Hunger Games*. Moreover, since science-fiction *nova* imply fictitious historical narratives, they can be connected to future-oriented activities developed by general conceptualisations of Global Education like "Future Timelines", "Drawing Upon the Future" or "Inventing the Future (Backwards)". [42] For example, students can create a timeline that reconstructs the development from the present US to Panem. They should mark the key moments in this development as mentioned in the text. A second step would be group work, in which two alternative timelines are to be added, one describing the development to the future that students consider probable, the other sketching a way to the future they wish for. After the presentations, the various probable and preferable futures should be compared to each other as well as to the future as projected in *The Hunger Games*. The discussion could then focus on the key moments that students believe to be decisive for the different developments.

5. Introducing Critical Terminology in the EFL Classroom: A Lesson Sequence

Topic	Lead-in to reading and discussing Suzanne Collins' *The Hunger Games* (2008)
Objectives	To develop and practise: • Speaking about prior knowledge • Reading: intensive reading and scanning

	• Vocabulary: critical terminology • Speaking: outlining content of texts, using categories and reflecting on them
Age	Secondary pupils (age 16 and above)
Level	CEF level B1 and above
Time	3 lessons (each 90 minutes)
Materials/media	Various books (science fiction and other) or pictures of book covers, board, whiteboard or overhead projector, *The Hunger Games* (novel), hand-out on technical terms on science fiction
Introduction	In this sequence, pupils will be introduced to critical terminology on science fiction, while starting to read *The Hunger Games*. The critical terminology they learn in this sequence can then be used in the further discussion of the novel.
1st lesson (90 minutes) Before reading 1	Present various book covers of science-fiction and other novels to the pupils and ask them whether the texts are science fiction and why (not). Collect their ideas in a mind map on science fiction. Ask pupils to develop their own definitions of science fiction in pairs, paying attention to differences from genres like crime stories, fantasy and horror. Give them some help by explaining definitions by genus and difference and present an example: "A bachelor is a man (= broader category) who is unmarried (= difference from other men)." Form groups of two former pairs in which pupils are supposed to compare their definitions and analyse some famous provocative and contradictory definitions of science fiction by writers (e.g. Robert Heinlein, Ursula Le Guin and Norman Spinrad). Ask them to discuss the famous examples and develop their own definitions further. At the end of the lesson, several presentations are discussed in class. If there is enough time, pupils can already begin to work on their homework. Homework: Let students think about their own habitat. What keeps you alive? What are your

	needs and how are they met? What places, people and things are essential to achieve that? Pupils can draw a map of their habitat or a diagram of the relationships that keep them alive. They can also describe their habitat on a special day in a short text.
2nd lesson Before reading 2 and while reading 1 Getting into the novel	Ask pupils to compare their homework in groups. Let them discuss which one visualises or describes the habitat best and should be discussed in class. Choose the groups to present randomly. During the presentation let pupils think about whether a person who lived two hundred years ago would have understood this presentation and why (not). Let them discuss how life today is different from life two hundred years ago. Ask pupils to read the first one and a half pages of *The Hunger Games*. They are supposed to find out what they get to know about Katniss' habitat and whether there are already any signals that this is a science-fiction novel. Let the class discuss the results and compare them to their homework for this lesson. Homework: Ask pupils to read the first chapter of the novel. They are to take notes on Katniss' habitat: What keeps her alive? What characters are introduced? What do we learn about the setting? Why is the day described in this chapter special?
3rd lesson While reading 2	Talk with your students about their reading experience, about their first impressions and difficulties that might have arisen while reading. Collect the results of their homework on the board. Compare Katniss' habitat with the habitat of the pupils. Hand out simplified formalist definitions of 'science fiction', 'novum', 'cognition effect', 'neologism', 'neoseme' and 'allusion' based on this chapter as well as the table of subgenres above. The hand-out should also contain a description of typical functions of *nova*. After reading the hand-out, pupils are supposed to work in pairs,

	compare the definition to their own, look for *nova*, neologisms and neosemes in the first chapter and try to identify subgenres of science fiction *The Hunger Games* might fit in. They can also already speculate about the possible functions of the *nova*. Let pupils discuss the results in class. In order to decipher the neologism 'Panem' and the neoseme 'Capitol', ask students to do research on the Internet. Speculate together about the functions of the *nova* and the neologisms. These speculations have to be referred to and reappraised later in the post-reading phase.

Table 2: Introducing Critical Terminology on Science Fiction and *The Hunger Games*

6. Conclusion

Learning critical terminology for its own sake would be demotivating and a waste of time. Critical terms are only relevant if they make meanings, connections and aesthetic phenomena manifest which would remain invisible or at least vague without them. Naming a formal element alone is not effective; English language teaching should always focus on the functions and effects that make the formal element important to the better understanding of the work of art. While teaching *The Hunger Games* to sixteen-year-old students at my grammar school in spring 2019, I noticed that students were fascinated by the possibilities to map genres and name aspects of science fiction that they had been exposed to for some time without really getting a grip on them. The sketch of a lesson sequence documents the beginning of our unit on the novel when I introduced some basic critical terms.

Suvin's *novum* is the key term when discussing the form of science fiction. Combined with Freedman's cognition effect, the *novum* can be used as the basis of an inclusive, neutral definition of the transmedial genre as well as of its subdivision in various subgenres. The polyvalence of many science-fiction *nova*, which formalist studies of science fiction have described, – as symbols, experimental hypotheses, intertextual references and core elements of fictitious future histories – facilitate teachers to identify where and why various approaches and types of tasks can be used in teaching units. Since science-fiction texts and films are frequently discussed in the advanced EFL classroom – and have been so for decades –, 'novum' should be a familiar critical term there – as familiar as 'personification', 'close-up' and 'omniscient narrator'.

Notes

1 See e.g. Hempel, Margit, and Frauke Matz (2013). "Ecodidactics im Englischunterricht der Oberstufe: Dystopian Fiction für ökologische Bildung." *Medien und Interkulturalität im Fremdsprachenunterricht: Zwischen Autonomie, Kollaboration und Konstruktion.* Eds. Maria Eisenmann, Margit Hempel and Christian Ludwig. Duisburg: Universitätsverlag Rhein-Ruhr, 169-181. Matz, Frauke (2015). "Alternative Worlds – Alternative Texts: Teaching (Young Adult) Dystopian Novels." *Learning with Literature in the EFL Classroom*. Eds. Werner Delanoy, Maria Eisenmann and Frauke Matz. Frankfurt am Main: Peter Lang, 263-280. Bland, Janice (2018). "Popular Culture Head On: Suzanne Collins' THE HUNGER GAMES." *Using Literature in English Language Education: Challenging Reading for 8-18 Year Olds*. Ed. Janice Bland. London: Bloomsbury Academic, 175-192.

2 See Le Guin, Ursula K. (2009). "The Year of the Flood by Margaret Atwood." *The Guardian* 29 Aug. 2009: n. pag. Web. 30 May 2019 <https://www.theguardian.com/books/2009/aug/29/margaret-atwood-year-of-flood >.

3 See Atwood, Margaret (2011). *In Other Worlds: SF and the Human Imagination*. New York: Doubleday, 5-7.

4 See e.g. Latham, Rob (ed.) (2014). *The Oxford Handbook of Science Fiction*. Oxford: Oxford University Press. Roberts, Adam (2016). *The History of Science Fiction*. London: Palgrave Macmillan. Rieder, John (2017). *Science Fiction and the Mass Cultural Genre System.* Middletown: Wesleyan University Press.

5 Rieder (2017), 14.

6 Lütge, Christiane (2018). "Literature and Film – Approaching Fictional Texts and Media." *Teaching English as a Foreign Language: An Introduction.* Eds. Carola Surkamp and Britta Viebrock. Stuttgart: Metzler, 177-195, 190.

7 See Nünning, Ansgar, and Carola Surkamp (2006). *Englische Literatur unterrichten: Grundlagen und Methoden*. Seelze-Veelber: Kallmeyer, 65-66.

8 See the analysis of teaching material in Wehrmann, Jürgen (2014). "Utopien, Dystopien und Science Fiction im Englischunterricht: Probleme und Perspektiven." *Englisch lehren, lernen, erforschen*. Eds. Wolfgang Gehring and Matthias Merkl. Oldenburg: BIS, 267-290, 269-270.

9 See e.g. Malmgren, Carl D. (1991). *Worlds Apart: Narratology of Science Fiction*. Bloomington: Indiana University Press, 76-83. Freedman, Carl (2000). *Critical Theory and Science Fiction*. Middletown: Wesleyan University Press, 80-86. Jameson, Fredric (2007). *Archaeologies of the Future: The Desire Called Utopia and Other Science Fictions*. London: Verso, xiii-xiv.

10 Suvin, Darko (2016) *Metamorphoses of Science Fiction: On the Poetics and History of a Literary Genre*. Bern: Peter Lang, 25-26.

11 Freedman (2000), 18.

12 Hegel, Georg Wilhelm Friedrich (1986). *Vorlesungen über die Ästhetik I: Werke 13*. Frankfurt am Main: Suhrkamp, 255-257.

13 See Penny, Laurie (2017). *Bitch Doctrine: Essays for Dissenting Adults*. London: Bloomsbury, 430-433.

14 See Malmgren (1991), 15-22.

15 Broderick, Damien (1995). *Reading by Starlight: Postmodern Science Fiction*. London: Routledge, 59-60.

16 See Suerbaum, Ulrich, Ulrich Broich and Raimund Borgmeier (1981). *Science Fiction: Theorie und Geschichte, Themen und Typen, Form und Weltbild.* Stuttgart: Reclam, 80-82.

17 See Freedman (2000), 38-42.

18 See Hallet, Wolfgang (2007). "Close Reading and Wide Reading: Teaching Literature and Cultural History in a Unit on Philip K. Dick's 'Minority Report'." *Amerikastudien* 52.3, 381-397.

19 Anon. (2012). "The Hunger Games: Who is Author Suzanne Collins?" *The Telegraph* 23 Mar 2012: n. pag. Web. 30 May 2019 <https://www.telegraph.co.uk/culture/film/film-news/9161107/The-Hunger-Games-Who-is-author-Suzanne-Collins.html>.

20 See Csicsery-Ronay, Istvan (2008). *The Seven Beauties of Science Fiction*. Middletown: Wesleyan University Press, 24-25.

21 *Ibid*., 19-20.

22 Juvenal (1993). *Satiren: Lateinisch – deutsch*. Ed. Joachim Adamietz. München: Artemis & Winkler, 206-207.

23 See e.g. Berkeley, George (2005[1752]). "On the Prospect of Planting Arts and Learning in America." Key *Concepts in American Cultural History: From*

the Colonial Period to the End of the 19th *Century.* Eds. Bernd Engler and Oliver Scheiding. Trier: WVT, 32.

24 Bordewich, Fergus M (2008). "A Capitol Vision from a Self-Taught Architect." Web. 3 June 2019 <https://www.smithsonianmag.com/history/a-capitol-vision-from-a-self-taught-architect-91773428/ >.

25 Murphy, Cullen (2007). *Are We Rome? The Fall of an Empire and the Fate of America*. Boston: Houghton Mifflin Harcourt.

26 Hartwell, David (2005). "The Golden Age of Science Fiction Is Twelve." *Speculations on Speculations: Theories of Science Fiction*. Eds. James Gunn and Matthew Candeleria. Lanham: Scarecrow, 269-287, 269.

27 See Bredella, Lothar, and Eva Burwitz-Melzer, (2004). *Rezeptionsästhetische Literaturdidaktik (mit Beispielen aus dem Fremdsprachenunterricht Englisch).* Tübingen: Narr, 93-97.

28 See Csicsery-Ronay (2008), 146.

29 See Delany, Samuel R. (2005). "Some Presumptuous Approaches to Science Fiction." *Speculations on Speculations: Theories of Science Fiction*. Eds. James Gunn and Matthew Candeleria. Lanham: Scarecrow, 289-299.

30 See in more detail Wehrmann, Jürgen (2018) "Thought Experiments with Science Fiction: Ursula Le Guin's The Ones Who Walk Away from Omelas." *Using Literature in English Language Education: Challenging Reading for 8-18 Year Olds*. Ed. Janice Bland. London: Bloomsbury, 193-208.

31 Suvin (2016), 88.

32 Byram, Michael (1997). *Teaching and Assessing Intercultural Competence*. Clevedon: Multilingual Matters, 44.

33 Kramsch, Claire (2011). "The symbolic dimensions of the intercultural." *Language Teaching* 44.3, 354-368.

34 Robert Heinlein was the writer who first became famous for this technique See Wolfe, Gary K. (2011). "Theorizing Science Fiction: The Question of Terminology." *Teaching Science Fiction.* Eds. Andy Sawyer and Peter Wright. Basingstoke: Palgrave Macmillan, 38-54, 52.

35 Collins, Suzanne (2013[2008]). *The Hunger Games*. Stuttgart: Klett. 47-48, 63-64.

36 Amis, Kingsley (1975). *New Maps of Hell: A Survey of Science Fiction*. New York: Arno Press, 152.

37 See Wehrmann (2014), 279-280.

[38] Cf. Freitag-Hild, Britta (2010). *Theorie, Aufgabentypologie und Unterrichtspraxis inter- und transkultureller Literaturdidaktik: British Fictions of Migration im Fremdsprachenunterricht*. Trier: WVT.

[39] See in more detail Wehrmann (2018).

[40] See for more on this method Hallet (2007).

[41] See e.g. Matz (2015), 268-269.

[42] Pike, Graham, and David Selby (2001). *In the Global Classroom 1*. Toronto: Pippin. 217-247.

Bibliography

Primary Texts

Battle Royale – Survival Program. Dir. Kinji Fukasaku. 2000. Toei Company.

Bradbury, Ray (1953). *Fahrenheit 451*. New York: Ballantine Books.

Collins, Suzanne (2013[2008]). *The Hunger Games*. Stuttgart: Klett.

Juvenal (1993). *Satiren: Lateinisch – deutsch*. Ed. Joachim Adamietz. München: Artemis & Winkler.

King, Stephen (1982). *The Running Man*. Pseudonym Richard Bachman. *New York: Signet Books.*

Takami, Koushun (2003[1999]). *Battle Royale*. Tokyo: Ohta Publishing.

The Running Man. Dir. Michael Paul Glaser. (1987). TriStar Pictures.

Wells, Herbert George (2009[1985]). *The Time Machine*. Ed. Stephen Arata. New York: Norton.

--- (1993[1898]). *The War of the Worlds*. London: Everyman.

Secondary Literature

Amis, Kingsley (1975). *New Maps of Hell: A Survey of Science Fiction*. New York: Arno Press.

Anon. (2012). "The Hunger Games: Who is Author Suzanne Collins?" *The Telegraph* 23 Mar 2012: n. pag. Web. 30 May 2019 <https://www.telegraph.co.uk/culture/film/film news/9161107/The-Hunger-Games-Who-is-author-Suzanne-Collins.html>.

Atwood, Margaret (2011). *In Other Worlds: SF and the Human Imagination*. New York: Doubleday.

Berkeley, George (2005[1752]). "On the Prospect of Planting Arts and Learning in America." *Key Concepts in American Cultural History: From the Colonial Period to the End of the 19th Century.* Eds. Bernd Engler and Oliver Scheiding. Trier: WVT, 32.

Bland, Janice (2018). "Popular Culture Head On: Suzanne Collins' THE HUNGER GAMES." *Using Literature in English Language Education: Challenging Reading for 8-18 Year Olds*. Ed. Janice Bland. London: Bloomsbury Academic, 175-192.

Bordewich, Fergus M. (2008). "A Capitol Vision from a Self-Taught Architect." Web. 3 June 2019 <https://www.smithsonianmag.com/history/a-capitol-vision-from-a-self-taught-architect-91773428/>.

Bredella, Lothar, and Eva Burwitz-Melzer (2004). *Rezeptionsästhetische Literaturdidaktik (mit Beispielen aus dem Fremdsprachenunterricht Englisch).* Tübingen: Narr.

Broderick, Damien (1995). *Reading by Starlight: Postmodern Science Fiction*. London: Routledge.

Byram, Michael (1997). *Teaching and Assessing Intercultural Communicative Competence*. Clevedon: Multilingual Matters.

Csicsery-Ronay, Istvan (2008). *The Seven Beauties of Science Fiction*. Middletown: Wesleyan University Press.

Delany, Samuel R. (2005). "Some Presumptuous Approaches to Science Fiction." *Speculations on Speculations: Theories of Science Fiction*. Eds. James Gunn and Matthew Candeleria. Lanham: Scarecrow, 289-299.

Freedman, Carl (2000). *Critical Theory and Science Fiction*. Middletown: Wesleyan University Press.

Freitag-Hild, Britta (2010). *Theorie, Aufgabentypologie und Unterrichtspraxis inter- und transkultureller Literaturdidaktik:* British Fictions of Migration *im Fremdsprachenunterricht*. Trier: WVT.

Hallet, Wolfgang (2007). "Close Reading and Wide Reading: Teaching Literature and Cultural History in a Unit on Philip K. Dick's 'Minority Report'." *Amerikastudien* 52.3, 381-397.

Hartwell, David (2005). "The Golden Age of Science Fiction Is Twelve." *Speculations on Speculations: Theories of Science Fiction*. Eds. James Gunn and Matthew Candeleria. Lanham: Scarecrow, 269-287.

Hegel, Georg Wilhelm Friedrich (1986). *Vorlesungen über die Ästhetik I: Werke 13*. Frankfurt (Main): Suhrkamp.

Hempel, Margit, and Frauke Matz (2013). "Ecodidactics im Englischunterricht der Oberstufe: Dystopian Fiction für ökologische Bildung." *Medien und*

Interkulturalität im Fremdsprachenunterricht: Zwischen Autonomie, Kollaboration und Konstruktion. Eds. Maria Eisenmann, Margit Hempel and Christian Ludwig. Duisburg: Universitätsverlag Rhein-Ruhr, 169-181.

Jameson, Fredric (2007). *Archaeologies of the Future: The Desire Called Utopia and Other Science Fictions.* London: Verso.

Kramsch, Claire (2011). "The Symbolic Dimensions of the Intercultural." *Language Teaching* 44.3, 354-368.

Latham, Rob (ed.) (2014). *The Oxford Handbook of Science Fiction*. Oxford: Oxford University Press.

Le Guin, Ursula K. (2009). "The Year of the Flood by Margaret Atwood." *The Guardian* 29 Aug. 2009: n. pag. Web. 30 May 2019 <https://www.theguardian.com/books/2009/aug/29/margaret-atwood-year-of-flood >.

Lütge, Christiane (2018). "Literature and Film – Approaching Fictional Texts and Media." *Teaching English as a Foreign Language: An Introduction.* Eds. Carola Surkamp and Britta Viebrock. Stuttgart: Metzler, 177-195.

Malmgren, Carl D. (1991). *Worlds Apart: Narratology of Science Fiction*. Bloomington: Indiana University Press.

Matz, Frauke (2015). "Alternative Worlds – Alternative Texts: Teaching (Young Adult) Dystopian Novels." *Learning with Literature in the EFL Classroom*. Eds. Werner Delanoy, Maria Eisenmann and Frauke Matz. Frankfurt a.M.: Peter Lang, 263-280.

Murphy, Cullen (2007). *Are We Rome? The Fall of an Empire and the Fate of America*. Boston: Houghton Mifflin Harcourt.

Nünning, Ansgar, and Carola Surkamp (2006), *Englische Literatur unterrichten: Grundlagen und Methoden*. Seelze-Veelber: Kallmeyer.

Penny, Laurie (2017). *Bitch Doctrine: Essays for Dissenting Adults*. London: Bloomsbury.

Pike, Graham, and David Selby (2001). *In the Global Classroom 1*. Toronto: Pippin.

Rieder, John (2017). *Science Fiction and the Mass Cultural Genre System.* Middletown: Wesleyan University Press.

Roberts, Adam (2016). *The History of Science Fiction*. London: Palgrave Macmillan.

Suerbaum, Ulrich, Ulrich Broich and Raimund Borgmeier (1981). *Science Fiction: Theorie und Geschichte, Themen und Typen, Form und Weltbild.* Stuttgart: Reclam.

Suvin, Darko (2016) *Metamorphoses of Science Fiction: On the Poetics and History of a Literary Genre*. Bern: Peter Lang.

Wehrmann, Jürgen (2014). "Utopien, Dystopien und Science Fiction im Englischunterricht: Probleme und Perspektiven." *Englisch lehren, lernen, erforschen*. Eds. Wolfgang Gehring and Matthias Merkl. Oldenburg: BIS, 267-290.

--- (2018). "Thought Experiments with Science Fiction: Ursula Le Guin's THE ONES WHO WALK AWAY FROM OMELAS." *Using Literature in English Language Education: Challenging Reading for 8-18 Year Olds*. Ed. Janice Bland. London: Bloomsbury, 193-208.

Wolfe, Gary K. (2011). "Theorizing Science Fiction: The Question of Terminology." *Teaching Science Fiction.* Eds. Andy Sawyer and Peter Wright. Basingstoke: Palgrave Macmillan, 38-54.

Contributors' Addresses

Grit Alter, Institut für Anglistik und Amerikanistik, Universität Regensburg, Universitätsstraße 31, 93040 Regensburg

Claudia Deetjen, Neuphilologisches Institut, Anglistik/Amerikanistik, Julius-Maximilians-Universität Würzburg, Am Hubland, 97074 Würzburg

Sarah Nele Geiger, Willy-Brandt-Realschule im Bildungszentrum Königsbach, Steiner Straße 48, 75203 Königsbach-Stein

Liesel Hermes, Institut für Mehrsprachigkeit, Fach Englisch, Pädagogische Hochschule Karlsruhe, Bismarkstraße 10, 76133 Karlsruhe

Nadja Heß, Institut für Mehrsprachigkeit, Fach Englisch, Pädagogische Hochschule Karlsruhe, Bismarkstraße 10, 76133 Karlsruhe

Peter Hohwiller, Institut für Anglistik und Amerikanistik, Department of English and American Studies, Universität Paderborn, Warburger Straße 100, 33098 Paderborn

Christian Ludwig, Fachbereich Philosophie und Geisteswissenschaften, Anglistik/Amerikanistik, Freie Universität Berlin, Habelschwerdter Allee 45, 14195 Berlin

Almudena Machado-Jiménez, Departamento de Filología Inglesa, Universidad de Jaén, Edificio D2, despacho 206
Campus Las Lagunillas, s/n, 23071, Jaén, Spain

Katalin Schober, Hermann-von-Helmholtz-Gymnasium, Europaschule, Kurfürstenstraße 53, 14467 Potsdam

Elizabeth Shipley, Institut für Mehrsprachigkeit, Fach Englisch, Pädagogische Hochschule Karlsruhe, Bismarckstraße 10, 76133 Karlsruhe

Jonathan Shipley, Fort Worth Country Day School, 4200 Country Day Lane, Fort Worth, TX 76109-4299, USA

Martin Štefl, Department of Language Studies, MIAS School of Business, Czech Technical University in Prague, Kolejní 2637/2a, 160 00 Prague 6, Czech Republic

Klara Stephanie Szlezák, Institut für Anglistik und Amerikanistik, American Studies/Cultural and Media Studies, Universität Passau, Innstraße 25, 94032 Passau

Jürgen Wehrmann, Graf-Anton-Günther-Schule, Gymnasium des Landkreises Oldenburg, Schleusenstr. 4, 26135 Oldenburg

Dennis Weißenfels, Institut für Anglophone Studien, Universität Duisburg-Essen, Universitätsstraße 12, 45141 Essen